ACCESS AND DELIVERY IN CONTINUING EDUCATION AND TRAINING

a guide to contemporary literature

Helen Bridge & Heather Salt

with

Mark Dale, John Davies & John Morgan

ACKNOWLEDGEMENTS

The authors are grateful to the Department of Employment, Resources and Strategy Directorate which commissioned and funded this research. In particular they would like to thank the Steering Group for their advice and support throughout the project. The Steering Group consisted of:

Don Brennan, Helen Bridge, Howard Capelin, Val Carroll, Stephen Creigh, Mark Dale, John Davies, Ann Greengrass, John Morgan, Jill Robson, Heather Salt, Joan Wilson and Mark Woods.

Many other individuals and organisations contributed generously to the project in terms of time, advice and materials. Sadly space precludes mentioning them by name but we are indebted to many of the organisations listed on pages 37-42. The library and information staff at the Department of Employment at Moorfoot, Sheffield and NIACE, Leicester deserve our special thanks for their help and support throughout the project.

At Nottingham University the authors were greatly assisted by staff of the Hallward Library and in particular the Education Librarian Peter Haywood. In the Department of Adult Education Ian Sherman advised and executed many of the tasks relating to the computing aspects of the project and Lynda Prescott has co-ordinated the printing and distribution of this volume.

Responsibility for the views expressed in this publication lies with the authors.

Printed by Quorn Selective Repro, Queens Road, Loughborough LE11 1HH

ISBN 1 85041 066 6

FOREWORD

I very much welcome this comprehensive review of the literature on access and delivery aspects of continuing education and training in Britain.

It is now widely accepted that encouraging individuals to continue to train throughout life is vital to our economic competitiveness. That is why the Government has identified as a strategic priority that 'providers of education and training must offer high quality and flexible provision which meets the needs of individuals and employers'. That means, among other things, continued progress in removing unnecessary barriers to access and increasing flexibility in delivery.

Much has been achieved, for example, through development in open and distance learning, the accreditation of prior learning, and credit accumulation and transfer systems. Much remains to be done, however, particularly at the practical level within individual institutions and organisations. I hope this review will be a valuable resource to all those involved in promoting new approaches or developing existing initiatives.

R.J. DAWE CB
DIRECTOR GENERAL
TRAINING, ENTERPRISE AND EDUCATION DIRECTORATE
EMPLOYMENT DEPARTMENT

CONTENTS

HOW TO USE THE BIBLIOGRAPHY

If you are looking for the work of a particular **author** or **organisation** look directly under that name in the bibliography which is arranged in alphabetical order by authors' surnames and by the names of organisations. The names of organisations are spelled out in full. For example NIACE is listed under National Institute for Adult Continuing Education. If you do not know the full name of an organisation look at the list of abbreviations at the beginning of the bibliography.

If you are looking for information on a particular subject look at the subject index at the back of the bibliography. Each item in the bibliography has been given a number. Here the numbers of books and articles on particular subjects are grouped together. These can then be looked up in the bibliography under their numbers.

For example if you are interested in women's access to Higher Education look in the subject index under the main heading women and then under the smaller heading access to HE which appears in the alphabetical list directly underneath.

women
    Access Courses, 150
    access to HE, 87, 320, 468, 485, 790
    accreditation of prior learning, 155
    adult education, 634

You would then look at numbers 87, 320, 468, 485 and 790 to find the information you need.

The report section at the front of the bibliography reviews the literature on access and delivery in continuing education and training. The most useful material on each subject is identified in the report by its number in **bold type**.

SUMMARY OF RESEARCH

This bibliography is an essential tool for anyone involved in practice or research in continuing education and training.

It is aimed at those seeking basic information as well as at the informed user.

It contains over 1200 entries and covers the leading material published on access and delivery in continuing education and training in the United Kingdom since 1985.

Each entry has a short annotation informing the reader what the publication is about.

Entries are arranged in an A-Z sequence by author so that readers can look up work by particular writers or organisations. A subject index also allows readers to look up particular subjects.

An overview of the literature is provided guiding the reader to the leading material on different themes and drawing out trends, gaps and areas where further research is needed.

The subjects covered in the report and bibliography include:

The barriers to education and training faced by groups with special needs such as:

- Women
- Ethnic Minorities
- People with Disabilities
- People lacking Basic Skills
- Ex-Offenders

The most relevant issues in continuing education and training including:

- Open Learning
- Distance Learning
- Accreditation of Prior Learning
- Quality
- Transferability
- Collaboration and Working Partnerships
- Funding
- Marketing
- Guidance and Counselling

ACCESS AND DELIVERY IN
CONTINUING EDUCATION AND TRAINING

Aims and Scope of Research

The aim of this research has been to produce a report and a select annotated bibliography to support the work of those with an interest in access and delivery in continuing education and training. We have assumed a broad definition of continuing education and training to refer to learning and training opportunities taken up after initial education has been completed. The research involved identifying literature, assessing its relevance and accessibility and reviewing its content. The research is concerned with literature relating to the United Kingdom which has been published since 1985 and which deals with the 18-55 age group.

Literature Search

An extensive literature search has been undertaken involving both manual and computer searches. An initial broad search on access has been followed by more specific in depth searches on individual themes. A substantial amount of research exists located within a variety of publications. Literature on specific themes often appears in research looking at wider aspects of access and delivery and many of the major themes are discussed with only slight changes of emphasis in different publications. The amount of research carried out in each area can vary dramatically and new issues are arising all the time. The review section of the report will pull the literature together and categorise it into relevant themes. This is primarily an 'informing' review, in which we have tried to show the trends, gaps and areas where further research is warranted.

The numbers in bold type refer to entries in the bibliography and direct the reader to the leading articles on the subject.

Introduction

Questions of access and delivery in continuing education and training have become a priority on a world wide scale. At the centre of the debate are economic and philosophical pressures for change. Increased access to and improved delivery of education and training are perceived as prerequisites for the creation of a flexible and adaptable workforce in a time of rapid technical and structural change. The link between the economic health of the nation and the performance of education and training has now become firmly rooted in the minds of both the public and the policy makers. Added to this is the notion that all members of society should have the opportunity to continue to learn and develop throughout life. This includes those members of society who have benefited least from compulsory education.

The mid-1980s witnessed a steady growth in alternative entry procedures into higher education, notably Access and Open College courses. Subsequent research has extended the range of debate surrounding the definitions and conceptualisation of Access, to focus on the notion of *'accessibility'*: that is the general 'opening up' and reform of education and training. This will encourage a flexible approach to learning and the delivery of education and training which will more effectively meet the needs of the economy. A number of initiatives which should help to facilitate access into continuing education and training (CET) include Access courses, open and distance learning, accreditation of prior learning (including experiential/work-based learning), modularisation, credit accumulation and transfer and NVQs. In addition there has been a progressive movement towards 'inreach' developments within the education and training sectors. Concern now focuses on the notion of 'employability', with the emphasis on updating and retraining, especially in high level technical and engineering skills. There is growing consensus that the development of the potential of existing staff at all levels, rather than looking to new employees, is necessary if a firm is to remain competitive.

Whilst a strong consensus supporting the development of effective training strategies emerges within the literature, often located within the wider context of the labour market (skills shortages and human resource management), research focusing specifically on employers' perceptions of the many innovations in education and training delivery is extremely sparse. A small amount of research on the training needs of employers at an individual level and the issue of training guidance for employers, especially for small and medium enterprises has recently emerged. However, research assessing both employers' and the wider public perception of changes in education and training is only just beginning to make progress.

We are witnessing a range of structural, attitudinal and cultural changes which in turn apply pressure to the education and training system and have caused a host of new initiatives and developments. In this report we identify such changes and developments and direct the reader to the leading material relating to them. We first consider the literature dealing with the pressures to widen access, remove barriers and improve the flexibility of delivery, looking in particular at the needs of non-participant groups. We then look at the developments and initiatives which support this process. Finally, sections on Northern Ireland and Scotland detail some of the different schemes and practices found in these areas.

1 Barriers to Access

Organisations such as ACACE, NIACE and the FEU have produced informative policy documents on the barriers which inhibit access to education and training and have highlighted the main ones as financial, domestic, geographical, situational and cultural. The groups most frequently hindered by such barriers are portrayed as those having benefited least from the education system and include women, ethnic minorities, people with special needs, ex-offenders and those people who lack basic skills. Many writers, whilst recognising that the people within these groups cannot be treated as homogeneous, have also highlighted the barriers common to all. McGivney systematically documents the barriers and motivational characteristics of non-participants (see: **723**). Much of the relevant literature suggests that complex interaction between barriers and cultural or attitudinal barriers usually *reinforce* all others.

Here we draw briefly on research making the most salient points on the barriers faced by each group.

1.1 Women

Research and subsequent literature identifying the barriers affecting women's educational and career development is extensive. These range from the largely theoretical contributions on women's economic marginalisation to the more accessible and general literature often drawing on case studies. Walby (1188) and Crompton and Sanderson (257) are useful in providing theoretical frames of reference which enables a deeper understanding of the mechanisms of inequality.

Much of the general literature suggests the demographic trends of the 1990s may provide opportunities for women starting or returning to work and the concept of 'returnism' is widely reported (see: Labour Market Quarterly Report (661); Hardill and Creen 530; Parsons and Berry-Lound 896; Deeks 275; Record 958 and Becton 79). A number of practical guides have also been published, for example NEC (842); Women Returners Network (1232) and Korving (655). However, much of the extant literature neglects to mention that many of these women will return to part-time, low paid work and/or experience downward mobility. With little or no chance of paid educational leave to update their skills they miss out on promotion to managerial positions (see: Brannen 125). Whilst writers have recognised that many women actively seek part-time work which will fit in with child care, the crucial issue is widely seen as one of freedom of choice: educational and training opportunities should be equally accessible to both men and women.

The most identifiable obstacles faced by women are portrayed as domestic and financial. In addition, women's career progression is hindered by the ambiguity of their role in society, their own self-image, discriminatory recruitment practices and lack of an effective equal opportunity policy (see: Straw 1078 for a good introduction to developments in the equal opportunities movement and future strategies and also Green (503) on sex discrimination in job related training).

Financial barriers are clearly discussed by Ames (26); Coats (191); EOC (365) and McGivney (720, 721, 723). Course fees, childcare fees, transport and stationery costs and lack of guidance and information on benefits and loans can prevent women returning to study. Single parent women on benefits and women with low paid partners are particularly restricted. Hyatt and Parry-Crooke (581) have produced a valuable report on the barriers single parents confront and argue work expenses should be disregarded from Family Credit if lone parents are to be re-integrated into the labour market.

The literature on domestic constraint is extensive and generally stresses the urgency for employers and educational institutions to provide accessible, good quality child care, career break schemes and flexible hours. A highly recommended report by the IPM *Work and the Family* (596) considers all aspects of the carers role and suggests enabling provision may be more attractive to employers and employees than fixed work place provision because of the complexity surrounding the laws governing quality of childcare provision (see: Women of Europe Supplement 1230; Working Mothers Association 1242; Glascock 486 and Falconer 382). For other valuable discussions on the issues of domestic constraint (see: McGivney 720-1 and Replan 969). The EOC continues to produce current, informative booklets and more detailed research projects which are widely quoted (see: EOC **360-369**; IDS **585-586** and the Economist **311-312**).

Lead companies who have introduced flexible working, job sharing, part-time work and child care facilities are often portrayed as models of good practice which those involved in CET could emulate (see: IDS **585-586**; White **1208**). Hull (**578**) and Buzzing (**157**) discuss the value of career break schemes and recommend certain steps to be taken if these are to be successful.

The literature which documents the difficulties and experiences of women in predominantly professional employment focuses on the lack of continuing education options. Men are more likely to gain access to training and management development schemes. Women who gain access to management, often meet an invisible barrier (the 'glass ceiling') which prevents their further rise to positions of seniority or high level executive positions. (see: Jackson and Hirsch **601**; Marshall **760**; Pickup in Progress **922**; Summers **1081**). The report by Spurling is particularly valuable in highlighting barriers faced by women wishing to gain positions of seniority within higher education institutions (see: **1061**).

Recruitment interviewers and those involved in admissions to CET may also be major barriers to advancement if not trained in equal opportunity matters. Collinson (**202**) shows how the personnel manager can act as a 'gatekeeper' to the enterprise. Povall (**937**) discusses the importance of monitoring the retention and career progress of female employees.

Calls for positive action strategies in the form of women-only training and education courses have met with some controversy and are open to claims of sex discrimination. However the benefits of women-only education and training courses have been extensively documented. (see: Evans **376**, Carter & Kirkup **165**; Kirkup **646**; EOC **366**; Pickup in Progress **922**; Povall **937**; Sharples **1019**). Those courses offered in areas typically classified as non-traditional can be beneficial (see: Burgen **150**; Willman **1216**; Warren **1193** and Cooke **221**). Others argue they should be an adjunct to the standard management courses if gender-related barriers are to be eliminated (see: Farrell **386**).

Specialist women's studies foundation courses can assist women in individually regaining a sense of identity and encourage them to continue in some form of further education. Excellent discussions are given by Bateson and Bateson (**75**) and Giles (**485**).

A recent report by the Hansard Society (**529**) concludes how little change has been made in women's access to senior positions because of a lack of training and promotion opportunities. Cooke draws similar conclusions (see: Cooke **222**).

The Training and Enterprise Councils (TECs) and local enterprise companies (lecs) in Scotland, which are new bodies formed by the government to improve the quality of training and promote enterprise also have a major role to play in promoting equality of opportunity. TECs have issued stringent guidelines on how providers of training can implement equal opportunity policies (see: TEC Director **1099**). A valuable introductory appraisal of the structure and functions of TECs is provided in IDS Study July 1991 (see: IDS **587**).

It is apparent that whilst a number of structural developments need to be made to overcome gender-related barriers, it is ultimately attitudinal change, whereby it becomes natural for men to have career breaks and share the caring role, that will facilitate women's access to education, training and employment. Reference is made to the need for a change in attitude by many of the above writers. Cockburn provides a more rigorous discussion of this issue (see: Cockburn **192**).

1.2 Ethnic Minorities

Two strands of argument, both of which affect access and delivery, are common to much of the literature on ethnic minority adults. First, there is the need to ensure that ethnic minorities receive a fair representation and share of the resources. Underpinning this is the need to combat racist attitudes and practices in institutions and individuals. The emphasis of the material which has been produced is very definitely on access to higher education and to a lesser extent further education. There is far less available on access to vocational training and still less on work based training. Much of the material available on training provision outside further and higher education seems to be in the form of reports on local schemes and initiatives (see: Fullerton **428**; Hagedorn **516**; Munns and Furnborough **812**). In addition a number of articles are beginning to appear which discuss the role of the TECs (see: Christians Against Racism and Fascism **183**; Spencer **1057**; Usher **1176**).

Many researchers have commented in general terms on the significant under-representation of ethnic minorities in continuing education. The collection of information on ethnic origin is a sensitive issue and the research to date has been hampered by the lack of any systematic and centralised data collection on ethnic minority participation in further and higher education. UCCA and PCFC have started to collect data on ethnic origin on the 1990 intake and the Further Education Statistical Review began to collect data in November 1990. When published this information should enable a more accurate picture to emerge.

The emphasis of much of the research is only on access. In particular, research on ethnic minority drop out rates and the particular problems faced by those whose first language is not English is very sparse. There is a need for more follow up work such as that undertaken by Brennan and McGeevor (**129**) and Johnes and Taylor (**611**) which looks at the experiences of ethnic minority graduates in finding employment and researches their subsequent performance in the labour market. Data on ethnic minority activity in the labour market is provided periodically in the *Employment Gazette* where the economic position of different ethnic groups is compared with that of white groups (see: Employment Gazette **343-346**).

Research has discovered both overt and covert racism in institutions and individuals. The Commission for Racial Equality in *Learning in Terror* (**204**) found numerous examples of racially motivated violence and harassment while Williams' review of equal opportunities policies showed that well over half of higher education institutions showed very little commitment to equal opportunities issues (see: Williams **1214**). In response to these issues a number of useful and practical publications have appeared such as the REPLAN/NIACE guide on providing effective educational guidance to black communities (**965**) and the work of UDACE on Black Community Access (**1166**). Both suggest ways of helping ethnic minorities to overcome the barriers to education and training.

1.3 Refugees

Very little has been written about the education and training of refugees in Britain. Part of the problem seems to be that refugees by the nature of their status remain a partially hidden group. The research which has been published has largely been undertaken by groups such as the British Refugee Council and the World University Service. The research all starts from the premise that education and training are of fundamental importance in enabling refugees to become self sufficient and settle in their country of asylum. The research to date has concentrated on identifying a number of key issues such as the provision of English language teaching and transferring previous educational and work experience to a sometimes unresponsive British system. This raises the issues of the recognition of foreign qualifications, professional requalification and the adaptation of existing skills. Other priorities relate to the need for specific funding and guidance provision for adult refugees.

All of these issues which are clearly spelled out in the work of the British Refugee Council are central to the education and training of refugees (see: British Refugee Council **136-137**). The research now needs to move on from the identification of the problems towards the investigation of practical solutions.

1.4 Special Needs

The literature on 'special needs' is extensive and there are some variations of definition. Many writers have used the term to refer to groups of people with physical, sensory or intellectual disabilities and those suffering from psychiatric illness. The Employment Department's *Good Practice Guide on Training and Special Needs* provides the following definition..."Special training needs arise from the specific problems that some people may have and which need to be dealt with alongside their occupational training. Just as anyone may need training to cope with a new task, so anyone may have a special training need. The problem may be big or small, long term or short term. Either way it needs to be met if the individual is to benefit fully from occupational training". The groups considered within this document are people with disabilities; those with literacy and numeracy problems, those with English as a Second Language training needs and those whose difficulties are caused by emotional or behavioural problems (see: NCVO Special Training Needs Task Force).

Whilst much has been written on learning difficulties in young people with disabilities, special education and the transition into college and work, there is a sparsity in the literature which focuses specifically on continuing education and training for adults. Indeed, as Brock has noted, whilst there has been a proliferation in the 'access to higher education' literature there is very little discussion of disability (see: Brock **139-140**).

More recent policy documents have begun to highlight a range of physical, material and dispositional barriers to participation for this group (see: Child **180**; DES **277**; McGivney **724**; UDACE **1165, 1167-1168**). Charities such as MIND (National Association for Mental Health) and the Rathbone Society are concerned with breaking down some of these barriers and have carried out practical study projects, with the objective of helping employment advisers, informing policy and advising TECs on appropriate 'special needs' training strategies (see: for example Rathbone Society **955-957**).

Educare, the journal of the National Bureau for Handicapped Students, reports on recent developments in education, training and employment opportunities for handicapped adults (see: Chapman **175**; Jones **625**; Lones **696** for a useful selection).

Clearly, there is a growing consensus that students with disabilities should be integrated into mainstream education and training courses (see: Cook **220**; Chapman **175**; Goulbourn **498**; Sutcliffe **1083**). Certain structural changes may be needed for this to be made effective but it is only through a change in attitude that integration will be totally successful. The FEU stresses that integration and choice are most likely to accrue if agencies and services work together (see: Child **180**; FEU **459, 432, 440**).

Studies which have examined training and employment prospects for people with disabilities have emerged and the resulting recommendations are of value (see: Griffiths **508**; Hewitson-Ratcliffe **556**; Jones **622**; Kettle and Massie **637**; Kuh **660**; Morrell **795**). Empirical research depicting case studies of organisations who have proactive strategies on the employment and training of disabled are especially important (see: Griffiths **508**; Kuh **660**). More research following these lines and including a gender dimension would be useful. Whilst Fry (**426**) has looked at the barriers to employment in the early stages of the recruitment process, some in depth research on the training and promotion prospects of people with disabilities is needed.

Whilst some research shows that training and education opportunities have increased, the proportion of young adults with disabilities who continue to be without work or employment training programmes is high. (see: Kuh **660**) The criteria of eligibility for disability benefits can deter people from embarking on training (see: Glendinning **488**). A consistent failure to enforce the Disabled Persons Employment Act is frequently mentioned (see: Employment Gazette **339; 342**; Jones **622**). Some controversy surrounds the Quota stipulation, persuasion tactics such as awards for employers, and financial incentives are often thought to be more appropriate than enforcement of the Act.

Employers need help in understanding the potential of people with disabilities and need to understand the benefits which can result in offering effective support, particularly during initial employment (see: Jones **622**; Kettle and Massie **637**; Morrell **795**; and Ramsay **953**). Colleges of further education can also help by offering awareness-training to industry. Clearly there is a need for disability equality training as an integral part of staff development (see: Boxer **115**; DES **277**; FEU **448**; McGivney **724**).

There remains an urgent need for documentary analysis, following the lines of Jenkins (**607**) and Brock (**140**) in which people with disabilities can relate their own experiences of access to CET. The monthly magazine *Disability Now* offers a forum for people with disabilities. However, it is essential that their views reach mainstream academic journals and other publications because there is a tendency for research to speak for this group.

1.5 Lack of Basic Skills

A lack of basic skills cannot be defined merely as problems with reading and writing. The term refers to a whole range of language, literacy, numeracy, communication and coping skills. The identification of needs and the provision of training are important at both an individual and a national level. For the individual basic skills can be seen as the gateway to education, training and ultimately employment. The attainment of competency levels and NVQs can now be added to these. On a national level it is now accepted that there is a need to strengthen the overall skill base of the workforce as a condition for international competitiveness and economic success.

A great deal of material has been produced about basic skills in recent years. However, a large part of it is concerned with teaching schemes and methods. There is much less material available which deals with the provision of training and the access of individuals to it. The literature which does exist is both practical and useful. Of particular note is the work of the Adult Literacy and Basic Skills Unit (ALBSU).

A key concern must be to identify and assess the level of need for basic skills training. Some work has been undertaken here mainly in relation to training schemes for the unemployed (see: ALBSU 10; ALBSU and MSC 8; Taylor 1094; Training Agency 1145). These all report on individual assessment programmes and procedures. This type of work needs to be extended to look at assessment for those already in work. In addition the accreditation of prior learning appears to be particularly relevant to this group (see: Chanda 174).

An important and topical issue is the role the TECs are to play in this sphere. An excellent ALBSU production entitled *Promoting basic skills: an information guide for TECs* (12) has been produced. This guide explains why basic skills training is such a vital part of the TECs work and aims to help them identify and evaluate high quality training. This document would provide a useful starting point for anyone with an interest in this area.

There is surprisingly little published material on access to basic skills training In particular research needs to be undertaken to discover the particular barriers which this group face. For example, the needs of those whose first language is not English, the particular needs of women returners and older workers could profitably be investigated as a basis for effective provision in the future.

1.6 *Ex-Offenders*

The barriers to CET are particularly acute for this group who must contend with problems often related to a lack of basic education, for example unemployment, poverty, homelessness and possibly re-conviction. There is evidence to support the claim that people are more likely to re-offend if they become unemployed on leaving prison (see: Lea-Wilson 675; NACRO Policy papers 823-829). These findings have stimulated interest in the value of education and training for ex-offenders. The issues have been given further prominence with the launching of An Offender Employment Charter, a national campaign designed to tackle the difficulties in this area of employment (see Pike 923).

The Apex Trust and NACRO are organisations actively seeking to break down barriers faced by ex-offenders and their publications are both concise and informative (see: NACRO 823-829; Apex Trust Review 31-33).

The HMSO Third Report (317) on prison education gives a high priority to education and training and illuminates the importance of transferability. That is, any new skills, including social and personal skills, developed whilst in prison should be accredited to enable ex-offenders to continue in some form of further education and training. For further discussions on the importance of the development of personal skills (see: Duguid **305**; Peaker and Vincent **905**; and Symonds **1087**).

Evidence from a recent study carried out by the Apex Trust (see: Symonds **1087)** clearly shows that many employers have no equal opportunity policy which includes the needs of ex-offenders. NACRO, the Apex Trust and the probation service have therefore, drawn up a statement outlining priorities for TECs on working with offenders. Further research could usefully monitor progress on this and the new Charter.

1.7 Summary

It is clear from a review of the material relating to barriers faced by *all* the social groups mentioned above, that employing organisations and providers of education and training, must establish Equal Opportunities Policies, which include effective monitoring of recruitment and retention for all previously disadvantaged groups. Valuable recommendations are given in the FEU's *Planning Human Resource Development through Equal Opportunities* (see: Warwick **1195**) and the *Report of the Special Training Needs Task Force* (see: NCVO **838**).

A crucial issue for providers of education and training is to adopt a flexible approach when delivering programmes. Delivery should examine the needs of non-traditional entrants (see: Coats **191**; Evans **374**; McGivney **723-4**; Wisker **1225**). Delivery should take into account the benefits of guidance and counselling, location, lack of financial independence and the design of application forms which should recognise unpaid work experience (see: Butler **155**; Dicken and Blomberg **300**; Hartresss **542**; Sheen **1020**).

2 Innovations in Lifelong Learning

2.1 Open and Distance Learning

The literature has developed some degree of convergence around the notion of lifelong learning as a necessary requisite for personal development as well as economic growth. Emphasis has been placed on the benefits to be gained from a flexible workforce. For a flexible workforce to emerge, the ability to 'learn how to learn' becomes a crucial issue. If this is to occur, adults need access to education and training courses which will fit their individual needs. A wider range of possibilities in the form and delivery of education and training is therefore important and the notion of flexible learning and training methods has gained credence and incorporates a number of new approaches. For example, open learning, distance learning and accreditation of prior learning have been well documented. For a good summary on flexible learning see the *Employment Gazette* (**348**). The notion of continuous progression, inherent in flexible learning, is mirrored by NVQs which are structured to enable a student to move from one level to the next (see: Gorringe **496-497**).

Open learning is the title given to more flexible methods of study and teaching in which there is openness in access, content, delivery systems and assessment. For good sources which offer precise definitions and an outline of the development of open learning (see:

NEC **841**; Bennett **83**; Open Learning Directory **874** and Scottish Committee on Open Learning **1007**).

Open Learning is seen as an attractive option by some UK companies and some interesting research has been carried out. For a valuable overview see the collection of papers edited by Paine *Open Learning in Transition: an agenda for action* (**887**), which offer informed analysis of current open learning initiatives in the UK. For other detailed studies which interleave theory with practice (see: Knapper **650**; Lengrand **678**; Molyneux **787**; Wagner **1186**; Withnall **1227**).

Employers are most likely to be interested in information which demonstrates tangible outcomes and case studies on organisations which have initiated an open learning programme can be useful (see: Cox and Davies **253**; Foggo **408**; Fuller and Saunders **427**; McGivney **722**; Mitchell **784**; Twining **1161**). Mann (**750**) presents the main factors which appear to have an impact on the individual's commitment to open learning. For guidelines on good practice (see: Windess **1223** and Crawley **255**). Crawley draws on the experience of Flexible Training Systems, a company which has been instrumental in introducing OL into a wide range of companies. Fricker clearly highlights both the advantages and disadvantages of the open learning method and articulates a number of recommendations to make such programmes efficient and effective (see: **423**). The Scottish Open Learning Consortium have also carried out work on flexible learning and have produced a useful guide consisting of case studies outlining different stages of development in flexible learning (see:**1013**).

It is important to distinguish open learning from distance learning. Distance learning covers a variety of forms. Students and tutor are separated by geographical distance and communication is through correspondence or other media. Distance learning may be favoured by employers because of its flexibility in overcoming the difficulties of releasing employees for long courses. There is a rapidly growing literature on this form of learning. A fully comprehensive text covering all aspects of distance learning is that by Keegan **630**. For other valuable sources (see: Bennett **83**; Birch **92**; Birchall **94**; Cooper **224**; Cox and Davies **253**; Dey and Harrison **298**). The reader may also be usefully directed to some of the comparative literature (see: the *European Journal of Education* **373** for three informative and different perspectives on distance education; and Hall **520**).

Many writers have concentrated on the motivational characteristics of students learning at a distance. The importance of a good support system is strongly emphasised. Pre-course counselling is especially important in order to prevent unnecessary wastage (see: Keegan **630**; Crawley **255**; Kirkwood **647**; Mann **750**).

Both open and distance learning systems use increasingly sophisticated materials and technology. It is crucial that materials are well structured and clearly delivered. For valuable case studies considering the delivery of open distance learning systems (see: Fuller and Saunders **427**; Cox and Davies **253**; Jefferies **605**).

2.2 *Accreditation of Prior Experiential Learning/Achievement*

This term covers schemes for giving students formal credit for prior or experiential learning as an alternative method of satisfying entry requirements into education and training. Recognition given to this form of learning has grown widely and this is reflected in a proliferation of literature appearing from 1983 onwards. In the earlier literature reference is usually made to accreditation of prior learning, but the terms experiential learning, prior work experience are also used and there has recently been a movement towards using the expression of prior achievements.

A considerable amount of research is being undertaken in the area of APL. Foremost is the work of Norman Evans for the Learning from Experience Trust, who has initially focused on APL in connection with entry to higher education. (see: Evans **375-378**). The collection of papers edited by Warner-Weil and McGill *Making sense of experiential learning: diversity in theory and practice* (see: **1192**) appraises a multiplicity of meanings and practices associated with experiential learning in an international context.

It is important to now place APL in a wider context because of the interest in flexible adult training and the structure of NVQs which are defined as a statement of competency (see Gorringe **496**). The movement towards the concept of accreditation of prior achievements, (APLA) which is meant to be a clearer definition is supported by the NCVQ and the FEU and suggests it is not the process of learning itself which can be assessed or credited, but what has been achieved by it. For a valuable introduction to and appraisal of APLA (see: *Coombe Lodge Report Vol 21 No 5* **521**; Gorringe **496**; also see FEU/LET **443**).

The NCVQ has stressed the importance of certificating prior learning achievements in the form of a National Record of Achievement for all levels of the workforce. This would enable learners to assemble credit towards a qualification over a period of time (see: Squires **1062**; UDACE **1170-1171**; LET **674**). For further useful discussions on the above (see: Jessop **609**; Barrett **70**; Withnall **1227**; Schuller **1002**; Fletcher **407**; Ingram **591**; NIACE **846**; Symonds **1087** and the Training Agency **1130**).

There is a growing consensus in the literature for a nationally coherent and flexible framework of accreditation and the harmonization of the approaches of NCVQ, CNAA, OU, Open College Networks and professional bodies (see: UDACE **1170-1171**; Squires **1062**; Toyne **1125**; Vaughan **1179**; IDS **587**).

2.3 *Work-based Learning and Training and Paid Educational Leave*

Work-based learning (WBL) and work-based training (WBT) are terms used inter-changeably within the literature but a distinction should be made between the two. WBL sees the learner as a whole and the education and training courses given are not necessarily job-specific. The concept behind Employee Development Schemes recognises the value of personal development, which should stimulate employee motivation. Research is progressing in this area and new schemes are likely to emerge. To date, the schemes feature predominantly in the motor industry (see Ward **1191**; TURU **1128**).

WBT training however is vocational and usually job-specific. Most companies which decide to invest in training and paid educational leave for continuous development relate their policy to business objectives (see Silver **1023**). Most of the training offered is vocational and job specific and is most often provided by large companies, many of which offer in-house specialist courses, utilise PICKUP and management development courses. For a useful and concise text on the benefits of continuous development and the initiatives taken by some lead companies see: Wood (**1234**). For other useful reviews (see: DES **281**; Ellis **327-8**; Hardy **531-2**; Hutchin **579**; Cridland **256**). Clendon and Yorke **188-189** have produced an influential study which documents the constraints on employers releasing personnel for training. Most small companies provide on-the-job training. This can be successful if implemented correctly but is not always easily accredited nor transferable (see: Blackburn **99**; Smith **1040** and Sloman **1034**). Interesting discussion on employers' attitudes towards training are those by Lowden (**701**) and Rosa (**991-992**).

Much of the literature discusses paid educational leave in relation to a structured career development programme predominantly for the skilled professional who needs to have access to updating courses in highly technical/scientific areas where skills quickly become obsolete (see: Hardy **531**; Horner **569**; Hutchin **579**; Garry and Cowan **471-472**; Robinson **987** Roweth **993**; The Guardian **511**).

A growing number of critical studies, drawing on empirical data, highlights the importance of paid educational leave for low paid, non-professional employees especially women (see: Field **394**; Mace and Yarnit **716-7**; Miliband **771**; NIACE **849**; Weatherall **1198**). These all agree that the retraining and utilisation of the potential of all employees at all levels makes sense economically and is socially just. The notion of learning contracts, that is an agreement among an employer, the employee and an academic institution, may extend training to the non-professional workforce. For a good discussion on learning contracts see Dearden **273**. For this to happen cultural change is needed which readily embraces 'lifelong learning' as natural and available to all. Further education, adult education and higher education institutions also have a part to play in recognising the importance of continuing education, deferred entry, part-time study and flexible admissions (see: Ball **55**; Ball and Eggins **51**; Fulton and Ellwood **429**). For other useful reading reinforcing the philosophy of education throughout life (see: DES **283-284**; Ball **55**; Duffin and Woods **304**; Employment Department **332**). For good discussions on the benefits of expanding part-time degree provision (see: Tight **1113- 1116**; Gallacher **463**).

From our review of the material looking at the development of structures designed to support continuing education and training, significant strides are being made. However, lack of public awareness into the many education and training initiatives means that the Training and Enterprise Councils have a large part to play in stimulating collaborative partnerships between education and industry and delivering training programmes relevant to local employers' needs (see: TEC Director **1102**; Davies **266**).

TECs should also be well-informed on skills shortages both on a national and local scale and initiate feedback among providers of education, employers and employees. Valuable general texts discussing skills training and the labour market both nationally and internationally can stimulate debate on how the needs of the individual, employers and the economy may best be accommodated (see: Stevens and Mackay **1071**; Gleeson **487**).

If employers are to adopt a pro-active approach to education and training they need to be convinced of the benefits of supporting individuals in their development, at all levels.

Hence, effective and coherent systems of guidance and information on training needs, a neglected area to date, must become a top priority issue.

2.4 *Quality Issues*

The notion of quality is one that has become increasingly important in the sphere of continuing education and training in recent years. Quality in this context is a difficult concept to define. It has a pervasive nature with different applications in different sectors of an organisation, and its achievement may be pursued in a variety of ways. Models which relate only to outcomes (such as qualifications attained) have been largely discredited as too simplistic (see: Cave and Hanney **169**; Gallagher **465**). The measurement, assessment and improvement of quality has become part of a complex balancing act between input, processes and outcomes. The need for the education and training sector to become more flexible and responsive to the needs of the economy is now accepted. The attainment of quality implies looking closely at aims and objectives and a move towards more effective and focused activity. In addition, financial pressures have given impetus to the need for accountability, or proof that public money is being well spent. As such, the increased emphasis on quality seen in industry and commerce in recent years is now being transferred to education and training.

Assessment of the quality of education and training inherently implies a system or mechanism for measurement, control and quality assurance and it is with these issues that much of the recent literature is concerned. There has been a proliferation of publications on the advantages and disadvantages of particular models such as the use of performance indicators (see: Cave and Hanney **169**) and the assessment of client satisfaction as a measure of quality. (see: Thompson **1107**). The TEC sector in particular has been concerned with the description and promotion of a number of initiatives such as BS 5750 (see: Foster **416-417**; Hazelwood **546**; Murphy **816**; Recruitment and Development Report **959**; Rees **961**; Transition **1149**); Investors in People (see: Drew-Smith **303**; Farmer **385**; Field **396**; Troth **1152**; Wolfson **1228**) and Total Quality Management (see: FEU **437, 456**; Tysome **1163**).

Measurable standards and qualifications play an important role in the achievement of quality as they act as the attainable and assessable targets against which performance can be measured (see: TEC Director **1101**). In particular, the notion of competence and the competency based National Vocational Qualifications are becoming increasingly important as their use becomes more widespread. A particularly clear and concise introduction to the work of the National Council for Vocational Qualifications (NCVQ) is provided in *Coombe Lodge Reports Vol 20 No 5* (see: Hall **521**).

One notable area of current debate is that of the dilution of quality of output in higher education by mass access and access for non-traditional students. A useful overview of the arguments is provided by Peter Wilson (**1219**). Some research has compared the performance of students without traditional qualifications in higher education with that of students with A levels and has found that quality of output has not been adversely affected. (see: Bolton **102**; Bourner **110**; Entwistle and Wilson **359**). Other research such as that by Smithers and Robinson (**1051**) has found that the standard of students entering higher education with BTec qualifications was below that of those entering with A Levels and that the drop out rate was significantly higher.

The assessment and improvement of quality in continuing education and training seems likely to become one of the central themes of debate and research in the 1990s. However, there seems to be relatively little research which investigates the links between quality and resources. From the literature which already exists it appears that the client centred approach used in total quality systems will become one of the central quality assurance systems to be applied in continuing education and training. As such, research which attempts to assess quality from the consumers point of view, such as students (including non-completers), employers and ultimately the economy, would be a useful contribution to the debate.

3 Collaboration and Working Partnerships

Collaboration or links between further and higher education, TECs and employers to ensure that progression routes for learners are open and flexible has become an increasingly pertinent issue.

The Employment Department actively promotes partnerships involving government, employers, the educational sector and the voluntary sector which is reinforced by the Department of Trade and Industry and the Council for Industry and Higher Education. These bodies have produced an important and accessible collection of policy documents intended to stimulate dialogue between all the major parties (see: DTI 295; CIHE 236-240).

The importance of closer communication is reflected in the emergence of a whole range of consortia arrangements bringing the relevant parties together. For example, University Enterprise Training Partnerships (UETPs), COMPACTs, TECs, Business/Education Partnerships, Learning Contracts, Enterprise in Higher Education, Workshadowing, New Training Initiatives, CATs, PICKUP, APL, ACCESS, CONTACT and the European Community COMETT programme for continuing education and training in technologies. (see: Schuller 1002; Watson 1197; Guy 512-513; Toyne 1125; Squires 1062; Contact 217). Linklater (689) is valuable for those interested in the developments in sandwich courses.

Race and Portwood (950) in a useful appraisal of some of the above, suggest many of these progressive initiatives can appear fragmentary and confusing to employers and will be more coherent and effective if developed and monitored through collaboration. Regional variations in the provision of links between business and education suggests TECs have an important role to play in coordinating existing provisions and stimulating new initiatives. Useful literature on TECs and partnership includes: (IDS 587; TEC Director 1102; Employment Gazette 349-350).

The earlier debates on links have focused on access to education and there has been a proliferation of studies stressing the importance of cooperation between further education and higher education if Access course initiatives are to succeed. Open college networks and credit transfer consortia are dependent on good working relationships (see: Slowey 1036; Parry 893). However, the issue of enterprise in education and various types of training consortia with local employers has recently taken precedence and the emphasis now appears to be on access to continuing education and updating of skills, especially in high level skills development, professional/managerial development and transferable skills.

Much of the earlier literature has also stressed the importance of collaborative research ventures. However, the notion of continuing education and training has now become the main focus in university-commercial collaboration. The growing status of continuing education and training in higher education institutions is reflected in the literature with the emphasis pointing to HEIs being encouraged to adopt a proactive stance towards CET, especially towards initiatives such as PICKUP, the expansion of work-related training schemes and increased access (see: Davies and Rispin 267; Schuller 1002; McIlroy 726; McNay 741; Knight 652; Massey and Goldsmith 765; DTI 297; CIHE 236).

Clearly, higher education institutions have the expertise to provide training and updating in technical, scientific and management skills and with better communication should be able to run effective programmes to tackle skill shortages tailored to meet the needs of individual companies by working with them to accredit in-house training (see: LET 674; Clendon and Yorke 188; Williams 1215 and Vaughan 1179).

A growing number of studies have focused on industry and higher education links. A useful starting point is Cerych's concise overview (see: Cerych 171; Loder 694; Stradling and March 1077). The international journals *Industry and Higher Education* and *CRE-action* offer a forum for all aspects of collaboration. For a useful selection (see: Bragg 120; Calman-Shaw 161; Connor 216; Laid 664; McCall 708; Coldstream 195; 197; Agnelli 19). Other good consultative documents are Ball (52) and Employment Department (338) which reinforce the general importance of such links.

Much of the extant research is descriptive rather than analytical, describing the various collaborative ventures being encouraged. However, those which inform policy makers by depicting the pros and cons, reasons for failed as well as successful ventures and obstacles preventing linkages can be useful (see: Kells 633; Connor 213-216; IPM 595; Cottam 234).

Cyrech (172) has usefully articulated the need for more in depth, rigorous analysis which would help in furthering the benefits of links, help prevent wastage through failed ventures, and would appeal to academics (see: CONTACT 217; Williams 1215).

4 Transferable skills

It is apparent that employers have become increasingly concerned with the relevance of those skills which can be transferred from education to employment. Many organisations have stimulated dialogue in this area and have produced valuable policy documents which they hope will stimulate feedback and inform debate. Some of the most frequently cited are RSA; Council for Industry and Higher Education; SRHE; Engineering Council; CBI; FAST and more recently TECS. For a useful selection (see: DTI 296; CIHE 239-240).

A recurring theme is the academic/vocational divide which has again become a top agenda issue. The White Paper *Education and Training for the 21st Century* focuses on the need for parallel academic and vocational education (see: **281**). The lower status of vocational skills however is deeply ingrained within the British culture. A number of studies has emerged which point up the need to eliminate this divide. However, few substantive measures for bridging the gap have yet emerged. Dialogue generated by more critical works is valuable (see: Hodgkinson **563**; Magee and Alexander **748** Gleeson **487**). These papers focus on the difficulties of studying both vocational and academic courses. The student must choose at sixteen to take one route or another and change-over is difficult. Wilson and West (**1217**) have recommended, and can claim support for, a unified learner-centred system of education and training throughout life.

Employers' needs in terms of the type of skills they wish to find in graduates form the basis of more recent policy documents (see; UDACE **1172**; DTI **296**; DES **286**; Brennan **130**; Finegold and Soskice **398**; Roizen and Jepson **990**; FEU/TA **461**).

Some consensus has emerged around 'knowledge-based' and personal transferable skills and usually stresses the key issues as: intellectual rigour, analytical ability, enterprise and personal skills, such as communication, flexibility and the ability to work in a team (see: Bradshaw **119**; Calman-Shaw **161**).

Some studies have adopted a more questioning approach towards crude and simplistic calls for more vocationally-orientated courses. Hitchcock (**561**) for example suggests such arguments need to be offset by a recognition of transferable skills obtained in most social science and humanities courses.

It is clear that personal skills may be enhanced via graduate work placements and work-shadowing schemes and research is beginning to emerge on the Enterprise in Higher Education initiative (EHE), the objective of which is to motivate institutions of higher education to produce graduates who are better prepared for the world of work. For informative discussions see: Bayliss **78**; Stern and Turbin **1070**; Kirby **644**; Barnett **66**; Training Agency **1142**).

Workshadowing is even less well developed in higher education institutions, hence very little research has appeared. One exception is the paper by Jack (**599**) who analyses a scheme at Cambridge University and stresses the benefits to participating companies as well as to students. The problems encountered usually centre around what the notion of workshadowing should be. As a learning process, it seems clear that workshadowing has a lot to offer and further research would be beneficial.

5 Widening Access

5.1 Funding

Arrangements for the funding of continuing education and training are obviously of central importance and this is reflected in the amount and scope of the literature which surrounds the subject. An important section of the literature which provides a useful starting point for those with an interest in this area is that which describes the current level and existing structures of funding for continuing education and training. A key work in this area is the Training Agency's *Training in Britain: a study of funding activity and attitudes* (**1143-1144**). There does not appear to be a comparable publication providing such a broad overview of funding activity in the further and higher education sectors. There is perhaps a need for a document providing a concise guide to the funding arrangements which exist in the further and higher education sectors and which brings together recent changes.

A considerable section of the literature deals with the impact of recent legislation on both institutions and existing and potential students. Of the changes in funding arrangements which have been introduced since 1985 that which seems to have caused the most reaction in terms of published material is the introduction of student loans. Research looked at how financial circumstances affect the situation of existing and potential students in terms of their access to further and higher education and their performance whilst in education (see: Ames **26**; Bourner **111**; Bryant **144-146**; Cornish **231**; Windle **1224**).

Cost effectiveness, efficiency and proof of a return on the financial investment made in education and training is a central theme of much of the work, particularly that which comes from official sources. Sir Christopher Ball's interim report *Learning Pays* (**52**) explores the concept that an investment in education and training is an investment in the future economic and social well being of the nation. However, in view of the sparsity of published evidence it appears to be extremely difficult to produce hard data which supports this thesis. Joan Payne (**901**) attempts to redress the balance in her study of adult off-the-job skills training in which she assesses the impact of such training on the individuals' subsequent performance in the labour market. In addition *Training in Britain* (**1143**) attempted to establish the link between high levels of funding and economic success. Also useful is the 1990 National Institute of Economic and Social Research Report *Productivity, Education and Training: Britain and other countries compared*. However, this is an area where further research is needed to assess the individual and national effects and to test the general consensus of opinion that adult training is effective both for the individual and the economy.

Of the research which still needs to be undertaken one of the most obvious areas is on how the proposed expansion of education and training is to be financed. Any changes which do occur will need to be carefully monitored and evaluated so there is also a need for ongoing research in this area. *Training in Britain* (**1143**) is a valuable piece of research, however its value would be greatly enhanced if it was part of a systematic and ongoing research plan in which developments are reported and assessed.

5.2 Marketing

In recent years marketing has gained acceptance as an activity relevant to education and training. In the past marketing in this sector has been somewhat narrowly defined as publicity and promotion and early work reflects the tension resulting from the perception of marketing as the wholesale commercialisation of education and training in which the ethics of business outweigh all others. However, more recent work reflects a wider and more positive interpretation of marketing as an overall approach which includes elements of market research, public relations and most importantly the effective matching of needs and delivery. It is seen to have an important role in improving communication and understanding between the education and training sectors and the world of work resulting in more effective education and training.

The literature produced since 1985 dealing specifically with marketing in continuing education and training falls into two broad categories. The first deals with why marketing is necessary and the second gives guidance on how to go about it successfully.

In the literature which concentrates on why marketing is necessary a number of key themes emerge. Some authors, particularly those writing about the higher education sector, concentrate on the debate surrounding the co-existence of marketing and academic principles arguing that marketing and academic objectives can and must exist alongside each other (see: Coldstream **196**).

Most importantly the research recognises the role of marketing in establishing and improving links between the providers and the consumers of education and training. Writers such as Coldstream (**196**) and Theodossin (**1105**) have recognised the value of market research in identifying the needs of employers. The key concern here is that the education and training sector becomes market led in terms of responding to the needs of employers and by implication the economy. It is widely accepted that if education and training are to play their part in reversing economic decline it must be viewed as a long term investment and marketing can be seen as a tool for setting long term objectives (see: Moore **791**).

The second set of literature relates to how marketing strategies should be developed and implemented. The common themes here are for coherent and systematically applied strategies based on careful market research. Writers such as Brain (**122**) have discussed the underlying concepts such as customer care and the need for a market led service. Also stressed is the need for the right marketing skills and adequate resources. Duncan (**308**) argues against the marketing techniques of manufacturing industry being crudely transferred across to education and training without refinement. Two bodies of literature lead in this field. That produced by the Further Education Unit (**450-1**) has a practical slant, often containing useful guidelines and checklists such as the 7 P's of marketing: Price, Place, Product, Publicity, Processes, People and Physical facilities. The Employment Department has produced a 'Developing Good Practice' Series aimed at the TECs one of which offers advice on how to make the most effective use of market research and marketing techniques (see: Employment Department **334**).

On all the issues discussed above *Higher Education Quarterly Volume 43 Number 2* is to be recommended. The whole volume is devoted to marketing and many of the issues are covered there.

5.3 Guidance and Counselling

To make effective use of the numerous education and training initiatives, a coherent and efficient system of guidance, counselling and information must be established. Lack of guidance and information on the available options for those wishing to return to study or re-train is a major barrier to increasing access. This is reflected in the burgeoning research and subsequent literature in this area.

UDACE lies at the forefront of research on guidance and has produced many informative policy documents offering good practice models which have influenced the development of services and initiated further research into this area (see: UDACE **1167, 1169**; Alloway and Nelson **23**; Alloway and Opie (**24-25**); Alldred et al (**22**) Oakeshott **870-71**). Alexander and Steward (**21**) usefully provide a comprehensive overview of the importance of guidance for adults.

There has been a definite shift in the literature away from a counselling model based on 'skill-deficiency' towards guidance as an 'educative' activity, which stresses the importance of 'self-management' and helps the client to develop the skills of acquiring and processing information (see: Killeen **640**; Imeson and Edwards **582**; UDACE **1165, 1168**; Bailey **44-45**; Evans **378**; Edwards **319**).

Whilst guidance must meet an individual's immediate needs there has been a progressive movement towards advocacy, that is the policy of negotiating directly with institutions or agencies on behalf of individuals or groups of clients (see: Hillier **560**) and feedback to education and training providers on unmet or inappropriately met need (see: Payne **903**; Oakeshott **870**; UDACE **1165, 1167-1168**).

The literature on feedback and advocacy predominantly focuses on access to further and higher education. There is now an urgent need to focus on feedback in relation to employers and the Training and Enterprise Councils if the training market is to deliver more effectively. It is clear that whilst educators have recognised the need to provide services to guide adults through the complex world of education, the needs of employers (especially small and medium sized businesses) and of individuals wishing to change career (either through redundancy, or choice) are somewhat neglected.

However, general themes have emerged from the small amount of research into guidance on employers' training needs. For example, Alloway and Opie (**25**) conclude from their survey of organisations providing guidance, that employers frequently complained of being bombarded with literature which they do not have time to analyse or which they perceive to be irrelevant to their organisation's needs. These claims are supported by Bailey (**45**); Clendon and Yorke (**189**); Maguire (**749**) and Rosa (**992**). Whilst many employers claim to be aware of local training provision this in reality is partial or out of date (see: Sunday Times **1082**; Employment Gazette **352**). TECs in response to employers' training needs' guidance have implemented a one-stop information and advice service and they promote a strategy for referral and collaboration between existing providers of information and advice. A major player in this area is the Employment Service whose advisers carry out around 7 million advisory interviews a year with unemployed people. This may lead clients to go on to review possible routes back to work on Restart Courses, or to look at alternative careers in the recently launched Job Review Workshops.

Although it is recognised that many adults are likely to face some form of career change within their lifetime, research considering this has tended to focus on the individual's resistance to change rather than the employers' response. There is also a tendency for research to focus on the needs of disadvantaged groups and neglect those already in employment, especially professionals, who would benefit from careers counselling. Exceptions are Lane (**669**) and Lancaster (**667**) who have produced valuable articles in this area.

From the material reviewed, there is clearly a consensus for a multi-agency approach if the activity of guidance and counselling is to succeed in helping to widen access and encourage employers to take continuing education and training seriously. Furthermore, the importance of training and development for all staff employed in guidance activities cannot be over-emphasised, especially support staff who can be neglected. Research is beginning to make headway in this area (see: Oakeshott 871).

Further investigation will be necessary using feedback from training provision. Information on the following areas would be useful: the extent of public awareness on training initiatives; the marketing of training; employers' attitudes towards training in relation to non-traditional recruits and the effectiveness of new guidance initiatives on training.

The emerging comparative literature usefully clarifies some of the above issues (see: Rivis 979 and Banks 62). For other useful reports (see: Lowden 701; Fazaeli 389; Munn and MacDonald 804).

6 Northern Ireland

Many of the issues which are raised in the literature on continuing education and training in England and Wales are also of concern in Northern Ireland. However, there are specific features of the situation in Northern Ireland which have attracted particular attention and are worthy of mention here.

The focus of the literature produced on Northern Ireland is very definitely on access to employment and on patterns of employment and unemployment, rather than on access to education and training (see: Eversley 379; Cormack and Osborne 227; Osborne and Cormack 877; Smith 1041). As Osborne and Cormack two of the leading writers in this field argue, there is a need for research which focuses on the 'tightening bond' between access to education, educational outcomes and employment (see: Osborne and Cormack *Unemployment and religion in Northern Ireland* 879).

A feature of the higher education situation which is currently attracting considerable political and media attention is the so called 'brain-drain'. A number of writers have produced evidence on the flow of well qualified Northern Irish entrants to higher education in the rest of the United Kingdom and to a lesser extent the Republic of Ireland without any corresponding influx of English, Welsh or Scottish students (see: Osborne 881; Birley 96; Cormack et al 228). Also of concern is the number who subsequently settle and work outside Northern Ireland. Obviously, this trend has implications both for the higher education system and the economy. The factors most often cited as causing this imbalance include relatively high unemployment, low incomes, geographical isolation and political instability. However, there seems to be little research which firmly establishes the link between the apparent causes and known effects.

Throughout this report we have referred to literature which deals with the problems faced by particular groups such as women, ethnic minorities and the disabled. In the Northern Ireland context the focus of the literature is on the experience of the different religious communities and again the emphasis is on patterns of employment and unemployment. A number of large scale studies and individual pieces of research have been undertaken in this area (see: Great Britain Standing Advisory Committee on Human Rights 502; McCormack and O'Hara 713; Eversley 379; Chambers 173; Smith 1041; Cormack and Osborne 227; Fair Employment Agency 381). Of particular interest is the work of the Fair Employment Agency which is a government financed but independent body which attempts to ascertain the extent of discrimination in the labour market against any minority group but in particular the Roman Catholic community. The research which has been undertaken centres on whether the concentration of members of the Catholic community in relatively lower paid and lower status jobs and their higher levels of unemployment are due to discrimination or to a combination of social factors such as geographical mobility, demography, high fertility and educational attainment. Again, there is a need for research which attempts to explain the labour market positions of the different communities in terms of their educational opportunities and of their ability to translate educational experience into jobs.

Much of the literature on continuing education and training in Northern Ireland reflects the issues raised by that relating to other parts of the United Kingdom. For example, the problems faced by women, prisoners and those requiring training in basic skills in Northern Ireland seem to be substantially the same as those faced by these groups in Britain (see: Murphy 817; Purcell 943; Northern Ireland Council for Continuing Education 868-869). However, there are a number of issues specific to Northern Ireland which warrant further research and where a useful comparative dimension could be incorporated.

The effects of the particular economic and social problems in Northern Ireland on continuing education and training must continue to receive careful monitoring. Such research is necessary for providing the evidence which could support calls for specific action in Northern Ireland. As one example, Cormack et al (228) argue that the student loan scheme does not adequately address regional variation. They believe that it will have a disproportionately negative effect on participation rates in higher education in Northern Ireland where parental support and graduate incomes are lower. The problem of migration to higher education institutions outside Northern Ireland has already been mentioned. One positive effect of falling numbers in Northern Ireland has been that the universities there turned to the 'non-traditional' sector for students much earlier than their counterparts in Britain (see: Osborne et al 882). There is undoubtedly much valuable experience which could be shared in this area. In addition, the establishment of the first trans-binary university in the United Kingdom through the merger of Ulster Polytechnic and the New University of Ulster to form Ulster University must provide useful evidence for mergers in Britain (see: Birley 96).

For an excellent introduction to many aspects of the education system in Northern Ireland Osborne et al *Education and Policy in Northern Ireland* (880) is highly recommended.

7 Scotland

Whilst there is less literature overall about continuing education and training in Scotland than in England and Wales, substantial strides have been made in recent years and the issues addressed and emergent recommendations are very similar.

It is worthwhile considering continuing education and training developments in Scotland separately because it is believed those initiatives being developed to facilitate wider access may be more readily accommodated due to the distinctive features of the Scottish educational system which appear to offer a more manageable environment for mature and non-traditional entry and the expansion of flexible learning and part-time degree provision.

Thus, any analysis of the growing range of learning opportunities available to adults in Scotland must be located within an institutional and cultural framework. For an introduction to some of the variations see Jordinson (626) who considers organisational issues and the development of Access. Niven's paper (865) is also useful for an appraisal of the post secondary vocational and technical educational system in Scotland. Gallacher and Osborne (464) provide a comprehensive comparative analysis of Access provision in Scotland and England. The Scottish Wider Access Programme (SWAP) is reviewed by Tuck in his article Quality Control in the Scottish Wider Access Programme in the *Journal of Access Studies, Spring 1991 Vol 6 No 1* , which discusses in some detail the future strategy and quality assurance arrangements. Clarke describes the role of central institutions and summarises the differences between these and the universities. For other useful discussions (see: Bone 103; DES 280; Horobin and Wilson 570; McLaughlin 737; Gerver 481).

By considering the variations in organisation, we can note that a distinguishing feature of the Scottish education system is its flexibility. Undergraduates take broad-based four year degrees and can defer specialisation for two years within a faculty. The school curriculum is also broader. SCOTVEC modules can be adopted to special needs and are available to anyone over the age of 16 and as Moore (789) has noted many adults returning to work after a break have found the modular system particularly suitable for part-time study and for sampling different vocational areas. For further discussion on SCOTVEC and modularisation (see: Gartside 474; Donaldson 302; Theodossin 1106; Cosgrove and McDonnel 233). Another unique feature attracting support is the use made of schools for adults returning to learning (see: Nicol 863 and MacIntosh 729).

It is also important to consider the cultural variations inherent in Scotland's education system. Milton's short article illuminates this well (see: Milton 781). He emphasises that the educational system is fundamental to Scotland's identity. The universities retain community links and teaching is highly valued. Higher education is therefore less rigid and attracts students from a wider social spectrum. Milton points out that since 1985 when modular national certificates were introduced almost every pupil who stays past 16 has left with a qualification and are much more likely to continue their education in some form. See Picard (919) for a review of the links between universities and the community.

The concept of self-improvement via night classes, or by studying for additional professional qualifications, for example the MBA, via distance learning or part-time study also has a long tradition in Scotland (See: Crozier **258**).

For more specific research on differences in education and training provision, recommended reading is (Lowden et al **701**; Alloway and Nelson **23**). For discussions on community education (see: Barr **68**; Burnes **151**; Alexander and Steward **21**).

Nevertheless, it is clear that many adults in Scotland continue to be sceptical of higher education and many are unaware of, or bewildered by, the diversity in forms of provision. A plethora of literature has emerged reflecting the need to break down barriers in order to attract the non-participant. Bown provides a very useful overview of the research so far completed in Scotland (see: Bown **114**). Much of the research on non-participation has emerged from the Scottish Council for Research into Education; the Scottish Institute of Adult Continuing Education; Scottish Community Education Council and Scottish Enterprise Foundation. For a good selection (see: MacDonald **715**; Munn and MacDonald **804**; Munn et al **807-810**; Lowden et al **701** and Rosa **991**).

Clearly, a lot of attention is given to the motivational characteristics of adults returning to learning and some interesting material has emerged on perceptions of education from the learners viewpoint (see: MacPherson **742**; Togneri **1122**).

One of the main conclusions reached from the research projects is the need for effective guidance and information both for the potential student and employers and this issue has formed the basis of later influential research. Scotland appears to be at the forefront of research which considers guidance for employers training needs (see: Alloway **23**; Docherty **301**; Rosa et al **992**). However, as Bown (**113**) has noted there is less research on other support services such as paid educational leave and childcare facilities.

Whilst research incorporating a gender dimension has a shorter history in Scotland, the demographic downturn and projected decline in the number of under twenty-five's entering the labour market is much larger in Scotland than elsewhere and this has been reflected in the growing literature on women returners and the education and training needs of women (see: Gerver **484**; Hanlow **528**; Hart **535-7**; Steele **1067**).

There is much less which focuses on continuing professional development for women wanting to reach senior managerial positions. One exception is Gerver and Hart *Strategic Women* (**483**) although this tends to emphasise personal attributes and characteristics of successful women rather than the barriers they face. Richardson and Hartshorn (**976**) have looked at gender-specific business training. Also see Roberton (**982**) on women and enterprise training. Further research on women's access to paid educational leave, and promotional prospects is necessary for a better understanding of women's position in the Scottish labour market.

There is also a paucity in the literature on the needs of the other groups we have considered in this report, particularly the needs of ethnic minority groupings and people with disabilities. This point is drawn out by Tuck in 'Quality Control in the Scottish Wider Access Programme' *Journal of Access Studies* Spring 1991; he notes that whilst the Scottish Wider Access Programme has successfully targetted those from socially disadvantaged backgrounds and women returners it has been much less effective in encouraging people with disabilities. Whilst some literature has appeared on access to education for these groups (see: Corner 229-230; Dept of Education Glasgow Division 294; Finn 402), access to training and employment is vastly under-researched which is comparable with the situation south of the border. However, whilst ethnic minorities have been targetted in England and Wales, this has not happened to the same extent in Scotland, perhaps because ethnic minorities are geographically more widely dispersed in Scotland. However, it would be useful to have a detailed picture of ethnic minority access to training and labour market position. A recent survey entitled *Ethnic Minorities in Scotland* published by the Scottish Office Central Research Unit, July 1991, is a useful project which makes a start in addressing this issue.

Research on adult basic education and the needs of offenders also lags behind. However it is clear that the SCOTVEC modules, if suitably adapted, will be invaluable to the needs of these groups. For general discussions on this (see: Hitt 562; Moore 789; Scottish Adult Basic Education Unit 1006; Pearson 907; and Jonathan 619). The education and training needs of prisoners has gained some prominence following the recent report produced by the Scottish Home and Health Department on education in prisons (see: Wright 1245; Henderson 548).

Some Local Enterprise Companies are now concentrating on special needs and high technology training so research which monitors progress will be useful to inform future provision.

Staff development is an area of crucial importance in Scotland (see: Barnes 65; Niven 866; Guy 513; Fordyce and Robinson 414; Cameron 162; Erskine 370; Gartside 473; Shanks 1016). Interest in open learning and flexi-study and the utilisation of public libraries for attracting people to open learning schemes is also growing (see: Scottish Committee on Open Learning 1007; Gellis 479; McElroy 718; Morris 796 and the Scottish Open Learning Consortium 1013.

Progress in the use of distance learning,especially for the rural population has emerged although more research is needed in this area. Some useful work has already appeared (see: Anderson 29; Craig 254; Kirkland 645; and Marker 756). Further research on the motivational characteristics of students undertaking distance learning, especially those in rural population is necessary.

Whilst interest is growing in credit accumulation and transfer and the granting of credit for appropriate prior learning and industrial training there is little in the way of rigorous analysis. However, the ideas behind SCOTCATS again compares with those south of the border. A useful paper addressing SCOTCATS is *Credit Transfer and Recognition Matters* by Harry Mitchell for the Council for National Academic Awards, June 1991. (Also see: CNAA leaflet on Scottish Credit Accumulation and Transfer Scheme 249 ; Baird 47 and Mitchell 784).

The issues currently receiving most attention in Scotland parallel those in the rest of the country: partnerships, enterprise, flexibility and quality. The Scottish Enterprise and Highlands and Islands Enterprise through LECs provide a new framework for training, enterprise and development. Little substantial research has been carried out in these areas but again, strategies tie in with national policies. For some flavour of Scottish developments (see: Scottish Education Department's *Fast Forward with Further Education* (**1009**) which gives a good overview of developments in relation to Local Enterprise Companies and PICKUP Scotland. Munro (**813**) also provides a useful introduction to the development of Local Enterprise Companies. For general discussions on enterprise and links (see: Brown and Fairley **142**; Hood **566**; Cole and Jack **198** and Scott **1003**).

In Scotland, as in England and Wales, there is growing interest in the expansion of part-time degree provision. Gallacher (**463**) provides a useful appraisal of current provision and argues for more research into this area, especially relating to institutional policies, funding and the monitoring of career development.

Our review of the Scottish literature on continuing education and training has shown that a progressive attitude towards initiatives to expand access and the cultural and organisational environment provides a good foundation for change. It will be interesting to monitor future progress and research.

Clearly, further research is needed on access and the impact on people with disabilities; ethnic minorities and the learning support for and career development of women.

To clarify some of the current issues the reader is directed to the comprehensive review of research *Adult Learning in Scotland* edited by David Hartley (**540**).

Conclusions and Further Research

The aim of this research has been to develop a guide to current issues and research on the accessibility and delivery of continuing education and training. This overview has attempted to draw out the conclusions from the recent literature. It is difficult to highlight one theme over another from the total range of research but some trends have emerged.

The barriers to continuing education and training are formidable for many women, ethnic minorities, those with special needs and other non-participant groups. Barriers such as funding are central to the problem of access but barriers operate in a complex, interdependent fashion. Despite a number of initiatives, the structure of continuing education and training still appears to favour those with a good record of traditional educational achievement and those in permanent full-time employment.

The literature has shown that rhetoric and tinkering with equal opportunities policies are not enough to widen access nor to give parity to non-traditional students and alternative modes of learning. When access provision is specifically made for special groups there is still uncertainty about the outcomes for individuals.

The literature survey demonstrates a growing awareness among traditional education institutions of the importance of vocational relevance and outcomes. What is less clear is to what extent employers have modified their recruitment, training and promotion policies to accommodate an increasingly diverse workforce. Without positive career outcomes, the motivation for reforming continuing education and training and the incentives for individual students are diminished.

The concept of lifelong learning seems to have gained wider acceptance and has expanded from the sphere of liberal adult education to the mainstream debate. Although investment in education and training is seen as essential to the long term health of the economy the precise nature and quantitative effects of this relationship are not properly understood.

These and other aspects of the continuing education and training debate have appeared as gaps in the existing literature. The following suggestions for further research may be helpful:

- access to vocational training for ethnic minorities.
- ethnic minority experience in continuing education and training and subsequent performance in the labour market.
- educational and training needs of refugees.
- the experience of adult special needs students in education and training.
- the career development of disabled people.
- the provision of and access to basic skills training.
- the assessment of basic skills needs for particular groups.
- the needs of those whose first language is not English.
- mature student access and outcomes.
- the impact of TECs on equal opportunities.
- guidance in vocational training and for career change.
- feedback on the training needs of employers, especially small and medium sized firms.
- open learning and Employee Development schemes especially in the public sector.
- the perception of quality amongst consumers and employers.
- the linkage between quality and resources.
- the effectiveness of workshadowing.
- drop out and outcomes at all levels of continuing education and training.
- access and outcomes for ethnic and religious minorities in Northern Ireland and Scotland.

LIST OF ABBREVIATIONS AND
ADDRESSES OF ORGANISATIONS

ABE   Adult Basic Education

ACACE   Advisory Council for Adult and Continuing Education (now NIACE).

ACOP   Association of Chief Officers of Probation - 20-30 Lawefield Lane, Wakefield. WF2
            8SP Tel: 0924 361156

AEU   Amalgamated Engineering Union - 110 Peckham Road, London. SE15 5EL
            Tel: 071-703 4231

ALBSU   Adult Literacy and Basic Skills Unit - Kingsbourne House, 229-231 High Holborn,
            London. WC1V 7DA   Tel: 071-405 4017

APEL   Accreditation of Prior Experiential Learning

APEX   APEX Charitable Trust Ltd - 31/33 Clapham Road, London. Tel: 071-582 3171

APL   Accreditation of Prior Learning

APLA   Accreditation of Prior Learning Achievements

BACIE   British Association for Commercial and Industrial Education - 16 Park Crescent,
            London. W1N 4AP   Tel: 071-636 5351

CATS   Credit Accumulation and Transfer Scheme

CBI   Confederation of British Industry - Centre Point, 103 New Oxford Street, London.
            WC1A 1DU Tel: 071-379 7400

CDP   Committee of Directors of Polytechnics - Kirkman House, 12-14 Whitfield Street,
            London. W1P 6AX   Tel: 071-637 9939

CEDEFOP   Centre Europeen de l'Education et Formation Professionelle - Publications c/o HMSO,
            Publications Centre, 51 Nine Elms Lane, London. SW8 5DR Tel: 071-211 5656

CERI   Centre for Educational Research and Innovation - OECD, Chateau de la Muette, 2 rue
            Andre Pascal, Paris 16e, France. Tel: 45 24 82-00

CES   Community Education Service

CET   Continuing Education and Training

CIHE   Council for Industry and Higher Education - 100 Park Village East, London. NW1 3SR

CIs   Central Institutions

CNAA   Council for National Academic Awards - 344-354 Gray's Inn Road, London. WC1X 8BP

COIC   Careers Occupational and Information Centre - Moorfoot, Sheffield S1 4PQ
            Tel: 0742 594563

COMMET	Community Programme for Education and Training in Technologies
CONTACT	Consortium for Advanced Continuing Education and Training - Enterprise House, Lloyd Street North, Manchester. M15 4EN Tel: 061-226 6586
CPD	Continuing Professional Development
CQSW	Certificate of Qualification in Social work
CRAC	Careers Advisory Committee
CRE	Commission for Racial Equality - Elliott House, 10/12 Allington Street, London. SW1 EHE Tel: 071-828 7022
CVCP	Council of Vice-Chancellors and Principals - 29 Tavistock Square London. WC1H 9EZ Tel: 071-387 9231
DE	Department of Employment - Caxton House, Tothill Street, London SW1H 9NF Tel: 071-273 3000
DENI	Department of Education for Northern Ireland - Rathgael House, Balloo Road, Bangor, County Down, Northern Ireland. Tel: 0247 270077
DES	Department of Education and Science - Elizabeth House, York Road, London. SE1 7PH Tel: 071-934 9000
DTI	Department of Trade and Industry - 1-19 Victoria Street, London. SW1H 0ET Tel: 071-215 5000
EC	European Community
ECCTIS	Educational Counselling and Credit Transfer Information Service - Fulton House, Jessop Avenue, Cheltenham. GL50 3GH
ED	Employment Department
EDAP	Employees' Development and Assistance Programme
EGSA	Educational Guidance Service for Adults - Room 208 Bryson House, 28 Bedford Street, Belfast. BT2 7FE Tel: 0232-232587
EHE	Enterprise in Higher Education
EOC	Equal Opportunities Commission - Overseas House, Quay Street, Manchester. M3 3HN Tel: 061-833-9244
ERA	Education Reform Act
ESL	English as a Second Language
ESOL	English for Speakers of Other Languages
ET	Employment Training
FAST	Forum for Access Studies - Derbyshire College of Higher Education, Kedleston Road, Derby. DE3 1GB Tel: 0332 47181

FE	Further Education
FEU	Further Education Unit - 2 Orange Street, London. WC2H 7WE Tel: 071-321 0433
FHE	Further and Higher Education
HE	Higher Education
HEI(s)	Higher Education Institution(s)
HITECCS	Higher Introductory Technology and Engineering Conversion Courses
HMSO	Her Majesty's Stationery Office - Queen Anne's Gate, London. SW1H 9AT
HNC	Higher National Certificate
HND	Higher National Diploma
IDS	Incomes Data Services Ltd. - 193 St. John Street, London. EC1V 4LS Tel: 071-250-3434
IMS	Institute of Manpower Studies
IPM	Institute of Personnel Management - IPM House, Camp Road, Wimbledon, London. SW19 4UW Tel: 081 946 9100
JUPITER	Joint Universities and Polytechnics Industrial Technology Education Research
LEA	Local Education Authority
LECs	local enterprise companies
LET	Learning from Experience Trust - Regent's College, Regent's Park London. NW1 4NS Tel: 071-436 7218
MBA	Master of Business Administration
MIND	National Association for Mental Health - 22 Harley Street, London. SW1H 9NF Tel: 071-213 4424
MSC	Manpower Services Commission
NACAB	National Association of Citizens' Advice Bureaux - 115-123 Pentonville Road, London. N1 9L7 Tel: 071-833 2181
NACRO	National Association for the Care and Resettlement of Offenders - 169 Clapham Road, London. SW9 0PU Tel: 071-582 6500
NAFE	Non-Advanced Further Education
NAPO	National Association of Probation Officers - 3/4 Chivalry Road, London. SW11 1HT Tel: 071-223 4887
NATFHE	National Association of Teachers in Further and Higher Education - 27 Britannia Street, London. WC1X 9JP Tel: 071-837 3636

NCDS	National Child Development Survey
NCVO	National Council for Voluntary Organisations - 26 Bedford Square, London. WC1B 3HU Tel: 071-636-4066
NCVQ	National Council for Vocational Qualifications - 222 Euston Road, London. NW1 2BZ Tel: 071-387 9898
NEGI	National Educational Guidance Initiative - Bowling Green Terrace, Leeds. LS11 9SX Tel: 0532 444414
NHS	National Health Service
NIACE	National Institute for Adult Continuing Education - 19B De Montfort Street, Leicester. LE1 7GE Tel: 0533 551451
NICEC	National Institute for Careers, Education and Counselling - Sheraton House, Gloucester Street, Castle Park, Cambridge. CB3 0AX Tel: 0223 460277
NORSWAP	North of Scotland Consortium of the Scottish Wider Access Programme - Summerhill Academy, Stronsay Drive, Aberdeen. AB2 6JA Tel: 0224 313391
NTS	National Training Survey
NUS	National Union of Students - 461 Holloway Road, London. N7 6LJ Tel: 071-272 8900
NVQ(s)	National Vocational Qualification(s)
OECD	Organisation for Economic Co-operation and Development - Directorate for Social Affairs, Manpower and Education, 2 Rue Andre-Pascal 75775 Paris Cedex 16, France. Tel: 010-33-1-4- 524 8200
OU	Open University - Walton Hall, Milton Keynes. MK7 6AA Tel: 0908 274066
PCFC	Polytechnics and Colleges Funding Council - Metropolis House, 22 Percy Street, London. W1P 9FF Tel: 071 436 4320
PGCE	Postgraduate Certificate of Education
PICKUP	Professional, Industrial and Commercial Updating Programme - Department of Education and Science, Elizabeth House, York Road, London. SE1 7PH Tel: 071-934 9790
PSI	Policy Studies Institute - Publications Dept, 100 Park Village East, London. NW1 3SR Tel: 071-387-2171
REPLAN	DES Programme for the Adult Unemployed [now defunct] - 19B De Montfort Street Leicester. LE1 7GE Tel: 0533 551451
RSA	Royal Society of Arts - 8 John Adam Street, London. WC2N 6EZ Tel: 071-930 5115
RVQ	Review of Vocational Qualifications
SABEU	Scottish Adult Basic Education Unit

SCEC	Scottish Community Education Council - West Coates House, Haymarket Terrace, Edinburgh. Tel: 031-313 2488
SCET	Scottish Council for Educational Technology - Dowanhill, 74 Victoria Crescent Road, Glasgow. G12 9JN
SCID	Scottish Council for Development and Industry - Campsie House, 17 Park Circus Place, Glasgow. G3 6AH Tel: 041 332 9119
SCOL	Scottish Committee on Open Learning - Dowanhill, 74 Victoria Crescent Road, Glasgow. G12 9JN
SCOTVEC	Scottish Vocational Education Council - Hanover House, 24 Douglas Street, Glasgow. G2 7NG Tel: 041 248 7900
SCRE	Scottish Council for Research in Education - 15 St John Street, Edinburgh. EH1 8JR Tel: 031-557 2944
SEB	Scottish Education Board
SED	Scottish Education Department - New St. Andrew's House, St. James Centre, Edinburgh. EH1 2SY Tel: 031-244-4492
SIACE	Scottish Institute of Adult Continuing Education (now defunct)
SRHE	Society for Research into Higher Education - University of Surrey, Guildford. GU2 5XH Tel: 0483 39003
SWAP	Scottish Wider Access Programme - 4-6 Nicoll Street, Dundee . DD1 1LY Tel: 0382 202904
TA	Training Agency
TAPs	Training and Access Points
TDIS	Training Development Information Service
TEC(s)	Training and Enterprise Council(s)
TEED	Training, Enterprise and Education Directorate - The Employment Department, Moorfoot, Sheffield. S1 4PQ Tel: 0742 753275
TUC	Trades Union Congress - Congress House, Great Russell Street, London. WC1B 3LS Tel: 071-636 4030
TURU	Trade Union Research Unit - Transport House, Smith Square, London. SW1
TVEI	Technical and Vocational Education Initiative
UCCA	Universities Central Council on Admissions - PO Box 28, Cheltenham, Gloucestershire. GL50 1HY Tel: 0242 222444
UDACE	Unit for the Development of Adult Continuing Education - Christopher House, 94B London Road, Leicester. LE2 0QS Tel: 0533 854436

UFC	Universities Funding Council - 14 Park Crescent, London. W1N 4DH Tel: 071-636 7799
UMIST	University of Manchester Institute of Science and Technology - PO Box 88, Sackville Street, Manchester. M60 1QD Tel: 061-200 3995
UNESCO	United Nations Educational, Scientific and Cultural Organisation - 7 Place de Fontenoy, 75700 Paris, France. Tel: 010-33-1-4 568 1000
VET	Vocational Education and Training
WEA	Workers' Educational Association - Temple House, 9 Upper Berkeley Street, London. W1H 8BY Tel: 071-402 5608
WI	Women's Institute
WISE	Women in Science and Engineering
WPRC	Women Prisoners' Resource Centre - 1 Thorpe Close, Ladbroke Grove, London. W10 5XL Tel: 071-968 3121
WRFE	Work Related Further Education
WRNAFE	Work Related Non-Advanced Further Education
YTS	Youth Training Scheme

BIBLIOGRAPHY

1   **Abilities not Disabilities** *Abilities not disabilities - video and training pack A staff resource* London Team Video Productions Ltd 1990
This video confronts the difficult issue of integrating people with disabilities in a natural and thought provoking manner. Taking the form of a documentary drama, the pack comes complete with training notes and checklists written by disabled people. The package will enable organisations to run staff training sessions to examine their existing situations and to plan for future developments. Address: Canalot, 222 Kensal Road, London W10 5BN

2   **Action on Long Term Employment** *ET: going for quality* London Action 1989 9 pages
Reports on a series of interviews with trainees on the Employment Training scheme which aimed to assess the quality of the training they had received.

3   **Adult Literacy and Basic Skills Unit** *After the act: developing basic skills work in the 1990's* London ALBSU 1988
Looks at the implications of the 1988 Education Reform Act for basic skills work. Considers how a framework for basic skills can be organised, established and funded within the post compulsory education system.

4   **Adult Literacy and Basic Skills Unit** *Basic education and unemployment* London ALBSU 1987 23 pages
Examines the links between problems with basic literacy and numeracy and unemployment.

5   **Adult Literacy and Basic Skills Unit** *Basic skills and schemes of delegation* London ALBSU 1989 24 pages
Analyses the impact of the 1988 Education Reform Act on the provision of basic skills teaching in the light of the Schemes of Delegation of Colleges.

6   **Adult Literacy and Basic Skills Unit and Manpower Services Commission** *Basic skills and unemployed adults: a report on ALBSU/MSC* London ALBSU 1987 24 pages
Reports on six projects conducted to help meet the basic communication needs of unemployed adults who embark on work-related training. Discusses new ways of assessing literacy and numeracy needs in a vocational context.

7   **Adult Literacy and Basic Skills Unit** *English as a second language: provision for adults in England and Wales* London ALBSU 1987 12 pages
Reports on data received from over 100 local education authorities about English as a second language provision in England and Wales. Suggests ways in which such provision should be developed.

8   **Adult Literacy and Basic Skills Unit** *Evaluating effectiveness in adult literacy and basic skills* London ALBSU 1987
Document aimed at local education authorities to enable them to monitor and evaluate their basic skills provision. Contains examples of good practice and a checklist for organisers.

9   **Adult Literacy and Basic Skills Unit** *Literacy and numeracy for work: case studies for training agents and training managers* London ALBSU 1988
Presents thirteen case studies which demonstrate good practice in the areas of organisation, assessment and delivery of basic skills training for the workplace.

10 **Adult Literacy and Basic Skills Unit** *Literacy, numeracy and adults: evidence from the national child development study* London ALBSU 1987 88 pages
Reports on the National Child Development Study - a study of people born in one week in 1958. Identifies those within this group who have problems with literacy and numeracy and looks at the special difficulties they face.

11 **Adult Literacy and Basic Skills Unit** *A nation's neglect: research into the needs for English amongst speakers of other languages* London ALBSU 1988 12 pages
Reports on an ALBSU survey which researched the degree and nature of the needs of those adults whose first language is not English.

12 Adult Literacy and Basic Skills Unit *Promoting basic skills: an information guide for TECs* London ALBSU 1991 36 pages
Outlines the importance of basic skills training in strengthening the overall skills base. The objectives of the document are to provide information about basic skills needs, offer models for the delivery of such training and discuss strategies to ensure high quality training in the future.

13 Adult Literacy and Basic Skills Unit *Publicising adult literacy and basic skills* London ALBSU 1985 60 pages
A practical guide aimed at the organisers of basic education which advises on the marketing and publicising of provision. Includes sections on the press, television, radio and the use of the printed word. Stresses the need for evaluation and monitoring of the process.

14 Adult Literacy and Basic Skills Unit *Resources: a guide to adult literacy and basic skills material* London ALBSU 1989 218 pages
A useful guide which gives details of over 400 published items and assesses their suitability for use in basic education work.

15 Adult Literacy and Basic Skills Unit *Resourcing adult literacy and basic skills* London ALBSU 1987 21 pages
Describes and discusses the level of funding needed to maintain high quality basic skills provision.

16 Adult Literacy and Basic Skills Unit *Setting up workplace basic skills training* London ALBSU 1987 64 pages
A handbook to support the work of those involved in basic skills training at work. Provides information on identifying training needs and marketing provision. Gives some accounts of this type of work in practice.

17 Adult Training Promotions Unit *New Training Initiatives* London DES 1990
A bulletin produced by the Adult Training Promotions Unit which reviews the latest developments in Local Collaborative Projects: partnerships between industry and training providers to make adult training relevant to the needs of local industries. *New Training Initiatives* looks at lessons that can be drawn from the programme gained from a number of case studies. The main points are conveniently summarized.

18 Adults Learning The impact of the community charge on adult education provision *Adults Learning* Vol 2 No 2 1991 34-36
Reports on a survey undertaken by NIACE which assessed the impact of the community charge and in particular charge-capping on the provision of adult education by local authorities.

19 Agnelli G. Industry's expectations of the university *CRE-action* 1988/9 11-17
An interesting article which stresses that the university, by long tradition, exists, and should continue to exist for pure research and academic investigation unlimited by time or purpose. However, whilst the university must retain its autonomy, the author asserts it must also reflect on the needs of a modern society and develop effective working methods and relationship with the outside world.

20 Aitken J. The access debate *Teaching News* No.31 July 1987 8-10
The main thrust of this concise report is the importance of attitudinal change and commitment towards widening access to higher education. Once the possible restructuring of provision is actually willed, then structural change should be sought.

21 Alexander D.J. and Steward T.G. Issues in the development of guidance on adult learning opportunities in Scotland *Studies in the Education of Adults* Vol 20 No 1 April 1988 29-48
An excellent in depth appraisal of developments in the field of guidance for adult learners. Documents the developments in adult continuing education and training, guidance and general education programmes in Scotland. Discusses the advantages of collaborative and multi-agency networks and records the experiences of Gorgie-Dalry Adult Learning Project and Linwood Information Centre (LINFO) which is held up as an excellent model of a shop-front, one-door entry agency. Concludes with some useful recommendations, notably the need for a National Unit for the Guidance of Adults.

22 Alldred J. et al *Managing information on educational guidance* NIACE/UDACE 1988 120 pages
This handbook is for those who provide adults with information about all kinds of opportunities for learning and provides details about all present information services operating and aims to help those developing their own local information files and databases by using the experience of those who have already done this.

23 Alloway J. and Nelson P. *Advice and guidance to individuals: a project report* Leicester UDACE 1987 66 pages
A major national survey into the guidance needs of adults about education and training, based on the views of 5500 people questioned by telephone questionnaire or in-depth interview. It addresses job change and career choice advice and stresses the importance of agencies knowing what adults and employers think about the services which exist.

24 Alloway J. and Opie L. *Setting up an educational guidance service: some ideas* Leicester UDACE 1987 34 pages
This booklet builds on previous reports and looks at some of the questions which need to be considered by those involved in planning a multi-agency guidance network. Social, political, economic and demographic factors will influence development and will lead to Local Educational Guidance units taking a unique form reflecting their environment.

25 Alloway J. and Opie L. *Understanding educational guidance* Leicester UDACE/NIACE 1988 50 pages
A picture of educational guidance development in response to local needs, with case studies providing practical illustrations.

26 Ames C. *Financial barriers to access* Leicester NIACE 1986 38 pages
Report of a project which considered the rules and regulations applying to adults in education and training. Looks at fees and concessions, awards and benefits and examines their effect on learners and potential learners.

27 Ames J.C *Administrative barriers to access. Second draft project report* 1986 54 pages

28 Anderson D. The Open University: a resource for training in community education *Scottish Journal of Adult Education* Vol 8 No 1 Spring 1987 35-38
Drawing on the proposals outlined in 'Training for Change' this article gives an indication of the possible links between the Training for Change Core Curriculum suggestions and relevant Open University courses. The paper suggests that the wealth of material in the Open University degree, associate and continuing education programmes can be adapted to any training system, especially individual patterns of training and professional development.

29 Anderson G. MBAs tailored to suit the company shape *Personnel Management* Vol 21 No 12 December 1989 71-73
Describes the University of Strathclyde's innovative developments in the structure of the MBA. Strathclyde was the first to offer the MBA by distance learning and is now designing a distinctive in-company MBA programme that will contain many of the elements which companies regard as important.

30 Anderson J.C. Management of professional training in higher education: challenges and opportunities *Educational Management and Administration* Vol 15 No 3 Autumn 1987 183-192

31 Apex Scotland *Apex Scotland - Annual Report 1990* Edinburgh Apex Scotland 1991 23 pages
This report usefully describes developments throughout Scotland in prison-based employment preparation courses, employment counselling centres, training workshops and job club facilities.

32 Apex Trust *Breaking the cycle* London Apex Trust 1990
This report focuses on the role which training and employment play in reducing the temptation of crime and the involvement which employers could and should have in this process. A number of valuable recommendations are posited.

33 Apex Trust Review 1990 *Time for action, time for change* London Apex Trust 1990 17 pages
This valuable review considers the Employment Impact Programme. Each Impact Centre can provide a resource bank on a whole

range of services: employment training, job search advice, employer liaison and work preparation. Apex Trust will be establishing a network of such centres throughout the country. Vocational skills training and job search assistance remain at the top of the agenda.

34 Arkin A. Giving credit to prior learning *Personnel Management* Apr 1991 41-43
Examines the issues surrounding accreditation of prior learning and the experience of two organisations which have already been involved in the area. The counsellor's role is portrayed as one of mediator who helps a candidate to review prior experience and match their likely competencies to the units or modules that make up an award which can be certificated.

35 Arkin A. Reskilling when disability strikes *Personnel Management* Vol 22 Issue 12 December 1990 53-54
Reviews Enham Village Centre, a charitable organisation which helps companies looking for ways of retraining staff who wish to return to work after a serious accident or illness. Enham's assessment programme uses real and simulated work to explore individuals' strengths and limitations.

36 Arnett J. Educating Peter *Adult Education* Vol 61 No 2 September 1988 115-117
The integration of adults with learning difficulties into mainstream provision is a desirable objective. John Arnett recounts his experience of attempting such integration with an individual student and the frustrations for the teacher of failing in the attempt.

37 Ashworth P. Is 'competence' good enough? *NATFHE Journal* Vol 15 No 6 1990 24-25
Argues against competence being the key to teaching assessment as the concept is unclear and the ideas superficial. Also, it seeks to describe human actions in an inappropriate and technically oriented way.

38 Ashworth P. and Saxton J. On 'competence' *Journal of Further and Higher Education* Vol 14 No 2 1990 3-25
Discusses the appropriateness of competence to describe aspects of human activity and the implications for education and training of using competence as a measure of outcome.

Argues that the notion of competence has not been clearly defined and that its use tries to oversimplify the complex processes at work.

39 Association of Chief Officers of Probation *Employment in prisons and for ex-offenders* London HMSO July 1991 100 pages
This paper draws on the submission by the Association of Chief Officers of Probation to the Employment Committee. Outlines the background to the Association's concern with employment issues, some of the measures that have been taken to tackle the problems faced by unemployed offenders and recommendations for future action by the key agencies who can contribute to improvements in the current situation both for offenders in custody and in the community.

40 Audit Commission *Obtaining better value from further education* London HMSO 1985 87 pages
Project in which auditors examined in detail the way resources are used in 165 polytechnics and colleges of further education.

41 Aughterson K. and Foley K. *Opportunity lost: a survey of the intentions and attitudes of young people as affected by the proposed system of student loans* London National Union of Students 1989 80 pages
Reports on research undertaken by the National Union of Students which surveyed the likely effects of the proposed system of student loans on the attitudes of young people who are considering entering higher education.

42 Avis J. White ethnicity white racism: teacher and student perceptions of FE *Journal of Moral Education* Vol 17 Jan 1988 52-60
Considers how race is perceived in a further education college through interviews with students and questionnaires with teachers. Discusses student attitudes to racism and teacher's attitudes to positive discrimination. Suggests there is institutional racism in further education. Argues that white ethnicity is not recognised in the same way as black ethnicity and therefore becomes normalised and powerful.

43 Bagchi A. Access courses and bilingual students *Journal of Access Studies* Vol 1 No 2 1986 62-67

Examines the relatively poor representation of Asian students on Access courses compared to Afro-Caribbeans. Considers the issues raised by offering a BEd Access course for bilingual

students in terms of recruitment, curriculum and the use of language.

44 Bailey D. *Guidance in open learning: a manual of practice* London NICEC/MSC 1987 204 pages
A training and reference resource intended to help those planning open learning schemes to link theory and practice about the guidance process.

45 Bailey D. Open learning and guidance *British Journal of Guidance and Counselling* Vol 15 1987 237-256
A valuable and in-depth account of the relationship between guidance and open learning which uses a framework based on the policy objectives of providers (enablement, enfranchisement, cost effectiveness) and on the components of learning (content, media, styles). The survey indicates a need for better evaluation strategies and a closer scrutiny of what is 'opened' for whom.

46 Bailey J. Adult training through college/company partnerships *Personnel Management* Sept 1986 38-41
A recent project between the Institute of Personnel Management and the DES, Professional, Industrial and Commercial Updating (PICKUP) unit examined how employers and colleges are working together to train adult employees. Data was gathered on 127 institutions. Results indicated the progressive higher education institutions can and do work effectively with employing organisations. However the two predominant learner types identified were managers/supervisors and engineers.

47 Baird G. Would you credit it? *Journal for Further and Higher Education in Scotland* vol 15 Part 2 1991 7-10
Describes the Accreditation of Prior Learning Service being introduced by a number of Colleges in the UK with particular reference to Elmwood College, a 'multi-tech' in Fife with a large emphasis on the education and training requirements of the rural community which is one of a number of colleges in Scotland piloting the APL service. The project based at

Elmwood was set up to evaluate the provision of the service to the Agricultural and Horticultural industries. Case studies showing effective recognition of skills and knowledge through APL are presented.

48 Baker C. and Thomas K. The participation of ethnic minority students in a college of further education *Journal of Further and Higher Education* vol 9 no 1 1985 47-55
Recognises lack of data on ethnic minorities in FE. Cites available research and summarises conclusions about relative under achievement and different performance by different ethnic groups. Research involved interviewing twelve Asian and West Indian students in an FE college about their reasons for taking post 16 education, for choosing an FE college, subject choice, parental support and career plans. Discusses factors affecting ethnic minority participation in FE including the British school system, unemployment, racial prejudice and stereotyping.

49 Ball C. *Aim higher: Widening access to higher education* RSA/Industry matters project Aim higher interim report London RSA 1989 43 pages
Interim Report for the Education/Industry Forum's Higher Education Steering Group produced as part of the Industry Matters campaign.

50 Ball C. *Fitness for purpose: essays in higher education* Surrey SRHE 1985 133 pages
A collection of twenty short essays on various aspects of the higher education system. The underlying theme is what the author sees as the unduly narrow purpose of much higher education and the disparity between the experience of higher education and the life and work faced by students after graduation.

51 Ball C. and Eggins H. (Ed) *Higher education into the 1990s* Milton Keynes SRHE/OU Press 1989 132 pages
This book considers the new dimensions being introduced into higher education which are likely to have marked effects in the 1990s, with special emphasis on changes in access patterns. It usefully brings together contributors with a wide range of expertise who point towards a future shape of higher education which will be more relevant and effective.

52 **Ball C.** *Learning pays: the role of post-compulsory education and training* London RSA April 1991 48 pages

This report gives many key leads on the importance of a learning society. The theme of cooperation between government, education and enterprise is evident throughout the document as an essential requisite for a learning society.

53 **Ball C.** The merging of the PCFC and the UFC: probable, desirable or inevitable? *Higher Education Quarterly* Vol 45 No 2 1991 115-117

Reviews the strategies applied to post-war funding of higher education. Considers the implications of the merger of the PCFC and the UFC and the reorganisation of research funding.

54 **Ball C.** *More means different. Widening access to higher education.* RSA/Industry matters final report London RSA 1990 76 pages

This report, based on wide consultation, offers recommendations for post-compulsory educational reform. The targets recommended here for higher education institutions are, as the author asserts, ambitious. The findings and major recommendations are conveniently summarized.

55 **Ball C.** Should education continue? *Adults Learning* Vol 1 No 1 Sept 1989 page 7

Suggests we must learn to recognise deferred progression into further and higher education as normal and sensible. The author advocates a learning society should be created in which lifelong learning is the norm, not the exception. Continuing education should become a mainstream and not a peripheral activity.

56 **Ball W.** Equal opportunities and post-sixteen education: strategies for institutional change, possibilities and constraints *Journal of Further and Higher Education* Vol 12 No 1 1988 54-69

Discusses the implications of Equal Opportunities policies in 16+ education. The article concentrates on local initiatives and provides a framework for interpreting policy. Taking a Midlands local authority as a case study it looks at Access courses and other initiatives.

57 **Ballard R. and Vellins S.** South Asian entrants to British universities: a comparative note *New Community* Vol 12 No 3 1985 260-265

Assesses the relative success of South Asian students compared with white students at British Universities using data from the 1981 census. Analyses Asian students by birthplace and gender and discovers great differences eg relatively high numbers of East African students and low numbers of Bangladeshis. Advances economic and environmental arguments for these different rates of achievement.

58 **Bamford C.** *Gender and education in Scotland - a review* Edinburgh SIACE 1988 86 pages

This review covers all aspects of education and is particularly useful for an overview on gender issues in adult and continuing education.

59 **Bamford C. and McCarthy C. (Ed)** *Women mean business - a practical guide for women returners* London BBC Books 1991 242 pages

Gives information and advice on all the areas that women who are planning to return to work need to tackle. The guide is both informative and accessible.

60 **Bamford C.** Initiatives in women's education: Canada and Scotland compared *Scottish Journal of Adult Education* Vol 8 No 3 Spring 1988 10-16

Compares and contrasts provision of courses specifically for women, in Scotland and Canada. These courses have grown rapidly in response to the growing awareness, in both countries, of the value of special initiatives to meet women's educational needs.

61 **Banking and Financial Training** Scottish Amicable Quality Programme *Banking and Financial Training* Vol 7 No 3 August 1991 page 32

Describes Scottish Amicable's effective 'quality and service initiative' which entailed the development of good training programmes and an evolution in culture. The training programme placed emphasis on personal development, positive thinking and the improvement of teamworking skills. Stresses the importance of being able to transfer learning to the workplace.

62 **Banks J.A.G.** et al *The single European market and its implications for educational and vocational guidance services.* CRAC occasional paper Cambridge CRAC 1989

This is a valuable and readable report of the Women in Higher Education project based in the King's College Research Centre. It consists of two parts: the first contains the findings and recommendations of the project, and the second presents material on the background to the project and the College's response to it. Using action research, the report highlights negative aspects of academic life at King's and its function is to serve as a basis for change within the College although the problems of women in higher education are considered in a wider context and the report will therefore be of interest to those concerned with higher education and education in general.

63 **Barden L.** UK polytechnic higher education: the essential role of competence *Industry and Higher Education* Vol 3 No 1 1989 37-43

Discusses the lack of any theoretical framework by which the higher education offered in polytechnics can be assessed. The author offers a model based on competence to ensure that polytechnics deliver the kind of education needed.

64 **Barnes A.J.L. and Barr N.** *Strategy for higher education: the alternative white paper* Aberdeen Aberdeen University Press 1988

65 **Barnes C.** Access and staff development *Journal of Access Studies* Vol 5 No 1 Spring 1990 93-99

The author, who is an Access course Development Officer presents a valuable review of a project designed to monitor and increase awareness of access by helping staff involved in receiving Access students to recognise these students may have different needs to non-Access students. The various work sheets and discussion groups are discussed and the points raised are used to develop new training programmes for staff.

66 **Barnett R.** Responsiveness and fulfilment: the value of higher education in the modern world *Higher Education Review* Vol 22 No 2 Spring 1990 59-69

Reviews recent developments in higher education: DES PICKUP, COMETT and the Enterprise Initiative and discusses some of the abilities and skills employers increasingly say they expect from graduates for example, oral skills, wider communication skills, interpersonal skills, creative problem solving, team working and an awareness of political and economic affairs. The author concludes this list is similar to the qualities which some current initiatives in higher education are seeking to foster as witnessed in the new vocabulary: enterprise skills, transferable skills, student competencies. The author argues however that starting from the viewpoint of the graduate in industry often neglects the qualities of human development which is an essential outcome of a degree.

67 **Barnett R.A.** The maintenance of quality in the public sector of UK higher education *Higher Education* Vol 16 No 3 1987 279-301

Describes the role of the CNAA and other agencies in determining the quality of education in colleges in the public sector. Comparisons are made between the ways in which courses are reviewed in colleges and universities.

68 **Barr J.** Keeping a low profile: adult education in Scotland *Adult Education* Vol 59 No 4 March 1987 329-334

An account of the current situation of adult education in Scotland and looks at the implications if provision is further reduced.

69 **Barr N.** *Student loans: the next steps* Aberdeen Aberdeen University Press 1989 87 pages

Criticises the governments proposed system of student loans. proposes a system of repayments linked to the national insurance system which the author argues would improve access and allow for the expansion of the higher education system without recourse to the Treasury.

70 **Barrett M.** *NVQs A report on the training for employment seminar* Nottingham University of Nottingham, Adult Education 1989 17-21

A succinct and useful introductory account describing the structure and role of NVQs.

71 **Barry M.** The unemployed: adult education consumers and producers *Journal of Further and Higher Education* Vol 10 No 1 1986 3-8

Examines the recent history and role of adult education in providing continuing education for the unemployed. Discusses this shift of what the author terms liberal to utilitarian adult education.

72   **Barry M.** The universities and continuing education *Adult Education* Vol 61 No 4 March 1989 352-355
Warns of the dangers of using continuing education purely as an income generator through self-contained updating units and argues it must also be seen as teaching and research in continuing education or may in a time of retrenchment go the way of extra mural departments.

73   **Basic Skills Accreditation Initiative** *Better basic skills better work: the basic skills initiative in the workplace* London BSAI 1990 19 pages
Reports on a joint Training Agency/ALBSU project to promote better basic skills training in the workplace.

74   **Bates S.** A step ahead and a step behind Europe *The Guardian* 27 August 1991 page 17
Summarizes findings of a series on education in EC countries. Education has become a top political priority across national borders and all countries are embarking on similar types of reform. Whilst the author concludes Britain does not compare as badly as is assumed to other countries it is clear that the comparisons of outcomes are not favourable. Discusses the low status of vocational education in Britain compared with other countries and is sceptical about rhetoric stressing the idea of developing comparability between academic and vocational qualifications.

75   **Bateson B. and Bateson G.** Women's education: definition and content *Adults Learning* Vol 1 No 4 Dec 1989 100-101
Discusses the aims of a curriculum for women's education. Argues women's education is fundamentally concerned with personal change: developing confidence and self-esteem. Women's education also provides the opportunity to collectively discuss common issues effecting women through case studies and personal experiences.

76   **Bathie D.** et al *The marketing of further education - a development model* Stirling The

Scottish Enterprise Foundation June 1988 90 pages
This study reports on the current and potential impact of marketing on the Further and Higher Education sector of Scotland. Reviews current marketing practices in a specific sample of colleges and attempts to determine their effectiveness. The study also compares the practices of the sector with standards of good marketing practices derived from elsewhere. The study pays particular attention to processes associated with building into College practice a marketing approach as well as identifying the resources needed to promote marketing development.

77   **Baxter C.** et al *Double discrimination: issues and services for people with learning difficulties from black and ethnic minority communities* London Commission for Racial Equality 1991 212 pages
Looks at the issues facing ethnic minority people with learning difficulties. Provides a starting point for planners, managers and providers who are developing anti-racist services.

78   **Bayliss V.** Doing good by stealth *Employment Gazette* July 1991 393-396
A useful article reinforcing the need for initiatives to increase the general level of education in the workforce in order to improve work satisfaction, increase flexibility and develop high-tech skills for the future. The Employment Department has developed a number of such initiatives which are systematically documented in this article.

79   **Becton K.** Women returners in employment training *Employment Training News* No 18 Feb/March 1990 20-21
Looks at the Women Returners course run by Mainport Training Ltd to prepare women to re-enter the labour market, and the back-up provided by the Employment Training programme.

80   **Bees M. and Swords M. (Ed)** *National vocational qualifications and further education* London Kogan Page 1990 223 pages
Describes the background and issues relating to the introduction of NVQs. Includes sections on TECs, marketing and special needs students. Also useful for those working outside the further education sector.

81 **Beloff, Lord** Universities and the public purse: an update *Higher Education Quarterly* Vol 44 No 1 1990 3-20
Discusses what the author sees as the basic incompatibility of the state funding of higher education and the autonomy of universities. Argues that the general public are not interested in university values and that this will hasten their decline.

82 **Benn R.** The need for a fourth recognised route into higher education *Journal of Access Studies* Vol 6 No 2 1991 210-215
Reviews the three generally recognised routes into higher education: traditional sixth form qualifications, vocational qualifications and access courses and questions the basic assumption that these are sufficient to cover all those with the necessary qualities to benefit from higher education.

83 **Bennett R.** Through the open door: today's revolution in open access and distance learning: introduction - what is open learning? *Journal of European Industrial Training (UK)* Vol 10 No 6 1986 3-7
A useful overview of open learning, when and where it is used and issues to consider when implementing open learning programmes.

84 **Berdahl R.O. et al** *Quality and access in higher education* Buckingham Society for Research into Higher Education 1991 176 pages
A collection of thirteen essays which explore the differences between the British and American systems of higher education through the themes of quality and access. The British system is seen to be highly selective and characterised by high academic quality while the American system is more accessible and marked by diversity of standards and delivery.

85 **Berlove S.** What kind of career counselling do women need? *Women's Education* Vol 4 No 2 Winter 1985 6-11

86 **Berry J.S. and Whitworth R.** Case study: access to engineering through HITECC *Educational and Training Technology International* Vol 26 No 1 Feb 1989 23-30
A valuable paper which explores the various routes to engineering and in particular the 'open access' route for mature students. Proposes the use of self-learning packages on access courses. The authors discuss HITECC courses which have proved successful to date, and the Advanced Physics Project for Independent Learning Scheme (APPIL).

87 **Berryman S.** Access to higher education: equal opportunities for women *Journal of Access Studies* Vol 2 No 2 1987 22-32
The importance of adult education and academic 'second chance' in furthering women's opportunities is now well understood. The author argues the need to translate verbal support, often expressed in equal opportunities statements, into practical action to rectify the imbalance between the use men have made of the education system at the higher levels and the failure of women to gain equal access. The purpose of this article is to place Access course development in the context of this change and to suggest how those working in the field might create a more 'women friendly' environment to take full advantage of the shift in outlook.

88 **Berry-Lound D.** Towards the family-friendly firm *Employment Gazette* Vol 98 No 2 1990 85-91
This article draws on a recent report examining child and elder care schemes to help employees combine professional and domestic responsibilities. The main recommendation is the need for an integrated approach if employers are to develop effective solutions. This would include flexible working systems, part-time career paths, formal career break schemes and re-entry, refresher training.

89 **Betts D. et al** Life after the Education Reform Act *Coombe Lodge Reports* Vol 20 No 11 1988 659-773
Collects together the sixteen contributions given at a series of seminars held by the Further Education Staff College on the impact of the Education Reform Act on further education.

90 **Bilborough B. et al** Developing the responsive college *Coombe Lodge Reports* Vol 20 No 10 1988
The whole issue is devoted to reporting on a further education marketing development initiative - the Responsive College Programme, which involved projects in 21 local authorities. It reports on the aims of the project and on initiatives on quality control, market research and customer communication. Two case

studies are used to examine the issues involved in implementing the proposals.

91   Bilham T. Two cheers for the UFC *PICKUP in Progress* No 19 Oct 1989 9-10
Examines the benefits and problems of the new UFC scheme for funding continuing education.

92   Birch D. et al Through the open door - today's revolution in open access and distance learning in further education *Journal of European Industrial Training* Vol 10 No 6 1986 23-30
Reviews the concept of 'open learning' and suggests open learning systems can be college based, local or distant. Open learning students must be mature enough to work on their own with learning materials. Concludes progress is slow due to lack of suitable learning materials and a general reluctance to innovate.

93   Birch W. Cloistered against the real world: lack of openness in the modern university *Times Higher Education Supplement* No 900 February 2nd 1990 page 18
Reports on the lack of openness in the modern university and argues there should be a constant search for a vigorous interactive relationship within a more open system. Such a relationship it is suggested demands a mutual respect for what the other does. Also discusses the need for a re-appraisal of undergraduate education to determine whether the prevalence of highly specialised honours degrees can meet the need of the great majority of students who take a degree in preparation for future employment.

94   Birchall D.W. Third generation distance learning *Journal of European Industrial Training* Vol 14 No 7 1990 17-20
Reports on Henley Distance Learning Ltd. who have become the major providers of distance education for managers in the UK and other countries. Also looks at Henley Extended Learning Programme which allows students and course administrators to communicate via personal computers.

95   Bird J. and Baxter A. The politics of access: access, students, loans and vocationalism *Journal of Access Studies* Vol 4 No 1-2 1989 43-51
Examines the implications of student loans for Access students through a survey of students in the Avon area. Researches their attitude to loans and assesses how likely they would be to undertake an Access course if their grant was replaced by a loan.

96   Birley D. Crossing Ulster's other great divide *Higher Education Quarterly* Vol 45 No 2 1991 125-144
An interesting account of the background to the formation of the first trans-binary university in the UK. The University of Ulster was formed by the merger of the New University of Ulster and Ulster Polytechnic. The attitude of the older Queen's University of Belfast to the new university is discussed. The article looks at some of the issues associated with the objectives and co-ordination of higher education in Northern Ireland both before and after the merger.

97   Bishop R. Part-time higher education in Northern Ireland *Open Learning* Vol 4 No 2 1989 21-25
Describes the history and current patterns of part-time higher education provision in Northern Ireland. Assesses the 'openness' of these learning opportunities many of which still require traditional qualifications. Outlines some of the access initiatives currently being undertaken. Calls for more co-ordinated planning of part-time higher education.

98   Black H. and Wolf A. (Ed) *Knowledge and competence* London COIC 1990 69 pages
A collection of papers exploring the issue of the role of knowledge and understanding in performance. It then discusses the implications of this in the use of occupational standards and training measures.

99   Blackburn R. and Hankinson A. Training in the smaller business: investment or expense? *Industrial and Commercial Training* Vol 21 No 2 1989 27-29
Small companies in particular suffer from shortages of skilled labour. Drawing on recent surveys of small companies the authors show that low participation in formal training was attributed to its expense and purported inappropriateness. The vast majority of training was on-the-job and informal.

100 Blin-Stoyle R. An alternative passport to higher education *Education* Vol 167 No 21 1986 473-474

Argues for a better way of selection than the rigid A-level grading system.

101 Boaden M. *Mature student finance: a study of discretionary grant and educational trust funding in higher education* Liverpool Polytechnic 1990
Reports on the financial circumstances of students on CQSW courses. The report examines changes in the allocation of discretionary LEA awards and looks at trends in the awards made to mature students by four educational trusts. Includes a list of recommendations focusing on the need for such vocational courses to be eligible for mandatory grants.

102 Bolton E. Quality issues arising from expanding access *Journal of Access Studies* Vol 1 No 1 1986 3-10
Discusses the maintenance of quality in the face of widening access to higher education to a non-traditional clientele.

103 Bone T. The Scottish dimension *Higher Education Quarterly* Vol 41 No 1 January 1987 43-56
This paper addresses in detail various models of educational guidance practice in access courses. The authors suggest that educational guidance could be formally integrated into courses through assessed and accredited modules and invite readers to regard educational guidance as fundamentally embedded within the access pedagogy rather than a 'bolt-on' activity. This follows the premise that learners need guidance prior to taking up access provision, while engaged in it and on exit. Recognising and accrediting experiential learning is at the heart of the access pedagogy.

104 Bonnerjea L. *Work base: trade union education and skills project: a research report* London ALBSU 1987 28 pages
Describes the work of workbase, a trade union project which provides and promotes basic education for manual workers.

105 Bonnerjea L. Training the invisible workers *Training and Development* Vol 7 No 14 1989 31-32
Argues that manual workers are invisible in terms of training priorities. Argues that they should be a key group on which training activity should focus.

106 Boot R. and Evans J. Partnership in education and change *Management Education and Development* Vol 21 No 1 Spring 1990 13-21
The author argues the case for both industrial organisations and universities to embark on significant internal change if they are to effectively respond to structural and demographic changes. This can be accelerated by working in partnership. Discusses the practicalities of such relationships.

107 Booth B. and Booth C. Planning for quality: advice respectfully tendered to the Polytechnics and Colleges Funding Council *Higher Education Quarterly* Vol 43 No 4 1989 278-288
Discusses the role of the PCFC in maintaining quality in the public sector of higher education. Offers advice on how the PCFC can ensure that quality is preserved and enhanced.

108 Borthwick A. et al *Planning NAFE. Equal opportunities for ethnic minorities. A handbook for senior LEA and college managers and Training Agency officers* London FEU 1988 46 pages
A handbook aimed at college managers and training officers relating to the provision of equal opportunities for ethnic minorities. Provides a checklist for action and implementation.

109 Bould D (Ed) *Developing student autonomy in learning* 2nd edition London Kogan Page 1987 74 pages
A review of case-studies of attempts to encourage student autonomy in learning in a range of higher and adults educational settings.

110 Bourner T. *Entry qualifications and degree performance: summary findings report* London CNAA 1987 16 pages
Reports on a project undertaken at Brighton Polytechnic on the relationship between access and performance in higher education. The degree results of those with entry qualifications other than A levels were compared with entrants with A levels. Overall the degree results of those accepted without A levels were marginally higher than for those with A levels.

111 Bourner T. et al *Part-time students and their experience of higher education* Society

for Research into Higher Education/Open Univ. Press 1991 146 pages
Present detailed analysis of the characteristics, motivations and experiences of part-time first degree students in British polytechnics and colleges in mid 1980s. Data obtained via questionnaire survey of nearly 3,000 students and course leaders.

112 Bousfield C. and Sherrard C. Equal opportunities and institutional racism: redesign of a comparative arts course for mature Access students *Journal of Further and Higher Education* Vol 15 No 2 1991 24-35
Describes attempts to incorporate an anti-racist initiative into a course aimed at mature Access students. Discusses the institutional racism which was encountered and the tensions which occurred when trying to implement initiatives without adequate resources.

113 Bown L. Implications of wider access for the higher education curriculum *Scottish Journal of Adult Education* Vol 8 No 4 Autumn 1988 24-35
This paper is based on the premise that wider access to higher education is a justifiable goal and that there are many people in Scotland not yet in the system who could benefit from higher education and contribute to it. The author indicates some of the implications for the curriculum if wider access becomes a reality.

114 Bown L. Research and policy in Scottish adult education: the state of the art in 1990 *Scottish Journal of Adult Education* Vol 9 No 4 Winter 1990 10-24
An excellent appraisal of the policy-orientated research which has been carried out in Scottish adult education. Describes the main agencies involved in research; the areas where Scotland leads the way and gaps which need to be filled in the 1990s. A useful reference source.

115 Boxer M. Learners with special needs - tutor awareness *Adults Learning* Vol 1 No 10 June 1990 274-276
Tutors' awareness and attitudes have a marked influence on access to mainstream learning opportunities for adults with special needs. This research report reveals the findings of a survey in Northamptonshire. Concludes there is a need for clear commitment from the centre

staff to overcome the subtle barriers as well as the obvious ones.

116 Boys C.J. et al *Higher education and the preparation for work* London Jessica Kingsley Publishers 1989 278 pages
This book is the outcome of interviews with forty nine departments in higher education institutions covering six academic disciplines. The author wished to illustrate how far there has been a shift from knowledge for its own sake towards the acquisition of knowledge and skills instrumental to economic and social objectives. Whilst the majority of academic staff recognised the relevance of academic experience to graduate employment and the importance of developing general enabling skills, it became clear that there was wide variation in opinion across disciplines in relation to curriculum changes and the involvement of outsiders.

117 Brace-Gough P. Training the trainers *Training Officer* Vol 25 No 9 1989 261-262
Pre-course counselling is invaluable for those about to embark on distance education courses. Several institutions provide assistance by means of materials in which a student-centred approach is adopted, some examples are discussed here.

118 Bradbury R. The image of the education of adults: extracts from an analysis of British press coverage, February-April 1985 *International Journal of Lifelong Learning* Vol 7 No 4 1988 301-315
Reports on research which analysed the coverage given to adult education in twelve British newspapers. Discusses the image which such coverage conveys to the public.

119 Bradshaw D. Transferable, intellectual and personal skills *Oxford Review of Education* Vol 11 No 2 1985 201-216
An interesting and detailed paper considering transferable intellectual and personal skills which should be cultivated through a degree course if employers' needs are to be satisfied when recruiting graduates. Skills in communication, cooperation and teamwork and positive personal qualities such as the will to set and meet objectives and to be innovative are deemed to be the most important.

120 Bragg S.L. The age of enlightenment: exploiting the expertise of Higher

Education Institutions *Industry and Higher Education* Vol 2 No 2 June 1988 76-79
This paper argues that many of the collaborative developments (industrial liaison, science parks) are facilitators only and that the real advance is the change of attitude of HEIs, who now positively want their expertise to be used. Argues the case for university companies.

121 Braid M. and Macaskill S. (Ed) *Workplace education: tapping your greatest asset in the 1990s. A handbook on education in the workplace* Edinburgh Scottish Community Education Council 1990 40 pages
The lack of research on mature graduate students outcomes makes this a timely and highly valuable report. The study explores the motivating factors which guided adults in their selection of degree courses and in their decisions after graduation. It is clear from the survey that employers continue to discriminate against older graduates because of preconceived, often negative, stereotypes. The author recommends the report be read by careers advisory staff, employers and mature students commencing their career search.

122 Brain G. Marketing or customer care? *Coombe Lodge Reports* Vol 22 No 5 1990 405-412
Argues that a cultural change is needed to ensure that the principles of customer care and a client centred approach underpin all marketing activities, particularly in an era of rapid changes and competition. Examines publicity, enrolment, induction and environment from the users point of view.

123 Brandon D. Thoughts on delivering a new Access course *Journal of Access Studies* Vol 2 No 2 1987 84-88
This short article summarizes some of the experiences of one lecturer involved in running an Access to Higher education course in its first year. Provides approaches to delivery of an access course and aims to help readers clarify their thoughts about such courses.

124 Brannen J. and Moss P. *New mothers at work* London Unwin 1988 200 pages
This book features the first-hand accounts of these women as they discuss the issues of why they decided to go back to work; how they chose the type of childcare and whether it proved satisfactory; the reaction of employers and colleagues; the role of husband and fathers. A picture emerges of a lack of co-ordinated support system for working mothers.

125 Brannen J. Childbirth and occupational mobility: evidence from a longitudinal study *Work, Employment and Society* Vol 3 No 2 June 1989 179-201
In Britain most women's employment careers are interrupted by childbirth; only a tiny proportion return to their pre-birth jobs and a considerable proportion experience downward mobility when they do return to work. Here evidence is presented from a longitudinal study of two groups of women in the first three years of motherhood: those who resumed their former jobs after maternity leave and those who resigned from the labour force.

126 Breinberg P. The 'black perspective in higher education' a question of conflicting views *Multicultural Teaching* Vol 6 No 1 1987 36-37
Examines different concepts of a 'black perspective' in groups of black and white students through observation, discussion and interview. White views concentrate on numbers of and access for black students. Black views related more to the curriculum and the way it is taught and the suitability of the books and materials used. Views were similar on the need for more black lecturers and examiners.

127 Brennan J. The charge for access *Times Higher Educational Supplement* No 721 29 Aug 1986 page 13
An informative report which draws on the conclusions of a survey of CNAA graduates. The focus of this study is the employment experiences after graduation and the extent to which undergraduate courses prepared students for work. Data from the survey has also been used to assess the 'capacity to benefit' of different groups of students.

128 Brennan J. *Employment of graduates from ethnic minorities: a research report* London Commission for Racial Equality 1987 77 pages
Compares samples of CNAA graduates from different ethnic groups in a study of pharmacy, electrical and electronic engineering. Findings show that ethnic minority graduates find it harder to gain employment in these areas than

white graduates. The report also offers some analyses of the effects of other forms of social disadvantage on ethnic minority graduates.

129 Brennan J. and McGeevor P. *Ethnic minorities and the graduate labour market* London CRE 1990
Detailed study of the graduate labour market revealed that while ethnic minorities benefit in personal and educational terms from higher education they experience greater difficulty in obtaining suitable employment than white graduates. Also the quality of their jobs and promotion prospects are likely to be poorer.

130 Brennan J. Preparing students for employment *Studies in Higher Education* Vol 10 No 2 June 1985 151-162
This paper explores some of the relations between degree-level higher education and employment. Argues that for a large number of graduates with unspecified degrees and competing in an open labour market, employers will be concerned with more general and transferable knowledge and skills.

131 Brennan J. Student learning and the 'capacity to benefit': the performance of non-traditional students in public sector higher education *Journal of Access Studies* Vol 1 No 2 1986 23-32
Discusses the notion of 'capacity to benefit' advocated by CNAA in relation to granting access to higher education. Argues for a change in higher education to meet the needs of non-traditional students.

132 Brewster N. National vocational qualifications *FEU Newsletter* Summer 1990 6-7
Looks at the work undertaken by the FEU to support further education colleges in the implementation of NVQs.

133 Bridge W. Trends in vocational education: the UK experience *Studies in Continuing Education* Vol 11 No 1 1989 1-13
A review of trends in vocational continuing education including a comparative dimension. Suggests that a key element in economic competitiveness, the expansion of vocational continuing education to match international progress seems unlikely without basic research on outcomes and benefits and a fundamental review of funding.

134 Brisenden S. Young, gifted and disabled: entering the employment market *Disability, Handicap and Society* Vol 4 No 3 1989 217-218
This article identifies the way systems and services designed to help disabled people simply act to increase dependency. Stresses the need to raise awareness about value of workers with disabilities to show that they do not present a problem but an opportunity.

135 Bristow R. Disabilities and special educational needs in post school education: a policy dilemma *Educare* No 30 1988 3-8
An interesting paper which urges the development of a comprehensive policy if real change towards the integration of people with special needs is to occur.

136 British Refugee Council *Providing access: the need for education and training* London British Refugee Council 1988/9 4 pages
A draft policy statement which stresses the importance of education and training to refugees in enabling them to become self sufficient. Calls for more English language provision, recognition of previous experience, professional requalification and more funding for further education, higher education and training.

137 British Refugee Council *Settling for a future* London British Refugee Council 1987
Proposals for a British policy on refugees including a section on education and employment.

138 Britton M.C. *Improved visibility: an international bibliography on the education of women and girls* Librarians of Institutes and Schools of Education 1991 380 pages
This is a useful bibliographical collection with extensive subject coverage. The section on stages of education provides valuable sources on women's vocational education and employment.

139 Brock S. More does not mean different: Access to higher education for students with disabilities *Journal of Access Studies* Vol 6 No 2 1991 165-176
This valuable article, drawing on case studies, attempts to stimulate those who may have the power or inclination to change the level of

visibility or inclusion of students with disabilities into educational debates and research. Briefly but usefully analyses an institutional view of the 'ideal' student and the student with a disability and then contrasts these two views with the students' own perception of their experience of institutional provision.

140 Brock S. The invisibility of disability *Journal of Access Studies* Vol 5 No 2 Autumn 1990 214-220

In this article, the authors shows that the invisibility of disability in the Access debates is not necessarily reproduced in institutional practices. Suggests the changing contemporary climate may introduce factors that will help to make people with disabilities more visible. Discusses some exceptional institutions who have, with little or no financial help, been innovative and expansionary in recruiting students with disabilities.

141 Brown A. and Webb J. The higher education route to the labour market for mature students *British Journal of Education and Work* Vol 4 No 1 1990 5-21

Examines the current position of students in the over 30 age group in UK universities with reference to their entrance qualifications, degree attainment and first destinations on leaving university.

142 Brown A. and Fairley J. Where the MSC left off: training for the nineties *Times Scottish Education Supplement* No. 1209 5 January 1990 page 16

Reports on the amalgamation of the Training Agency and the Scottish Development Agency into to a new body called Scottish Enterprise. Rather pessimistically concludes that Scottish Enterprise will have a difficult job modernising VET in Scotland because it will not have a clean sheet to develop the programmes best suited to Scottish conditions.

143 Brown G. Typecast *Training Officer* June 1991 12-13

The author considers the wasted talent of many secretaries, who if offered training and structured career development could move into managerial positions. Unfortunately, the author depicts the secretary as 'she' throughout and implicitly reinforces gender stereotyping.

144 Bryant R. and Noble M. *Education on a shoestring: a survey of the financial circumstances of students at the long term residential colleges* Oxford Ruskin College 1989 42 pages

Looks at the financial problems experienced by students who are undertaking courses at the eight long term residential colleges and assesses the effects of financial hardship on the students performance. The implications of student loans for the students based at the colleges are discussed.

145 Bryant R. Grants, debts and second chance students Adult *Education* Vol 61 No 4 1989 336-341

Reports on a survey of students at Ruskin college which examines the financial difficulties experienced by second chance students in gaining discretionary grants. Discusses the negative impact this has on recruitment and the student's experience of the course.

146 Bryant R. Loans and adult students *Adults Learning* Vol 2 No 2 1990 40-41

Examines the impact of the student loans scheme on mature students. Argues that due to age and domestic commitments mature students are more likely to suffer financial difficulties which have a negative effect on their studies.

147 Bryson J. From concept to practice: implementing a competence based programme in a college hairdressing curriculum *Vocational Aspects of Education* Vol 42 1990 113-118

Describes the way in which a further education college in Northern Ireland revised a course curriculum to meet the requirements of NVQs. Discusses the changes required in delivery systems and the traditional role of lecturers to meet the needs of competency based qualifications.

148 Buckle J. *A learning introduction to building on your experience* London Learning from Experience Trust 1990

This publication is of value to tutors wishing to develop schemes for the assessment of prior learning and can be used as a workbook for students.

149 Bull D. *Refugee education in the UK: a strategy ?* London World University Service 1989 7 pages
Policy statement for the World University Service which outlines the particular problems facing refugees such as legal status, professional requalification and finance. Includes a list of recommendations.

150 Burgen S. Building blocks *The Guardian* 3 April 1991 page 33
An interesting article which reports on the Women into Architecture and Building access course founded 1985. This day-release course for mature students has proved most successful. Those who complete the course are able to enter the School of Architecture at Polytechnic North London or other polytechnics and research shows an unusually high level of achievement among those who enter via the access course. This is a good example of a positive action policy of having a 'woman only course'.

151 Burnes L. The training of volunteers: a case study of Volunteer Development *Scottish Journal of Adult Education* Vol 17 No 2 Autumn 1985 37-43
Discusses the importance of training for volunteers. Presents a wide range of training opportunities and types of training for volunteer workers. Training for Change included positive recommendations that community education training modules should be open to voluntary workers. The author discusses the possible effects.

152 Business in the Community *Putting the enterprise into Training Enterprise Councils* London Business in the Community 1989 9 pages

153 Butcher B. Community education in inner city areas: views of potential and existing users *Journal of Access Studies* Vol 5 No 2 1990 133-143
Summarises the findings of a project which looked at the educational needs of women living in inner city areas, where the Black and Asian communities are concentrated. Makes recommendations for improving access to education and training for such women.

154 Butler L. *Information and technology in educational guidance for adults* Leicester UDACE 1986 58 pages

Calls for a national response to the need for development of common standards in information systems on learning opportunities. In the light of the number of separate experiments being undertaken, many of which have ceased to operate, it stresses the urgency for detailed technical and organisational studies.

155 Butler L. Accrediting women's unpaid work and experience *Adults Learning* Vol 2 No 2 1991 198-199
Discusses unpaid work competence which can be accredited towards the same vocational qualification as competence acquired in paid work. Competence is defined as the ability to perform in work roles to the standard required, not where or how competence/skill is acquired.

156 Butler L. The educational guidance service for adults (EGSA) movement: a review *Adult Education* Vol 57 No 1 1984 7-11
This article charts the current state of the EGSA movement. Educational guidance emerges as a complex, labour intensive task which should be taken seriously by all those involved in continuing education.

157 Buzzing P. *Keeping in touch with teaching: how to use the career break to prepare for your return* London Equal Opportunities Commission/HMSO 1989 51 pages
This report considers the benefits of support during career breaks in the education sector. Discusses other studies which indicate that those who want to return after a career break may benefit from a chance to maintain contact, opportunities to refresh/update skills, which can help in regaining confidence.

158 Buzzing P. Equal opportunities - creating returner-positive schools *Management in Education* Vol 4 No 3 1990 18-20
Looks at the characteristics of a returner-positive school. Stresses the importance of positive support from senior management towards career breaks. Offers suggestions to potential returners.

159 Caird S. Enterprise education: the need for differentiation *British Journal of Education and Work* Vol 4 No 1 1990 47-57
Explores the characteristics of enterprise education and argues for a distinction to be

made between the occupationally focused small business courses and more 'progressive' forms of enterprise education which may be more correctly called competency education initiatives.

160 Caldwell B. Access: changing the face of A-levels *Journal of Access Studies* Vol 5 No 1 Spring 1990 89-99
An interesting article which assesses the motivational characteristics of Access and A-level adult students. The results presented here, show that Access students are more likely to attend courses for personal development and as a requisite for entry to higher education, rather than specific career goals. Adult students perceived Access courses as most appropriate to their needs.

161 Calman-Shaw J. Knowledge-based skills: integrating practical skills in higher education *Industry and Higher Education* March 1991 7-14
Argues compartmentalisation of education and training into 'knowing about' and 'knowing how to do' certain things is unhelpful and the success of skilled professional practitioners requires a fully integrated programme balancing both elements. The author describes the 'apprenticeship model' which he believes provides an appropriate and well-tested framework of such integration and which is found in medicine, law, accountancy.

162 Cameron A. Lifelong learning but not for the educators: poor quality of inservice training *Times Educational Supplement Scotland* No. 1121 29 April 1988 page 2
Whilst the philosophy behind lifelong learning and need for retraining to keep abreast of technological developments has been widely accepted it appears little attention has been paid to the needs of educators themselves. This article strongly asserts the need for good quality in-service training and staff development for teachers. Calls for teachers to have access to expertise and support and be able to negotiate their own training needs.

163 Careers and Occupational Information Centre *Sponsorship 91* Sheffield COIC 1991 37 pages
Directory of sponsorship offered to students by employers and professional bodies.

164 Carroll S. et al *Access to learning and accreditation* London FEU 1991 70 pages

165 Carter R. and Kirkup G. Redressing the balance: women into science and engineering *Open Learning* Vol 6 No 1 Feb 1991 56-58
The Initiative Women into Science and Engineering (WISE) is appraised. WISE seeks to increase the participation of women at all levels in technology, engineering, science and maths; women continue to be under-represented in these areas.

166 Castelino C. and Munn P. *An evaluation of training modules for part-time workers in community education* Project Report No.19 Edinburgh Scottish Council for Research into Education 1990 53 pages
This project evaluated three modules which were developed to meet key basic training requirements common to part-time workers in different branches of community education. Draft modules were sent to about forty individuals or organisations in the field for comment on their structure and relevance. In addition, a sample of the participants and all trainers were interviewed. Overall perceptions were positive and these are highlighted in the report as well as some of the problems with the modules.

167 Castling A. RVQ: a way into the maze *NASD Journal* No 16 1986 13-16
Outlines the work involved in the Review of Vocational Qualifications. Assesses the major weaknesses of the present system and discusses how a national framework will bring improvements.

168 Caudrey A. The third route *New Society* Mar 1988 14-15
Discusses the role of Access courses in breaking the cycle of educational disadvantage. Argues that the Education Bill by removing Polytechnics from LEA control will break links with FE colleges and co-operative Access courses. Includes some discussion with black students about their experience on the Access course which are very positive.

169 Cave M. and Hanney S. *The use of performance indicators in higher education: a critical analysis of developing practice* 2nd Edition London Jessica Kingsley 1991 160 pages

Provides an overview of the development and use of performance indicators in higher education and compares the British experience with that of higher education overseas. Different types of performance indicators are classified and their various inadequacies discussed. Important issues are raised such as the danger of teaching to get a ' good score' and the need for performance indicators to be adaptable to changing goals and values. The book is useful in bringing together much of the information and argument on this subject.

170 Cawthorne M. Careers guidance at a distance *Open Learning* Vol 2 No 3 1987 30-34
This article considers how careers guidance, which in conventional institutions relies so much on personal contacts can be adequately provided for distance students. The use of printed materials, the telephone and computers is reviewed.

171 Cerych L. Collaboration between higher education and industry: an overview *European Journal of Education* Vol 20 No 1 1985
An excellent overview appraising collaboration between higher education and industry. It is suggested a network of relationships rather than a single link appears to be a key to successful university-industry collaboration. The author points out that to date, many university and industrial staff prefer informal links because of a belief that formulated contracts may result in a lack of flexibility.

172 Cerych L. University-industry collaboration: a research agenda and some general impacts on the development of higher education *European Journal of Education* Vol 24 No 3 1989 309-313
A valuable article suggesting the need for more rigorous social scientific research into the area of university-industry collaboration. Those which are available are descriptions of numerous cooperative schemes and new pilot projects. Presents a Research Agenda setting out some issues where analysis could be useful.

173 Chambers G. *Equality and inequality in Northern Ireland: Part 2 : the workplace* London PSI 1987 250 pages
Part of a large scale research project undertaken by the PSI to review the coverage

and effectiveness of laws and institutions involved in securing equality of opportunity and freedom from discrimination in Northern Ireland. This section involved surveying and interviewing staff at 260 work places in an attempt to investigate policies and practices in employment.

174 Chanda N. *Assessment of prior learning: a common sense approach for ABE and ESOL* London ALBSU 1990 7 pages
Argues in favour of the assessment of prior learning and offers advice on how this can be done with adult basic education students and English as a second language students.

175 Chapman L. Disabling services *Educare* No 31 1988 15-20
This paper is an edited version of the FEU document 'A Curriculum Perspective on Adults with Special Needs' (1988) and considers the transition to adulthood and services designed to help. The author suggests that many disabled adults would, if asked, reply that many of these services in fact constitute a handicap because they reinforce dependency. Suggests adult and continuing education can offer flexibility, offer scope for innovation and a new kind of relationship with professionals in which they are equal partners. Concludes every LEA should enact a stated policy on adult education and special needs.

176 Chapman M.E.A. Marketing the college: some benefits and barriers *Education Management and Administration* Vol 14 No 2 1986 107-111
Examines the benefits to a college of applying a coherent marketing strategy. Argues that this offers the opportunity to formally consider the needs of the consumer, long-term planning and analysis and the effective use of resources.

177 Chapman P.G. The crisis in UK adult training policy: 1981-1990 *Studies in the Education of Adults* Vol 23 No 1 April 1991 53-60
This paper describes and comments on the main adult training employment schemes in the eighties. A discussion of the economic rationale of these policies follows. Finally, the paper examines the nature of adult training in the eighties and some recommendations are presented.

178 Charnley A.H. and Withnall A. *Developments in basic education: special development projects 1978-1985* London ALBSU 1989 115 pages
Reports on the lessons learned from a series of special development projects undertaken by ALBSU and its predecessor the Adult Literacy Unit. Provides useful background information on the aims, structure and organisation of adult literacy and basic skills work in Britain. Includes sections on facilitating access, publicity and promotion and types of provision. It also deals briefly with specific target groups such as the unemployed, the disabled and women.

179 Chigwada R. Black women's unequal performance of prison education *Gender and Education* Vol 1 No 2 June 1989 199-201
Although education in prison is supposed to improve inmates' socio-economic mobility following release, interview data obtained from ten black women inmates who had tried to further their education revealed that racism hindered their efforts. Several recommendations are offered to alleviate this situation, emphasising that education provides such women with the means to earn a living and consequently reduces recidivism.

180 Child D. *Access to higher education: students with disabilities at the Open University* London Further Education Unit 1989 6 pages
This publication is part of a series of studies entitled 'Working together'. It was undertaken for the UK contribution to the OECD/CERI disabled action programme.

181 Chivers G.E. *Staff development for continuing education in the universities* London DES Adult Training Promotions Unit 1989

182 Chivers G.E. Developing continuing education and training providers: implications for UK higher education institutions *Industry and Higher Education* Vol 4 No 3 September 1990 197-203
Examines the staff development needs of UK higher education providers of continuing education and training for industry. The author points out that whilst all kinds of structures may be established to encourage stronger links between industry and HE, the venture will not be successful unless efforts to develop staff are made.

183 Christians Against Racism and Fascism Racism in employment training *Searchlight* No 179 1990 page 17
Report of an Action Against Racism in Training conference of 7.4.90. Evidence of racial discrimination in ET was reported in terms of black people being excluded from the most popular schemes and non implementation of equal opportunities policies. Concern expressed about the role of TECs in such schemes as black people are largely excluded from such organisations.

184 Claridge M. and Brew A. New kids on the block: providing access opportunities for young adults *Journal of Access Studies* Vol 6 No 2 1991 190-204
This is an interesting paper based on an investigation carried out in Portsmouth Polytechnic which was set up to consider the feasibility of a degree programme designed to attract capable young people (targeting those aged 18-21) who had not previously considered higher education. Here the findings of the feasibility study and the model of the degree programme based on partnerships which emerges are presented in some detail.

185 Clarke K. *Women and training: a review* Manchester Equal Opportunities Commission 1990 94 pages
This is a current and valuable report which examines women's access to training over the working lifetime and includes both the full range of initial training at the end of compulsory education and continuous training up to retirement. Access to training is considered for three groups - young women making the transition from full-time education to employment; adult employees and women who are not in employment. A broad definition of training is used encompassing vocational and academic education.

186 Clarke P. Central institutions and their place in higher education in Scotland. Information paper 19. *Scottish Educational Review* Vol 19 No 1 May 1987 50-54
A valuable paper which describes the role of the Central Institutions and summarises the differences between these and the universities in the areas of vocational aims and objectives,

teaching and validation, student applications, funding and staff establishment.

187 **Clayton K.** Trends in funding arrangements *Higher Education Quarterly* Vol 42 No 2 1988 134-143

The author examines trends in the funding of higher education since 1974. Considers the role of the University Grants Committee and the National Advisory Body.

188 **Clendon R. and Yorke D.** *Towards effective contact* Manchester CONTACT/DES September 1986 91 pages

A nationally acclaimed study of the constraints on employers releasing personnel for training, and employer and employee views on ways of relaxing these constraints and designing and delivering the training they want from academic institutions.

189 **Clendon R. and Yorke D.** Adult training: the employers' viewpoint *Education and Training* Vol 29 No 1 Jan/Feb 1987 10-12

The authors carried out research into sixty six companies and their training strategies. One of the main conclusions reached focuses on the absence of any coordinated help and advice for employers about their training needs and how to arrange training for new skills.

190 **Cliff R. et al** *Identification and assessment of basic skills needs: PSS report to the literacy and numeracy working group* Sheffield MSC 1987 37 pages

Report on a project which aimed to identify the extent and nature of the literacy and numeracy problems of long term unemployed adults involved in the Restart programme and to assess the adequacy of the support systems and training available to them.

191 **Coats M.** Support for women learning: requirements and resources *Adults Learning* Vol 1 No 4 Dec 1989 104-105

Argues that institutions and organisations which want to attract women learners must identify their specific needs and provide education which is relevant to women who wish to return or continue. Those requirements may involve extra resources for women.

192 **Cockburn C.** Equal opportunities: the short and the long agenda *Industrial Relations Journal* Mar 1989 213-225

This paper considers the reasons for the current disillusionment of many concerned with 'equal opportunities' policies in employment and reviews the potential of an equal opportunities orientation for progressive change.

193 **Coffield F.** From the decade of enterprise culture to the decade of the TECs *British Journal of Education and Work* Vol 4 No 1 1990 59-78

This is a highly recommended article which appraises the rise of the enterprise movement in the 1980s and the establishment and performance of TECs. Both strategies are thought to be part of an ideological project of the Conservative Government to transform Britain's economy and education by means of the enterprise culture. The main initiatives designed to promote such a culture are described, the concept of enterprise as used on enterprise courses is examined and the conclusion drawn that there is no generic skill of enterprise the essence of which can be distilled and taught. A number of crucial issues in relation to TECs (the need for a national plan for education, training and employment, the commitment of employers etc) are discussed and constructive suggestions made.

194 **Coffield F.** The year 2000: inventing the future *Scottish Education Review* Vol 21 No 2 November 1989 77-86

Offers pertinent reflections on an under-educated society, management in the UK and the education, training and employment needs of young adults. Concludes by highlighting the main issues which have to be tackled throughout the 1990s and beyond.

195 **Coldstream P.** Campaigning for partnership: the British experience *Industry and Higher Education* Vol 4 No 4 1990 257-261

Charts the development of industry-higher education partnership in the UK from the vantage point of the Council for Industry and Higher Education.

196 **Coldstream P.** Marketing as matching *Higher Education Quarterly* Vol 42 No 2 Spring 1989 99-107

Discusses the need to match the activities of higher education to the needs of society and the economy in terms of output and recruitment. Calls for higher education to break into the mass market and achieve access for non-traditional learners.

197   Coldstream P. The university-industry dialogue in the UK *CRE-action* No 83 1988 35-44

Discusses the role of the Council for Industry and Higher Education (CIHE) and draws on the main proposals contained in the paper 'Towards a partnership: HE, Government and Industry by CIHE'. A main conclusion of the Council's enquiries is the desire of the business world to focus attention on the value of teaching and not just on that of research.

198   Cole B. and Jack B. Case study: the Glasgow college - Scomagg Ltd Teaching Company Scheme *Industry and Higher Education* Vol 2 No 3 September 1988 178-181

199   Cole N. No longer a job for life *Director* Vol 42 No 3 1988 110-114

This article looks at career change among executives and draws upon information from the Vocational Guidance Association. Outplacement specialist firms are discussed.

200   Collins M. Prison education: a substantial metaphor for adult education practice *Adult Education Quarterly* Vol 38 No 2 Winter 1988

This study shows how education and training in prison is essentially accommodative. The analysis informed by critical theory perspectives and on-site investigations with both inmates and prison educators, yields disturbing insights on the kind of power relationships and coercive structures that impinge on prison education and also shape much of the modern practice of adult education, e.g. self-directed learning.

201   Collins T. *Development of adult guidance within the Careers Service* National Association of Educational Services for Adults, Bath Conference National Association of Educational Services for Adults Spring 1990 page 3

Argues for more communication between Careers Services and Educational Guidance Services and stresses the importance of a client-centred rather than blanket interview technique. Recommends the training for careers officers should include more adult-based skills.

202   Collinson D. Poachers turned gamekeeper: are personnel managers one of the barriers to equal opportunities? *Human Resource Management Journal* Vol 1 No 3 Spring 1991 58-76

Draws on EOC research which suggests UK Personnel Managers fail to implement equal opportunities in recruitment because they are often too subordinated to line managers or are untrained and uncommitted to the principles and practices of professional human resource management. In the case of women personnel managers who knew that their credibility was even more 'on the line' and open to the critical gaze of other managers than their male counterparts, the pressure to subordinate occupational and gender identity to conform to organisational demands concerning short-term production and profit was much greater.

203   Commission for Racial Equality *Code of practice for the elimination of racial discrimination in education* London CRE 1989

Aimed at those with responsibilities at all levels of education. Outlines the practical implications of the 1976 Race Relations Act.

204   Commission for Racial Equality *Learning in terror: a survey of racial harassment in schools and colleges in England, Scotland and Wales 1985-1987* London CRE 1988 37 pages

Report concluding that racial violence and harassment is widespread in education. Gives numerous examples of such cases and criticises LEAs for their failure to respond.

205   Commission for Racial Equality *Medical school admissions: report of a formal investigation into St. George's Hospital Medical School* London CRE 1988 23 pages

Investigation revealed that a computer programme dealing with UCCA applications gave less favourable weighting to women and non-whites thereby making it less likely that they would be called for interview. CRE found that St. George's had directly discriminated on racial grounds.

206 Commission for Racial Equality *Positive action and equal opportunity in employment* London CRE 1985 39 pages
Defines and explains the importance of positive action and outlines the measures allowed under the 1976 Race Relations Act.

207 Commission for Racial Equality *Positive action in local authority employment* London CRE 1987 29 pages
Report from a conference of Northern local authorities which discussed ways of implementing positive action policies. Includes discussion on the role of Access courses and training schemes aimed at ethnic minorities.

208 Committee of Directors of Polytechnics and Committee of Vice-Chancellors and Principles of the Universities of the United Kingdom *Financing the expansion of higher education: report of the joint CVCP/CDP working group on funding mechanisms* London CVCP/CDP 1990 8 pages
Report which starts from the premise that the expansion of higher education is necessary for the economic and social well being of the country. It discusses the problems of funding such expansion from the institutional point of view. Possible sources of increased funding are considered.

209 *Computer Weekly* 1st Feb 1990 page 106
A report by the Institute of Manpower Studies, 'Good practices in the employment of women returners', argues that women returners are ideal for managing the changes in the employers' policies caused by skills shortages in the 1990s and are forecast to account for over 80% of the growth in the labour force.

210 Connelly B. Access or access: a framework for interpretation *Journal of Access Studies* Vol 6 No 2 1991 135-146
Discusses the current political support for access. The author suggests the government's view of access as an important part of its strategy for influencing change in higher education policy, practice and curriculum has become the central focus for debate on the role of access.

211 Connolly M. Achievement of access and non-access students on a BEd course *New Community* Vol 12 No 1 1984-85 33-51

Addresses the need for more ethnic minority teachers and the consequent need for enabling those without traditional qualifications to undergo teacher training. Examines the achievement rates of access and non-access students on a BEd course at the Polytechnic of North London.

212 Connolly M. Achievement of access and non-access students on a BEd course: addendum *New Community* Vol 12 No 3 1985 273-4
An addendum to the preceding entry in which the author compares the two groups in their third year in terms of passes, merits and distinctions.

213 Connor A. and Wylie J.A Academic industry liaison in the UK: economic perspectives *Higher Education* Vol 15 No 5 1986 407-420
This paper draws on some relevant areas of economic theory to analyse the relationship between Higher Education Initiatives and industrial organisations. It is argued that liaison can frequently strengthen the traditional functions of higher education institutions by contributing to teaching and research. Advocates an institution-wide liaison centre which offers 'facilitation' services to individual academics and departments, to encourage them to operate within the institutional system of information and control.

214 Connor J. *The Carousel skills group: a case study in widening access to training, education and community involvement for unemployed adults* London Employment Unit 14 pages

215 Connor S. and Wylie J. Post experience vocational education: an investigation of its role in linking colleges, universities and business *Scottish Journal of Adult Education* Vol 7 No 2 Autumn 1985 14-22
This article discusses a research project which assesses the provision of post experience vocational education (PEVE). Using a mixture of quantitative and qualitative methodology, the perceptions of academic staff based in three Scottish central institutions and from industrial, commercial and public sector organisations are presented.

216 Connor S. et al Technology transfer between industry and higher education:

the UK Teaching Company Scheme *Industry and Higher Education* Vol 5 No 2 June 1991 97-104

A review of the Teaching Company Scheme which is a technology transfer system devised to encourage the two-way flow of advanced technology between higher education and industry. Reports on a number of case studies on the programme and draws conclusions about the effectiveness of the scheme.

217 **Consortium for Advanced Continuing Education and Training (CONTACT)** *Contact Newsletter* no 5: continuing education and training - then and now Manchester CONTACT October 1990 23 pages

A useful newsletter, produced by Universities of Manchester and Salford, UMIST, Manchester Polytechnic and Manchester Business School and available on request. Provides up-to-date information on TECs in north west region, business-education links, CET, and European matters.

218 **Conti G.J.** *Dialogue on issues of lifelong learning in a democratic society Working Papers from a British and North American Faculty Exchange* Texas A. and M. University 1985 103 pages

Consists of twelve papers which are largely theoretical with an interconnecting theme: all adults have the potential to develop. Challenges in the continuing education field and women's training needs are documented.

219 **Cook K. and Crook G.** in Raggatt P. and Unwin L. *Change and intervention: vocational education and training* London Falmer Press 1991 220 pages

Reports on a case study on the ways in which a community college has responded to changes in funding policies and the impact this has had on its delivery of vocational education and training.

220 **Cook P.M.** Integration - a two way street *Adult Education* Vol 61 No 1 June 1988 33-35

Peter Cook, who is himself visually handicapped, reminds us that if integration is to work as a practical measure, then disability awareness must become a mainstream topic in education and training.

221 **Cooke A.** Meeting the challenge: women's training and development *Journal of European Industrial Training* Vol 10 No 7 1986 3-9

Discusses the Women and Training Group. This Group encourages organisations and the individuals within to view women's training and development in a different way.

222 **Cooke A.** Training for change *Training Tomorrow* Jul/Aug 1991 21-22

Discusses equal opportunities in companies and argues that a major cultural change which will challenge the stereotypical images of women's work is needed. Appraises recent developments in Catalyst - Training for Change, which is committed to providing the information base on equal opportunities issues. Concludes training is the key to change.

223 *Coombe Lodge Report* Provision for students with special needs: Part 1 and Part 2 Vol 18 No 10 and 11 1986

These are valuable reports which examine the practical alternatives to LEAs, colleges and schools in seeking to offer adequate, effective and appropriate education and training to students with special needs. Part 1 addresses broad issues associated with organisation, planning, management and resources. Part 2 considers more specific curricular issues to do with curriculum design, delivery and support.

224 **Cooper A.** Distance learning and management education *Media in Education and Development* Vol 18 No 1 March 1985 25-28

Briefly discusses traditional management education methods and the move towards distance and open learning schemes. Describes, by way of example, Henley Distance Learning Ltd's distance and open learning scheme for management education and outlines two newly developed courses.

225 **Corbett J.** An experience of in-service training: introducing the support network for students with special needs *Educare* No 32 1988 39-43

The author discusses her experience of developing and implementing a short course of in-service provision at the North East London Polytechnic, for those working with students with special needs. The author convincingly proposes that any in-service course must include the opportunity to visit a variety of setting. Only through experiential learning and sharing of skills, she concludes, can improvements in the quality and efficiency of further education practices be made.

226 **Cormack R.J.** *Education reform in Northern Ireland* Belfast DENI 1988 18 pages
Contains the government's proposals for education reform in Northern Ireland. Includes a section on further education outlining proposals for the financial delegation of individual further education colleges.

227 **Cormack R.J. and Osborne R.D.** Employment and discrimination in Northern Ireland *Policy Studies* Vol 9 No 3 1989 49-53
The authors respond to criticism of their work on patterns of Catholic and Protestant employment and unemployment. Some of the work undertaken in this area is briefly reviewed.

228 **Cormack R.J. et al** Student loans: a Northern Ireland perspective *Higher Education Quarterly* Vol 43 No 3 1989 229-245
The authors argue that the student loans scheme does not adequately address regional variations and that the scheme will have a greater impact on participation rates in higher education in Northern Ireland. Argues that the higher proportion of students from manual backgrounds with little financial support from parents and the lower wages of graduates will make it more difficult for students to undertake courses and to pay off loans afterwards. Some useful data is given on participation rates in higher education in Northern Ireland compared to the rest of the United Kingdom.

229 **Corner R.** *Take-up of further education and youth training by ethnic and a linguistic minority youth* Glasgow Glasgow University 1988
The aim of this project is to analyse the take up of further education provision by ethnic and linguistic minority group school leavers in Strathclyde. Case studies using interview data with those students entering the local further education college which is making some special provision are presented.

230 **Corner T.** *Ethnic monitoring of the training of teachers* Glasgow Glasgow University August 1989
The aim of the project was to survey colleges and departments of education in Scotland to ascertain the extent of current participation by ethnic and linguistic minorities; review their equal opportunities strategy and obtain evidence as to the extent of multicultural education courses.

231 **Cornish J.W.P. and Windle R.E.** *Undergraduate income and expenditure survey 1986/87* London HMSO 1988
Aimed to provide factual information on undergraduate sources of income and patterns of expenditure to assist the DES in the development of policy on student financial support. The research which was conducted through interviews and diaries of expenditure was based on students taking first degrees at British universities and polytechnics.

232 **Corrie M. and Zaklukiewicz S.** Leaving special education: issues for research *Scottish Educational Review* Vol 16 No 1 May 1984 10-18
This paper discusses the difficulties faced by handicapped school leavers and the limitations of existing research related to the transition of handicapped students from special education to adult life. Suggests future research directions and priorities especially with regard to provision.

233 **Cosgrove D. and McDonnel C.** *Post 16 developments in continuing education in Scotland in the 1980s.* Dundee Dundee College of Education 1984 80 pages
This book is the second in a series of volumes published by Dundee College of Education on the broad themes of current development in lifelong learning in Scotland.

234 **Cottam D.** University-industry collaboration: overcoming the barriers *Industry and Higher Education* Vol 4 No 4 December 1990 238-243
Previous studies, the author argues have emphasised the barriers to the successful commercial exploitation of university research by industry. In this paper, the barriers to collaboration prior to commercial exploitation are examined. It is argued that the 'soft' human-orientated barriers are at least as important as the more obvious 'hard' technical

and contractual barriers. Both types of barrier need to be effectively handled in the preliminary stages of collaboration.

235 **Council for Continuing Education** *Programme for progress: report of the Northern Ireland Council for Continuing Education* Bangor Council for Continuing Education 1986 30 pages

A short report on learning opportunities for adults in Northern Ireland which summarises the work of the council for continuing education. The patterns of provision are briefly described and those groups requiring particular attention are highlighted.

236 **Council for Industry and Higher Education** *Collaborative courses in industry and higher education: expanding the partnership with industry* London CIHE 1990 63 pages

This publication is about a partnership between industry and education. Through specific examples, it illustrates the mutual benefits that can flow when academic and business organisations learn to pool their expertise. The paper shows how, in practice, firms and higher education institutions can successfully collaborate in the production of degree courses which will make those who take them more effective in their industrial and commercial careers.

237 **Council for Industry and Higher Education** *Towards a partnership - higher education-government-industry* London CIHE Spring 1987 22 pages

This is the pioneering paper which proposes objectives for developing higher education into the next century and outlines some implications for achieving them. The Council invited feedback from government ,institutions of higher education and from companies in order that future developments could be effectively planned.

238 **Council for Industry and Higher Education** *Towards a partnership: the business contribution to higher education* London CIHE July 1991 19 pages

This paper is a first attempt to measure industry and higher education collaboration. Points out that whilst companies must never substitute for governments in funding the mainstream of higher education, they are growing and willing, contributors.

239 **Council for Industry and Higher Education** *Towards a Partnership: the company response* London CIHE 1988 19 pages

Provides the first picture of UK companies' present approach to higher education and outlines their chief areas of concern. It is aimed at those managers asked to assemble policies for their own companies.

240 **Council for Industry and Higher Education** *Towards a partnership: the humanities for the working world* London CIHE 1990 11 pages

This paper is intended to encourage debate within the academic community which will reaffirm what the humanities, part of mainstream education, should continue to offer society and to their students. The report points out that many employers have stated that some of the best and most creative recruits in many departments have educational backgrounds in the arts and whilst agreeing that a rise in the number studying engineering and science is a high priority, the message here is that graduates usefully educated in the humanities disciplines are also welcomed.

241 **Council for National Academic Awards** *Access courses to higher education* London CNAA 1989 140 pages

A guide to access courses and providing institutions. Usefully offers general information of access, broad trends and definitions and advice on other routes into higher education.

242 **Council for National Academic Awards** *Access courses to higher education: a framework of national arrangements for recognition* London CNAA 1989 2 leaflets

This paper is a report on progress and a statement of intentions, addressed primarily to providers of Access courses and those responsible for the admission of students to higher education.

243 **Council for National Academic Awards** *Access courses to higher education: development of a database* Series No. 17 London Council for National Academic Awards 1989 6 pages

A Report arising from a CNAA Development Fund Project at Bedford College of Higher Education in conjunction with the Forum for Access Studies.

244 Council for National Academic Awards *The accessibility of higher education: a case study in improving access networks and curricula* Report no. 27 London CNAA April 1990

An overview of the CNAA Development Fund project by Manchester Polytechnic in conjunction with 3 further education and community colleges. This report and checklist for action arise from the project's fieldwork which examined the experiences of mature students from Manchester Open College Federation accredited Access courses, who were non-traditional entrants on the courses offered by the Polytechnic. The project's rationale was that the more we know about adults' experience in higher education, the better their needs will be served. Also concerned itself with the attitudes of the polytechnic staff towards mature entrants.

245 Council for National Academic Awards *Credit Accumulation and Transfer Schemes: a guide for students registered centrally with the scheme* London CNAA 1989

Provides guidance and information for students registered with the CNAA Credit Accumulation and Transfer Scheme.

246 Council for National Academic Awards *Credits for change: the CNAA Credit Accumulation and Transfer Scheme and the universities* London CNAA 1989

Reports on a conference held in 1988 concerned with the role of the CNAA Credit Accumulation and Transfer Scheme within the universities.

247 Council for National Academic Awards and UDACE *Guidance and counselling for students in higher education* CNAA/UDACE Ends December 1991

This project aims to develop models for a coordinated advisory and counselling service geared to the needs of non-traditional students by promoting collaboration with guidance facilities outside the higher education institutions. Other work will focus on raising higher education staff awareness of the different perceptions and experience of mature non-traditional students and will investigate ways for tutors to develop their guidance role.

248 Council for National Academic Awards *A survey of access courses to higher education: analysis and prospects* London CNAA 1990 9 pages

This paper offers a background to the development of the Access database and the Access to Higher Education courses directory. It provides a presentation and analysis of data and issues arising from the data and the directory.

249 Council for National Academic Awards and Scottish Office *Scottish Credit Accumulation and Transfer Scheme* Glasgow CNNA Scottish Office 1990 4 pages

An outline of the Scottish Credit Accumulation and Transfer Scheme.

250 Council of Europe *Prison Information Bulletin* Jun/Dec 1990 28 pages

This is a special issue devoted to the theme of education in prison and stresses the importance of structured post-release courses and continuation of education and training opportunities when back in the community.

251 Council of University Classical Departments *Classics in the market place* London The Council of University Classical Departments 1990 17 pages

An interesting report which considers the relevance of a classics degree in today's labour market. The general conclusion is that the rigorous study of the languages, literature and society of the ancient world provides those 'transferable skills' which employers need and value.

252 Cowper H. Why the open college deserves to prosper *Times Educational Supplement Scotland* No. 1067 17 April 1987 page 2

Appraises the success of the open college to date and strongly supports its further development.

253 Cox S.M. and Davies D.T. Information support for using open learning materials within engineering education *European Journal of Engineering Education* Vol 12 No 2 1987 173-177

Reviews current trends in engineering education, particularly open and distance learning. A case study is presented which shows a recent move toward relevant and up-to-date courses materials in the area of Advanced Manufacturing Technology for undergraduates through collaboration between academic and library staff.

254 Craig D. Higher certificate in library and information science - a distance learning course for senior library assistants *Learning Resources Journal* Vol 4 No 3 October 1988 113-122

The Higher Certificate in Library and Information Science, which is a distance learning course for senior library assistants is described. Considers the reasons for choosing the distance learning mode; the course structure; higher certificate; student and employment profile and issues and problems arising from the implementation of this type of course.

255 Crawley R.C. Flexible training systems: breaking the mould of training in Britain In *Open learning in transition: an agenda for action* Paine N. Cambridge National Extension College 1988 253-263

This paper draws on the experience of Flexible Training Systems - a company which has been instrumental in introducing open learning into a wide range of companies throughout Britain - to examine how successful open learning has been as a training method in companies, and whether it is truly revolutionary.

256 Cridland J. Promoting careership through working life In *Training and competitiveness* Stevens J. & Mackay R. National Economic Development Office Policy Issue Series 1990 229-241

The CBI Task Force Report 'Towards a Skill Revolution' sets out a new framework for the development of training in Britain. It places greater emphasis on the role of the individual in updating the skills of the UK workforce. CBI's Careership proposal seeks to improve foundation skills as a basis for lifetime learning. This paper develops these ideas further. The central themes consider how the UK can ensure skills are enhanced and updated throughout working life and how those outside employment be given the opportunities to improve their skill base.

257 Crompton R. and Sanderson K. *Gendered jobs and social change* London Unwin Hyman 1990 203 pages

A systematic exploration of the changing structure of women's paid work in Great Britain since the second world war. Empirical work drawing on case studies is set within a context of discussion relating to current theoretical debates concerning gender occupational segregation and class and stratification theory.

258 Crosier K. Scotland: a learner's market *Marketing* Vol 28 No 12 1986 55-56

Discusses management education, with special reference to the value of Scottish marketing degrees. Shows how the MBA and self improvement via night classes are prominent features in Scottish education.

259 Cross M. The black economy *New Society* Vol 81 24.7.87 16-19

Argues that as resources are channelled out of the inner cities here 80% of ethnic minorities live, they are bearing a disproportionate share of the negative effects of unemployment. Positive action policies in some professional jobs are creating a black middle class but little is being done for the urban poor. The author calls for quality training which will be saleable in the labour market.

260 Crossland B. Industrial collaboration in engineering education in the United Kingdom *European Journal of Engineering Education* Vol 10 No 2 1985 109-118

Discusses developments in industrial collaboration in engineering education with particular reference to Queen's University Belfast. The particular problems of severe industrial decline in Northern Ireland are discussed and the importance of collaboration between industry and education in rebuilding the economy is noted.

261 Cross-Durrant A. Quality matters *FEU Newsletter* Summer 1990 July 1990 4-5

Looks at the different interpretations which can be applied to the notion of quality within the further education sector. Discusses some of the models available for quality assurance and describes the FEU's role in keeping the further education system informed of progress in this area.

262 Curran J. and Stanworth J. Training for enterprise: approaches to small business education *Business Education* Vol 8 No 1 1987 20-27

There is clearly a need for a wide range of possible training programmes geared to the multiple needs of potential and existing small owners. The authors describe one of the longest established and best known small business training courses in Britain - the London Enterprise Programme, which they believe can act as a useful role model for others. Offers some guidelines on training for small businesses and concludes there is a need to specify the target audience and plan the detail of the course accordingly.

263   **Currell B.R. and Randall G.K.** The Thames Polytechnic Credit Accumulation and Transfer Scheme *Industry and Higher Education* Vol 3 No 1 1989 46-48
Reports on a Credit Accumulation and Transfer Scheme in operation at Thames Polytechnic.

264   **Dale R.** *Education, training and employment: towards a new vocationalism?* Oxford Pergamon Press Ltd 1985 129 pages
This reader consists of a collection of articles, the primary concerns of which are the policy responses to pressures to bring the education system into closer alignment with the priorities of employers.

265   **Davies D.** The FE route to adult education *Adult Education* Vol 61 No 4 1989 342-346
Argues that the further education sector must concentrate on the issues of collective educational needs, mass access, special needs and the role of work in society to ensure its central role in the extension of learning opportunities.

266   **Davies D.** TEC development and new times *Adults Learning* Vol 1 No 6 February 1990 161-162
Review of TECs and the importance of adapting to change. Argues industrialists and educators must develop new ways of thinking and relating to each other and points to the example of Clywd who have achieved a successful record of partnership between business and public sector education.

267   **Davies H. and Rispin M.** The role of academia in providing training for industry *Journal of Further and Higher Education* Vol 11 No 1 Spring 1987 45-57
This paper attempts to look outside the educational institutions at the perceived needs of industry and at employers' perceptions of the educational sector drawing upon work carried out for the Humberside small-scale local collaborative project. It aimed to improve the delivery of PICKUP-type activities by bringing together the two institutions of HE, the five colleges of FE and a group of six major local employers. One of the main conclusions suggests that if the marketing of training by academic institutions is to be effective, then, it must not be simply 'promotional' but must actively assist organisations to identify their training needs in detail.

268   **Davies P. and Scribbins K.** *Marketing further and higher education: a handbook* York Longman 1985 77 pages
Provides guidance on marketing concepts and techniques which can be applied within the further and higher education sectors. It examines the nature of the market and discusses the principles that can be applied to market research, product, place, price and promotion.

269   **Davies P. and Scribbins K.** Marketing FHE post-ERA: routes to salvation *Journal of Further and Higher Education* Vol 13 No 2 1989 11-21
Provides guidelines on marketing concepts and techniques which can be applied within the further and higher sectors. It examines the nature of the market and discusses the market research stage before considering the four P's: Product, Place, Price and Promotion.

270   **Davies P.** Marketing further education to adult learners *Adults Learning* Vol 13 No 2 1989 11-12
A useful article providing a checklist of marketing components with practical examples based on the principle of customer care. Lists the seven P's needed to make a marketing package: Product, Place, Price, Promotion, People, Physical facilities and Processes. Stresses the need for professional marketing skills, the commitment of senior management and the involvement of all staff.

271   **Davies P. and Yates J.** The progress of former access students in higher education *Journal of Access Studies* Vol 2 No 1 1987 7-11
This paper draws on some of the findings of a project designed to monitor the progress of former Access students in higher education

courses. Overall, conclusions suggest there is a complex pattern of personal, institutional and external factors contributing to the progress and performance of the former Access students on their courses in higher education.

272   De Wit P. Students and the institution in a university-access scheme *Journal of Access Studies* Vol 3 No 2 Autumn 1988 21-28

This is an interesting article which describes a well-established access scheme at the University of Birmingham and draws attention to some questions raised by mature students' experience of the university whilst initially taking the access courses and when they enter a regular BA course. The focus is on integration into the student community at university and certain problems faced specifically by mature students are highlighted.

273   Dearden G. *Learning while earning: learning contracts for employees* Learning from Experience Trust London 1989

Describes the procedures involved in learning contracts which are agreements between an employer and the employee and an academic institution about a work based learning programme for the employee.

274   Debling G. Developing Standards In: *Change and intervention: vocational education and training* Raggatt P. and Unwin L. London Falmer Press 1991 220 pages

Chapter exploring the background to the introduction of standards within an education and training context. This is related to government policy aimed at creating an effective workforce. The implications of the use of occupational standards for post compulsory education and training are discussed.

275   Deeks G. Too old at 40? Now in 1995 *Training Officer* Vol 25 No 8 Aug 1989 248-249

Discusses the need to plan for the training of older workers and women returners who will be needed to fill the employment gap created by the falling numbers of young people in the 1990s.

276   Department of Economic Development *Fair Employment (Northern Ireland) Act* c.32 Belfast Dept. Economic Development 1989 55 pages

Act which placed duties on employers to ensure the active practice of fair employment in Northern Ireland. Employers are required to monitor and report on the participation in employment of members of the Catholic and Protestant communities. Also establishes a Fair Employment Tribunal for Northern Ireland.

277   Department of Education and Science *Abilities not disabilities* Manchester REPLAN/DES 1990 16 pages

This checklist is not intended for 'special needs units', providers are asked to answer the questions as they relate to their 'mainstream' provision. Contents include sections on access and facilities, problems of transport, targeting publicity, guidance and advice, employment of people with disabilities.

278   Department of Education and Science *Academic validation in public sector higher education* London HMSO 1985 115 pages

Report of the committee appointed to enquire into academic validation of public sector degree courses with a view to ensuring the maintenance of academic standards. Discusses the historical background, the main methods of validation and suggests the principles for future developments.

279   Department of Education and Science *The contribution of further and higher education to professional, industrial and commercial updating* London HMSO 1988 19 pages

This report presents the findings of a survey of courses of professional, industrial and commercial updating (PICKUP) designed for adults in employment and of the organisation and management structures devised by colleges to promote PICKUP. A lack of information and guidance being provided to PICKUP students was noted; furthermore, many of the students were in fact unemployed and would have benefited from guidance and library services available to students on mainstream courses.

280   Department of Education and Science *Development of higher education into the 1990s* Cmnd 9524 London HMSO 1985 59 pages

This paper is about higher education policy in all parts of the UK. Most of the policy questions addressed are of general application, but differences do arise because of historical and organisational variations in parts of the UK and these are noted. The underlying theme is one of enhancing access without dilution of quality.

281 **Department of Education and Science** *Education and training for the 21st century* Cmnd 1536 London HMSO 1991 39 pages
Sets out the government's proposals on the future organisation and funding of education and training. In particular, the White Paper proposes the removal of further education colleges from local authority control and the establishment of councils to oversee the colleges.

282 **Department of Education and Science** *Education Reform Act* London HMSO 1988 284 pages
Major legislation dealing with all aspects of education provision, organisation and funding.

283 **Department of Education and Science** *Education (student loans) Act* London HMSO 1990 7 pages
Introduces the Governments legislation dealing with the student loans scheme.

284 **Department of Education and Science** *Higher education: a new framework* Cmnd 1541 London HMSO 1991 42 pages
Sets out the government's policy on the future organisation and funding of higher education. In particular it aims to abolish the binary line between the universities and other higher education institutions.

285 **Department of Education and Science** *Higher Education: meeting the challenge* Cmnd 114 London HMSO 1987 45 pages
Introduces the Government's proposals in funding and national planning for higher education. Includes the setting up of the Universities Funding Council and the Polytechnics and Colleges Funding Council.

286 **Department of Education and Science** *Highly qualified people: supply and demand* London HMSO 1990 68 pages
This report concentrates on the inter-relationship between higher education and employment. Draws together information about the supply of and demand for newly qualified graduates including the largest ever survey on this subject.

287 **Department of Education and Science** *Managing colleges efficiently* London DES 1987
A joint report by the Department of Education and Science and the Local Authority Associations which is concerned with cost effectiveness in further education colleges. Includes a list of recommendations.

288 **Department of Education and Science** *Report by HM Inspectors on a survey of higher introductory technology and engineering conversion courses* London HMSO 1989 11 pages
This is a useful survey offering an evaluation of higher introductory technology and engineering conversion courses. Issues included are structure of the courses, students' experiences, resources, environment, student support and aspects of management and organisation. The overall conclusion suggests these courses have provided a stimulating and successful contribution to widening access to engineering higher education.

289 **Department of Education and Science** *Student grants and loans* London DES 1991 27 pages
A concise guide to the student support system from grants and loans.

290 **Department of Education and Science** *The student top up loans scheme: an outline* London DES 1990 10 pages
Provides a concise guide to the system of student loans.

291 **Department of Education and Science** *Top up loans for students* Cmnd 520 London HMSO 1988 48 pages
Presents the case for change and outlines the mechanism of the student loans scheme. Attempts to answer questions about how it will affect the decisions made by potential students and in particular groups such as women, ethnic minorities and mature students.

292 **Department of Education and Science** *Universities in the training market: an evaluation of the University Grants Committee PICKUP selective training funding scheme* London DES/PICKUP 1989 44 pages

293 **Department of Education for Northern Ireland** *Higher Education in Northern*

Ireland: the future demand Bangor Dept. of Education and Dept. of Finance and Personnel 1985 22 pages
A discussion document which aimed to support the planning of higher education in Northern Ireland until the end of the 1990s. It provides some useful background information on the system and forecasts future demand.

294 **Department of Education, Glasgow Division** *Meeting the educational needs of a multi-cultural society* Glasgow Department of Education, University of Strathclyde December 1984
This report seeks to describe the efforts made by the Glasgow Division to meet the developing educational requirements of a multi-cultural and multi-racial society and to indicate directions in which it is hoped that future action may be possible.

295 **Department of Trade and Industry and Council for Industry and Higher Education** *Continuing education and training: collaboration between business and higher education* London HMSO 1990 41 pages
This booklet, one of a series on good practice in collaboration, aims to demonstrate how collaboration between business and higher education can bring about more effective continuing education and training. It is written for a mixed audience from both business and higher education and thus aims to explore both perspectives.

296 **Department of Trade and Industry** *Getting good graduates* London HMSO 1990 54 pages
A report designed to help those in business who are concerned with forming more effective links with higher education in order to enhance their ability to recruit and retain graduates who best meet their needs. Includes a useful selection of case studies depicting successful collaboration and advice on how these were established.

297 **Department of Trade and Industry** *Research and development report* London HMSO 1990 57 pages
Continuing the series on collaboration, this report provides practical information and guidance to those in business and higher education who are planning to work together on research and development projects and

programmes. It is aimed particularly at those who either have already formulated a conscious policy and strategy for collaborative research activity and are now setting out to implement them, or who are already involved in such activity and looking to review and improve their performance. Some chapters are directed more specifically to either higher education or the business reader.

298 **Dey I. and Harrison J** *Distance education and training for small firms (UK)* European Centre for the Development of Vocational Training Berlin CEDEFOP 1988 122 pages
This document describes some of the vocational training options available to small and medium sized business enterprises in the UK. A useful overview of distance education and training from a national context is provided and a selection of case studies is presented.

299 **Diamond J. and Kearney A.** Access course development: a case study *Journal of Further and Higher Education* Vol 11 No 2 Summer 1987 51-57
This article describes one particular model of adult provision - South Manchester Community College Access courses. The purpose of the article is not to generalise the appropriateness of such a model to other areas, rather to demonstrate the need for adult provision to be flexible in response to the local community in which it is based and to stimulate debate about the issues raised by Access provision.

300 **Dicken B. and Blomberg R.** Evaluating volunteer experience of women re-entering the workforce *Personnel Journal* Vol 67 No 12 Dec 1988 94-99
Women who have been active community volunteers and who are re-entering the job market are a valuable resource to employers. Active volunteer participation indicates self-motivation, high energy and a wide range of interests.

301 **Docherty A.** *Local educational guidance services for adults in Scotland* Edinburgh Scottish Institute of Adult and Continuing Education March 1988 35 pages
This study surveys current provision of guidance for adults at local level in Scotland. It

suggests that, while policies for guidance and even specific projects are developing, there appear, so far, to be insufficient resources allocated to enabling adults to make fully informed choices about education and training. Recommendations are made for the establishment of a national Scottish adult guidance initiative to provide advisory, consultancy and training services to support local and national developments.

302 Donaldson J.T. Scottish education: the 16+ development programme *Educational Management and Administration* Vol 14 No 1 Spring 1986 9-15
The Scottish 16+ Plan has been singled out as the most significant development in British education in the 1980s. Its objectives and characteristics are described in this article. The essence of the Action Plan is that it allows for rapid updating, preparation of new material to meet new demands within a standard format and rapid adjustment to the needs of industry.

303 Drew-Smith S. Investors in People: the employers view *TEC Director* Issue 7 1991 22-23
Reports on a series of case studies of British companies to assess their views of the benefits and drawbacks of the Investors in People standard. Stresses that companies which decide to implement the standard will look to the TECs for much of their support.

304 Duffin L. and Woods M. *Lifelong learning: Britain's future* Oxford Conference Report University of Oxford 1991 44 pages
With an introduction by Christopher Ball, this conference report is a valuable contribution to the philosophy behind lifelong learning. The Executive Summary depicts the main findings and recommendations for central action and action to be taken by higher education and TECS. The presentations on good practice are significant and summaries of the pre-circulated papers are attached.

305 Duguid S. What works in prison education *Adult Education* Vol 58 No 4 1986 page 329
The author argues that prison educators should concentrate on 'outcomes' - the desired behavioural and attitude changes in their students. It is not enough just to supply

prisoners with remedial, vocational or post secondary education.

306 Duke C. Post-16 Partnerships *Adults Learning* Vol 2 No 8 April 1991 233-235
Reviews continuing education. Argues adult continuing education stands to gain much from closer and more effective partnership with industry.

307 Duncan C. Racism in education, training and employment in Ranson S. *The revolution in education training* London Longman 1986 109-120
Provides some definitions of racism and examines their effects in education and employment focusing on the particular difficulties faced by ethnic minorities.

308 Duncan J.G. Marketing of higher education: problems and issues in theory and practice *Higher Education Quarterly* Vol 43 No 2 Spring 1989 175-188
A largely theoretical discussion about the state of marketing in higher education. Argues that much of the marketing which takes place is unsophisticated, being transferred into higher education without refinement.

309 Eagleson D.E. The educational counselling of unemployed adults *International Journal for the Advancement of Counselling* Vol 12 No 4 1989 273-279
Describes the background, aims and work of the Educational Guidance Service for Adults which is based in Belfast. Its role in providing information on learning opportunities and support to unemployed adults in Northern Ireland is discussed.

310 Eaton C. Retraining women to meet changing needs - is anyone really interested? *Women and Training News* Issue 29 Winter 1987 page 4
Considers the economic and social benefits which could accrue from retraining, to recognised standards, existing female employees to fill technician/technical engineer skill shortage occupations.

311 Economist Britain: women at work - paying for happier families *The Economist* Vol 31b No 7664 21 July 1990 56-57

This article looks at the initiatives taken by some companies to attract mothers back to work. Boots the Chemist for example, is offering a term-time working contract that leaves women free during school holidays.

312 Economist Childcare: the servant problem *The Economist* Vol 314 No 7646 17 March 1990 59-60
Companies believe that tax relief on childcare is needed because cheaper childcare would expand the supply of labour. In much of Europe, state provision increases the supply and lowers costs.

313 Education Competence and Assessment *Education* No 6 Oct 1988 4-8
Part of a series of short articles on research and experimental work which has been carried out so far on the viability of assessment and accreditation of prior learning.

314 Educational Counselling and Credit Transfer Information Service *Access to higher education courses directory 1989* Cheltenham ECCTIS 1989
A guide to courses throughout the UK, especially designed for adults who want to enter higher education and do not have the normally required entry qualification.

315 Educational Counselling and Credit Transfer Information Service *Educational Credit Transfer 1989/1990* Cheltenham ECCTIS 1990
A guide to credit transfer opportunities offered by advanced, further and higher education institutions in UK. Includes EGSAs who conform loosely to a list of criteria, which centre on the client-centred approach and whose main function is the provision of educational guidance.

316 Education, Science and Arts Committee **Second Report** *Prison Education* London HMSO March 1991 30 pages
The changing attitude towards the purpose of imprisonment is the overriding theme of this report. The prime importance of education and training is stressed and a number of recommendations concerning certificated achievements and the possibilities of continuing education and training outside prison are discussed.

317 Education, Science and Arts Committee Third Report *Prison Education* London HMSO June 1990 8 pages
This report discusses the necessity of a positive regime in prison which would enhance the role of education and training. Recommends that more workshops be brought into use with the industrial activity being used as the basis for vocational training.

318 Edwards J. *Evaluation in adult and further education* Liverpool WEA 1991
A practical handbook aimed at teachers and organisers involved in adult and further education. Offers advice on how to develop and implement ways to evaluate and improve the quality of the service on offer. Also discusses the staff training this will involve.

319 Edwards R. *An open learning pack* Milton Keynes Open University 1990
This pack enables those with an interest in adult educational guidance to locate the sources of influence on the guidance worker/client relationship and chart those factors which both enable and constrain the outcomes for learners. Stresses the importance of understanding the shared context guidance workers and clients work within as an essential component of good practice.

320 Edwards R. Access and assets: the experience of mature mother students in higher education *Journal of Access Studies* Vol 5 No 2 Autumn 1990 188-202
The research on which this paper is based was concerned with mature mother students, across race and class. A sample of mature mother students were interviewed to establish their feelings about the effects of studying upon relationships within their families and social groups. The results are fairly pessimistic. The students, having gained access, felt factors surrounding gender, race and class continued to prevent equality of experience.

321 Edwards R. Where is the DOE taking us: further education into the 1990s *Adults Learning* Vol 1 No 9 May 1990 253-254
An appraisal of skills training. Argues training must include broad based transferable skills which enable workers to cope with change.

322 **Edwards R.** Women, education and family life *Training and Development* Vol 9 No 2 Feb 1991
Describes some of the findings from research which addresses the implications for mature women students who have families.

323 **Eggins H.** Humanities and employment: disseminating innovation in the UK *Industry and Higher Education* Vol 4 No 2 1990 125-130
This article concerns higher education and the world of work. Argues that effective encouragement of changes within the humanities curricula and their dissemination throughout higher education can only be brought about by an informed understanding of how the higher education system works.

324 **Eggleston J. et al** Assessing and evaluating curriculum for unemployed adults from the black communities *Multicultural Teaching* Vol 9 No 1 1990 21-24
Report of an FEU project which looked at ways of meeting the needs of black adults with particular reference to successful black led community based projects. The findings are based on contact with the groups and interviews with the students and staff. Black led groups provide the right environment for the black unemployed to rebuild self esteem and gain employment. The problems of funding, pressure of external values (from government/industry), organisation and staffing are analysed. Concludes with a set of recommendations, the major of which concerns financial support, to DES, local authorities, industry and training agencies.

325 **Eldred J.** The experience of non-participant long-term unwaged adults and their attitudes towards continuing education *SERCH* No 10 1988 19-21

326 **Elking L.** Competency based human resource development: making sense of the ideas *Industrial and Commercial Training* Vol 22 No 4 1990 20-26
Discusses the growing use of competence in education and training and outlines the different definitions of competence which have been used.

327 **Ellis P. and Gorringe R.** Continuing education and training through competence based vocational qualifications *Education and Training Technology International* Vol 26 No 1 1989 7-13
Describes the establishment of the NCVQ and the introduction of NVQs. Discusses the effects of this in promoting greater flexibility in education and training and looks at the responses of staff and institutions.

328 **Ellis P. et al** Continuing education *Educational and Training Technology International* Vol 26 No 1 Feb 1989 7-38
Case studies examining continuing education are illustrated. Included are PICKUP; retraining in software engineering; Higher Introductory Technology and Engineering conversion course (HITECCS) training needs in manufacturing and the Seafish Open Learning Project.

329 **Employment Department** *Employment for the 1990s* Cmnd 540 London HMSO 1988 60 pages
Outlines proposals for a new system of industry led Training and Enterprise Councils which will be responsible for planing and delivering most of TEED's training and enterprise programmes.

330 **Employment Department** *Employment training for people with disabilities* London Employment Department 1990 108 pages
This consultative document is about how best to help people with disabilities find, keep and advance in work, so that society can draw more effectively on their talents and skills.

331 **Employment Department** *Lifelong learning - Britain's future: executive summary* Sheffield Employment Department and University of Oxford 1990 2 pages
In December 1990 heads of TECs and Higher Education Institutions and other senior figures attended a conference at the University of Oxford, Department for Continuing Education to discuss the issues surrounding the theme of 'lifelong learning'. This summary conveniently sets out the main recommendations. The need for TECs and HE to work together to pursue common goals in partnership is highlighted.

332 Employment Department *Lifelong learning: Britain's future: conference report: recommendations for action* Oxford Employment Department and University of Oxford 1991 44 pages

This report draws out the key concerns and recommendations from the 1990 Conference at University of Oxford, Department for Continuing Education on Lifelong Learning. See also Duffin L. and Woods M.

333 Employment Department National Institute of Adult and Continuing Education and REPLAN *New approaches to adult training* Leicester NIACE/REPLAN 1991 64 pages

Includes two sections on assessment and accreditation and evaluating quality. The first looks at the accreditation framework established by the NCVQ and assesses the impact it has made on assessment methods. The second focuses on the internal quality controls of training providers and discusses ways of monitoring performance.

334 Employment Department *Planning TEC market research* Sheffield Employment Department 1990 15 pages

Guide which aims to show TECs the central importance of a coherent marketing strategy as a basis for planning and evaluating activities. Deals with assessing information needs, ensuring the necessary resources and skills, and monitoring and evaluating the strategy and results. Part of a series of good practice guides.

335 Employment Department *Skills in focus* Occasional papers Sheffield Skills Unit, Employment Department 1990 7 pages

A useful series of occasional papers intended to offer a convenient briefing on specific skills and enterprise topics.

336 Employment Department *The training and development of trainers* Sheffield Employment Department 1990

This report by the PSI spells out what the successful companies are doing to train their trainers in order to develop the talents needed for the opportunities of the nineties.

337 Employment Department *Training and enterprise councils: a prospectus for the 1990s* Sheffield Employment Department 1990 21 pages

This prospectus describes TEC's principle objectives; their breadth of responsibility; how they will operate, be staffed and financed.

338 Employment Department *Training in Britain - employers' activities: a research report* Sheffield Employment Department 1989 99 pages

This report provides information gained from field research on the extent to which employers train and why they train. The main results are documented in the executive summary. It is clear from this that very few companies had a formal training strategy but those establishments which are growing fastest are the ones providing higher levels of training than the rest of British industry.

339 Employment Gazette Attitudes the key to more jobs for the disabled *Employment Gazette* Vol 98 No 8 August 1990 page 380

Reports employers' attitudes are the key to opening up productive job opportunities for people with disabilities. This is the fundamental message running through the consultative document *Employment and Training for People with Disabilities* published by the Employment Department. Here, the various measures to encourage employer's understanding are usefully summarised.

340 Employment Gazette Business leaders vie for TECs *Employment Gazette* Vol 97 No 6 1989 page 275

Reports on the response from employers for funding to establish TECs and establish business development plans.

341 Employment Gazette Contact makes enterprise work *Employment Gazette* Vol 97 No 7 1989 page 346

Describes the launch of Enterprise Works, the marketing campaign of the local enterprise agency networks.

342 Employment Gazette Disabled employees in the public sector *Employment Gazette* Vol 96 No 2 1988 79-83

This article shows the latest figures for a wide cross section of public sector employers whose individual quota positions have been disclosed with their agreement.

343 **Employment Gazette** Ethnic origin and the labour market *Employment Gazette* Vol 98 No 3 March 1990 125-137
Based on the Labour Market Survey, this article looks at the position of different ethnic groups in the labour market.

344 **Employment Gazette** Ethnic origin and the labour market *Employment Gazette* Vol 96 No 3 March 1988 164-178
Based on the Labour Market survey the article examines the economic position of different ethnic groups and draws comparisons with the white population. Includes data on economic activity, work status, unemployment and qualifications.

345 **Employment Gazette** Ethnic origin and the labour market *Employment Gazette* Vol 96 No 12 Dec 1988 633-646
Based on the Labour Market Survey this article looks at the position of different ethnic groups within the labour market and compares it with that of the white population.

346 **Employment Gazette** Ethnic origin and the labour market *Employment Gazette* Vol 99 No 2 Feb 1991 59-72
Looks at the position of ethnic minorities in the labour market. Identifies differences and similarities between different economic groups and compares them with the white population.

347 **Employment Gazette** Ex-offenders need better deal on jobs *Employment Gazette* Vol 98 No 8 August 1990 page 378
Draws attention to the pamphlet *Releasing the potential'* published by consultants Next Step Training Ltd. which considers the job prospects for ex-offenders. The pamphlet says that employers should have a written and regularly reviewed policy for employment of ex-offenders as part of their Equal Opportunities Policy. This could, in effect, restart access for a significant pool of potential and able employees.

348 **Employment Gazette** Learning to learn *Employment Gazette* Vol 99 No 3 March 1991 page 108
A useful review of the Flexible Learning Framework, launched by the Employment Department as a national strategy for education and training in the 1990s. Flexible Learning is about enabling the student to 'learn how to learn' as well as learning specific

subject knowledge and the principles can be applied to education and training at any age.

349 **Employment Gazette** New body to build school-industry links *Employment Gazette* Vol 98 No 11 November 1990 page 529
Reports on the Foundation for Education and Business Partnerships funded by TA, DES and range of blue chip companies. Among its priorities will be to persuade businesses to draw up a policy statement on partnership.

350 **Employment Gazette** New funds for school-industry links *Employment Gazette* Vol 99 No 1 January 1991 page 3
Reports on nationwide network of school-business partnerships due to be set up later this year. A range of activities could include: work experience placements for teachers and students; employer involvement on major education and training developments like NVQs, student, teacher and employee visits and exchanges including work-shadowing and more relevant careers advice.

351 **Employment Gazette** News brief: graceful CVs *Employment Gazette* Vol 99 No 2 Feb 1991 page 49
A very short discussion of the work of Harriet Grace who has set up a counselling service for women returners. This service is designed for women who have a clear idea of which career they wish to enter and help is given on CV compilation.

352 **Employment Gazette** News brief: more help with job search - plus more flexible training next year *Employment Gazette* Vol 98 No 12 Dec 1990 page 585
Considers how TECs will be able to tailor courses to provide help with rebuilding confidence, act as a short refresher or provide customised training linked to local employers experiencing recruitment problems.

353 **Employment Gazette** News brief: revamp for training information service *Employment Gazette* Vol 99 No 1 Feb 1991 page 49
This article considers the Training Development Information Service (TDIS) which provides a wide range of information covering all aspects of training and concludes with some pessimism that the service is not being used to

full effect. Some future developments are explored, notably rationalisation of the present database and also the incorporation of local records and information to the TDIS network in the hope of attracting more users.

354 **Employment Gazette** TEC News *Employment Gazette* Vol 99 No 2 Feb 1991 page 51

A round-up of some of the latest developments from the network of eighty two TECs up in operation. The TECs discussed here are portrayed favourably and have strong information and advice services on training and enterprise matters. For example, the Manchester TEC has access centres which will offer provision designed to help those whose needs are acting as a barrier to their provision.

355 **Employment Gazette** TECs and their partners *Employment Gazette* Vol 99 No 6 June 1991 page 334

Reports on a seminar by Chief Executive of North Nottinghamshire TEC on subject of TECs, their future and likely partners. The most commonly recognised partnerships involving TECs are education/business partnerships but this article shows other important partners will be local district council, environmental groups and industry training boards.

356 **Employment Gazette** Employment Training in Britain: key statistics *Employment Gazette* Vol 96 No 3 March 1988 page 130

This article presents key statistics on training and related topics. It is argued that all agencies involved in training need reliable information to judge the amount and type of training being undertaken.

357 **Engineering Council** *Continuing education and training: a national system for engineering* London Engineering Council 1988

This consultative document outlines proposals for a national system of continuing education and training for engineers and technicians.

358 **Engineering Council** *A national system for continuing professional development: a framework for action* London Engineering Council 1991 18 pages

This is an up-to-date consultative document which considers a national system of continuing training and education within the engineering industry.

359 **Entwistle J. and Wilson P.** Access and quality: two responses *Journal of Access Studies* Vol 2 No 1 1987 82-93

The paper presents two responses to the question of quality control in the Access route to higher education in the light of concern about the effects of non-traditional entry on standards. Argues that the evidence shows that quality is not being adversely affected but this is not perceived by many both inside and outside education.

360 **Equal Opportunities Commission** *The key to choice: an action plan for childcare: A discussion paper* Manchester EOC Oct 1990 48 pages

This paper which is both practical and forcible argues childcare cannot be tackled satisfactorily by employers and private providers alone. Suggestions for the main statutory functions of an Independent National Childcare Development Agency are highlighted.

361 **Equal Opportunities Commission** *Equal opportunities - a guide for employers* Manchester EOC Aug 1990 24 pages

The guide that explains the employment provisions of the Sex Discrimination Act to employers.

362 **Equal Opportunities Commission** *Positive action in vocational education and training* Manchester EOC Aug 1990 8 pages

A leaflet explaining section 47 of the Sex Discrimination Act to institutions of further and higher education, employers and other training organisations who may want to take positive action. Information is also given about funding and about existing positive action training initiatives.

363 **Equal Opportunities Commission** *Recent developments in childcare: a review* Manchester EOC 1988 99 pages

Reviews the quality of childcare. Concludes government policies have substantially hindered both local authorities and the voluntary sector in their efforts to respond to parental demand for more childcare of a higher quality. Case studies included.

364 Equal Opportunities Commission *Signposts* Manchester EOC Aug 1990 28 pages

A guide for women returning to work or learning. It helps them to find out what the choices are - how to find their way through the world of education and employment - how to find out what is available - and where to go for help.

365 Equal Opportunities Commission *A sound investment? The treatment of women by financial institutions* London HMSO 1989 64 pages

Results of this research suggest that financial institutions are often biased against women. This discrimination may be direct or indirect, most notably when giving bank loans. Amongst the recommendations made here is the importance of staff training which breaks down stereotypes about women customers and reflects the changes in women's employment status and lifestyles.

366 Equal Opportunities Commission and BBC *Women, training and tomorrow* London EOC/BBC 1991 12 pages

This booklet describes a practical example of how one organisation has encouraged women to enter a technical area of work. It is hoped that this will act as a blueprint and stimulate other organisations to introduce similar training schemes and/or to find other ways of enhancing the employees.

367 Equal Opportunities Commission *Women's business matters* Manchester EOC Nov 1989

Good practice guidelines for providers of training advice and finance to women entrepreneurs.

368 Equal Opportunities Commission for Northern Ireland *Annual Report* 1990 Belfast EOC Northern Ireland 1990 54 pages

Provides some useful background and statistical information on the position of women in the Northern Ireland labour force. The aims of the commission in relation to adult education and training are spelled out.

369 Equal Opportunities in Britain *Women and men in Britain* 1991 London HMSO 1991 37 pages

A review of the current position of women and men in contemporary Britain to inform the debate on equal opportunities. This edition is particularly concerned with the EOC's priority issues of earnings without discrimination, part-time work, social security and pensions. Included are sections on training and who is most likely to have access to job-related training and women in management.

370 Erskine S. Teacher education and professional development *British Journal of In-service Education* Vol 14 No 2 Spring 1988 113-116

Discusses the importance of professional development in relation to the further education of teachers in the form of in-service training; access to courses leading to further professional qualifications and access to degree courses.

371 European Centre for the Development of Vocational Training *Equality of opportunity and vocational training: creation and management of enterprise by women: the situation in the UK* Luxembourg CEDEFOP 1988 76 pages

This report is the result of a survey conducted throughout all twelve countries of the European Community to identify the vocational training needs of women in order to provide assistance for the improvement of training provision.

372 European Communities Committee Twenty-first report - *Vocational training and re-training* Warwick University of Warwick 24 July 1990 29 pages

Reviews the FORCE programme which is the Community action programme for the development of continuing vocational training. The aim of FORCE is to improve vocational training and re-training in the community. This report illustrates a national strategic framework for vocational training.

373 European Journal of Education Key issues in distance education *European Journal of Education* Vol 24 No 1 1989 11-46

Distance education is looked at from three perspectives: the academic, industrial and government viewpoints. The three papers have look at the main developments in distance education across Europe, the paper by Fox, seconded from the UK Training Agency to

COMETT Technical Unit is a particularly useful overview of European Distance Education programmes which uses examples in the UK and France to illustrate national strategies in this field.

374   Evans J. The benefits of women-only courses (in management) *Transition* April 1987 16-17
The first women-only management course at Ashridge Management College is reviewed, together with an analysis of leadership skills. The author believes women-only management courses should be encouraged as they can help many potential women leaders in their personal development.

375   Evans N. *Assessing experiential learning: a review of progress and practice* York Longman Resources Unit for FEU 1987 30 pages
This report is primarily concerned with ways of assessing the experiential learning that is undertaken in educational institutions. Provides a summary of current practice which should be a useful source of information for those involved in implementing the proposals of the RVQ Working Group and NCVQ. Will also be useful for tutors/trainers who can draw on the experience of others as they devise schemes to meet their own particular requirements.

376   Evans N. *Assessment of prior experiential learning* London Council for National Academic Awards March 1988 4 pages
This is a report of a CNAA Development Fund project by the Learning From Experience Trust directed by Norman Evans. The objectives of the project were 'to negotiate, establish, monitor and appraise schemes for the assessment of prior experiential learning in polytechnics and colleges'.

377   Evans N. *Collaboration between employment and education: staff development* London LET June 1990 page 3
Discusses a new initiative which offers an approach to collaboration which would enable academic staff and company staff to be placed on the same development programme.

378   Evans N. Assessing prior experiential learning *Industrial and Commercial Training* Vol 21 No 1 1989 3-5

All learners, particularly older learners, bring a wealth of knowledge and skills with them when they engage in additional and formally organised learning. It is in everyone's best interest to obtain an accurate account of what that knowledge and those skills, competencies and capabilities are. The assessment of prior experiential learning (APEL) can offer guidance and counselling, a general preparation for and access to further study, and advanced academic or professional standing in relation to a particular qualification being sought.

379   Eversley D. *Religion and employment in Northern Ireland* London Sage 1989 256 pages
An important work which reports on research commissioned by the Fair Employment Agency for Northern Ireland. The research aims to explain some of the differences in local or community unemployment rates by reference to demographic factors, sex, age, educational attainment and the structure of the labour market. The educational and training opportunities open to the local communities are examined. Much useful statistical information is provided. There is also an extensive bibliography.

380   Fage J. Vocational guidance provision: an international survey *Open Learning* Vol 3 No 1 Feb 1988 53-55
This article covers the results of an international survey of the provision of vocational guidance in distance education and recognises the diversity of vocational guidance strategies in different countries.

381   Fair Employment Commission *A profile of the workforce in Northern Ireland: a summary of the 1990 monitoring returns* Belfast Fair Employment Commission 1991 57 pages
This report is based on the returns which monitor the religious composition of the workforce in Northern Ireland under the Fair Employment (Northern Ireland) Act of 1989. The report concentrates on the distribution of members of the Protestant and Roman Catholic communities by occupation.

382   Falconer H. Children at work *Personnel Today* 3 April 1990 page 14
The author suggests that the Government response of removing the tax employees must pay on employers' provision on workplace

nurseries does not go far enough; argues cash allowances and voucher schemes are also needed.

383   **Falconer H.** Women talk money *Personnel Today* 1989 page 8
Reports that the TUC wants to place equal opportunities for women higher up the bargaining agenda. A set of guidelines for negotiations on equal opportunities issues 'The Charter for Women at Work' has been drawn up after wide consultation among trade unions. Aims to raise awareness especially among male negotiators, of women's issues.

384   **Farley M.** Let's make new friends: the training and enterprise councils *Education* Vol 17 No 3 19 Jan 1990 58-59
A Report on TECs and their importance in strengthening education-industry links. TECs are also encouraged to support the enterprise in higher education initiative and help them to form the necessary EHE partnerships with employers and encourage links between local employers and HE in developing provision to meet specific local needs and feedback of labour market information.

385   **Farmer T.** Why does a businessman invest in people *TEC Director* Issue 7 1991 18-19
The chairman of Kwik-Fit Plc discusses the value to his business of investing in its staff and argues for the use of the Investors in People standard.

386   **Farrell P. et al** Training for women and men working together *Journal of European Industrial Training* Vol 10 No 7 1986 34-43
There are several reasons why courses are needed to train men and women to work together. These are thoroughly explored in this article. Attitudinal factors must be changed to eliminate barriers to women's advancement and development.

387   **Farren S. and Todd M.** *Adult literacy and adult basic education in Northern Ireland: 10 years on* Dublin Reading Association 1986 12 pages
Reports on a study which examined the ways in which adult literacy provision in Northern Ireland has developed since 1975. Questionnaires were distributed to organizers

and tutors to determine the patterns of provision.

388   **Fatchett D.** Education and training: the Labour view *Transition* Vol 89 No 9 October 1989 9-11
Sets out the Labour Party's proposals on education and training. This aims to expand full-time, post-16 education and improve the quality of technical education and training. It is designed to make possible an improvement in vocational training standards and to remove the differentiation between the academic and the technical.

389   **Fazaeli T.** *Innovation in access:* 1: The overview 2: Case studies 3: Case studies Leicester UDACE/NIACE 1991
These three volumes are the result of a project which set out to examine approaches to improving access to education and training for adults by studying the work of thirteen very different agencies and institutions in GB. The overview presents the issues and themes emerging from the studies. The second and third volumes contain the detailed case studies. The 'whole institution' approach to access is influential throughout. The issue of guidance was perceived by all providers to be of great importance but at present it seems guidance within courses is not approached systematically by any one case-study institution.

390   **Felton D.** Skill shortages reflect lack of investment in training *Employment Bulletin and IR Digest* Vol 4 No 12 1987 3-4
Claims that growing skill shortages will convince employers that they must invest in training.

391   **Fennell E. et al** The analysis of competence: current thought and practice *Competence and Assessment* Issue 1 1989 1-20
The whole issue is devoted to an examination of how occupational standards are being used in the field. Includes contributions from a variety of occupational backgrounds on the analysis of standards in their area.

392   **Ferrar P.** Open learning *Training and Development* Vol 9 No 4 April 1991 36-40
Explains how the Bradford and Bingley Building Society set about implementing an

open learning programme which won a National Training Award.

393 **Fey S. and Davey M.** *Preparing proposals for funding: basic guidelines for adult education* London Educational Centres Association 1986 36 pages

Brings together information on funding for adult education from external agencies. Contains lists of addresses and contacts and worked examples of funding proposals.

394 **Field J.** What workers, what leave? Changing patterns of employment and the prospects for paid educational leave In: *Learning for Life* Molyneux F. et al (Ed) Croom Helm 1988 63-75

Discusses paid educational leave in the context of a rapidly changing labour market. Argues that continuing education at present reinforces existing inequalities resulting in a growing divide of core and periphery workers. If training is to be taken seriously, the author suggests that employers incorporate training as well as educational leave.

395 **Field J. et al** *Struggling to learn: the financial situation of access students* Forum for Access Studies 1990 33 pages

Report dealing with the extent and the nature of the financial pressures faced by Access students which stop them from achieving their aims. It looks at sources of finance and credit and the main costs and areas of financial difficulty experienced. Gives possible additional sources of support for Access students.

396 **Field R.** The National Training Awards: a personal perspective *TEC Director* Issue 7 1991 24-25

The chairman of Sheffield TEC describes his involvement in the National Training Awards. Discusses the positive role they can play in encouraging business to invest in training and to emphasise the support that TECs can offer.

397 **Finch J. and Mason J.** Gender, employment and responsibilities to kin *Work, Employment and Society* Vol 4 No 3 Sept 1990 349-367

This article based on empirical research surveys the competing demands of employment commitments and family responsibilities. Concludes respondents rarely made stark choices between family and job but tended to rely on compromise situations such as the sharing of caring responsibilities with a spouse or siblings, or working part-time.

398 **Finegold D. and Soskice D.** The failure of training in Britain: analysis and prescription *Oxford Review of Economic Policy* Vol 4 No 3 1988 21-53

Highlights the need for policy makers and academics to take account of the two-way nature of the relationship between education and training and the economy. Argues that GB's failure to educate and train its workforce to the same level as its international competitors has been both a product and a cause of the nation's poor relative economic performance.

399 **Finegold D. et al** *A British baccalaureate - ending the division between education and training* London Institute of Policy Research 1990 60 pages

An informed and highly relevant discussion on all aspects of post-16 education with special emphasis on the value of vocational education, training and tertiary colleges.

400 **Finlayson B.** Economic awareness and enterprise education in Scotland *Economics* Vol 24 Part 4 Winter 1988 172-174

401 **Finn E. and Bocock J.** Poor relation status: the enemy of quality *NATFHE Journal* Vol 10 No 7 1985 12-13

Assesses the impact on the quality of education of the increase in the student staff ratio in the public sector of higher education.

402 **Finn G.P.T.** Multicultural anti-racism and Scottish education *Scottish Educational Review* Vol 19 No 1 May 1987 39-49

Discusses racism and its influences on educational thinking and approaches including some forms of multiculturalism. Calls for the development of multicultural anti-racism to combat Scottish racism.

403 **Finn R.** Distance learning: the palatable training tonic *Works Management* Vol 44 No 2 1991 41-45

The author considers how distance learning may fit into a company's training strategy. The central thrust of the article is that as no two companies will have identical training needs, individual firms need help in assessing their own training programmes and will probably benefit more by using a range of training methods rather than reliance on one method. Provides an example of one company who introduced distance learning and concludes if this method is to succeed then on-site tutorials or access to counsellor/tutor/support group is essential.

404 **Fisham N.** Our customers want seamless excellence in their training *Journal for Quality and Participation* Dec 1990 24-27
Argues that a successful training programme must incorporate a quality control mechanism.

405 **Fiske P.** *Developing educational guidance* Leicester UDACE/NIACE 1989 38 pages
Gives a snapshot of what happened in eleven English LEAs who received Educational Support Grants for educational guidance over two financial years. They report that funding has stimulated both development and expansion, although this has been very varied, reflecting a host of local circumstances and needs.

406 **Fitzgerald M.J.** Teaching English as a second language to bilingual adults in Britain *British Journal of Language Teaching* Vol 23 No 1 1985 42-51

407 **Fletcher S.** Accreditation of prior learning: a contribution to national economic objectives *Journal of European Industrial Training* Vol 14 No 9 1990 8-11
Assesses the potential role of APL in making maximum effective use of existing national resources and in encouraging adults to acquire new skills.

408 **Foggo T.** Open learning in ICI *Open Learning* Vol 1 No 1 February 1986 13-15
Open learning embraces advances in educational theory, technology and practice. The primary emphasis is on meeting individual needs by allowing flexibility of pace, and learning opportunities in relation to work routines. This article looks at ICI's open learning programme and using this example concludes any open learning initiative needs to be based on a sound foundation of good training and development practice and an awareness of what constitutes good learning material. Clear line management, commitment and advocacy must be combined with an understanding and awareness of the consequences for the organisation of changes in training and development practice.

409 **Fonda N. and Hayes C.** Is more training really necessary? *Personnel Management* Vol 18 No 5 May 1986 47-50
The authors consider the literature received by employers from the government and other bodies informing them they need more and better training. They conclude that such literature is not always perceived to be relevant to employers' needs. Employers, wish to know how their 'own' organisation would be more effective and successful if more training was given.

410 **Forbes A.** The Open University: my great hope *Multicultural Teaching* Vol 8 No 3 Summer 1990 36-37
A black woman describes her experiences as an Open University student. She experienced alienation as the only black student in white middle class tutorials and summer schools. She questions equal opportunities and staff training and the lack of anti-racist perspective within the Open University.

411 **Ford G.** The Careers Service and the adult guidance dilemma *Careers Journal* Jan 1987 31-37
Looks at the questions raised for the Careers Service with the increasing demand from adults for guidance. It is likely to have even greater impact as more authorities adopt tertiary and community orientated solutions to 16 plus provision. Argues information provision is one essential role for the Careers Service of the future, or for the emerging education-based guidance and counselling service into which it may be incorporated.

412 **Ford G.** Meeting the vocational education, training and guidance needs of adults *Adult Education* Vol 58 No 7 June 1985 35-38
Outlines some of the issues raised within a Leeds Education Authority Report on adult vocational education, training and counselling requirements. Discusses the need for a coordinated strategy which would encompass essential unity of need and impartiality of choice.

413 **Ford R.** Going to market *Training Tomorrow* Sept 1989 17-18

Recognises the difficulty of marketing training as the benefits are hard to identify. Offers advice to training companies selling services to organisations such as TECs and suggests ways of bringing training into the public eye.

414   Fordyce D. and Robinson S. Professional education in civil engineering: a specific example *European Journal of Engineering Education* Vol 15 No 2 1990 105-115
Describes a professional development programme at Heriot-Watt University. Recommendations are provided.

415   Forrest A. Women in a man's world *Journal of Management Development* Vol 8 No 6 1989 61-68
This article describes management career development and argues the pressure to conform to a corporation's timetable for success discriminates against the female manager. Preconceived notions about women's and men's career values often mean women who want to succeed are not given due respect.

416   Foster A. Explaining quality systems *Training Tomorrow* Sept 1990 38-40
Discusses the application of the quality assurance standard BS 5750 to organisations involved in training.

417   Foster A. Up quality street *Training Tomorrow* May 1991 19-21
Examines the potential benefits and problems associated with the application of BS 5750 to training.

418   Foster P. Information Paper 11: adult basic education in Scotland *Scottish Educational Review* Vol 15 No 1 1983 52-59
Describes the evolution and success of Scotland's adult basic education programme, staffed with paid and volunteer tutors in literacy, numeracy, social and other skills. Illustrates regional differences in adult basic education skill offerings. Stresses the underlying adaptability of adult basic education to student needs.

419   Fowler G. The vocational route to higher education *Education and Training* Vol 32 No 4 1990 20-22

The author argues that the Government's under funding of the higher education sector is preventing the widening of access. Argues for the vocational route to higher education to be accepted.

420   Frankel A. and Reeves F. Educational access: strategies in a movement for expanding participation in further and higher education *Journal of Access Studies* Vol 6 No 2 1991 124-134
This paper discusses a number of different strategies which co-exist under the 'access' title and which have in common the objective of expanding participation in further and higher education provision. Particular emphasis is given to the notion of access and equality of educational opportunity.

421   Freeman R. The National Extension College: open learning in the making *Open Learning* Vol 3 No 1 1988 42-44
Describes the history and growth of the National Extension College. Traces subsequent developments in open learning back to the establishment of the NEC.

422   Freeman R. Open learning: taking stock *Open Learning* Vol 5 No 3 Nov 1990 3-9
Discusses NVQs which bring with them assessment of prior learning. As NVQs grow so will provision for accrediting prior learning and for recording individual units of competence. That is the smallest component of learning that the NCVQ requires. Makes the point that routes in to university, apart from A-levels for example, are poorly publicised. Looks at the notion of 'choice' and argues that choice is not something the market offers, we demand it of the market by our purchasing decisions and suggests we should do the same in education.

423   Fricker J. Open learning: what's in it for business? In: *Open learning in transition: an agenda for action* Paine N. (Ed) Cambridge Cambridge National Extension College 1988 264-273
An excellent discussion of the advantages and disadvantages inherent in open learning. The key points for open learning in industry are conveniently summarized.

424   Fritchie R. How to design women's training that gets results *Journal of*

European Industrial Training Vol 10 No 7 1986 10-14

Although women make up 44% of the total working population, they continue to work in predominantly low paid, low status jobs which are not seen to require much training and development. This paper suggests why training for women employees is necessary and offers practical suggestions for designing training programmes.

425   Froggatt P. Higher education in Northern Ireland: a Queen's University perspective *In: Osborne R.D. et al (Eds) Education and policy in Northern Ireland* Belfast Policy Research Institute 1987 219-229

Describes the development of higher education in Northern Ireland since the Lockwood Report of 1965. Examines the effects of restructuring on Queen's University in terms of funding, student mix and co-operation between institutions. Discusses the problems faced by Queen's as a large civic university in the national system but also as a partner in higher education in a society which the author regards as socially and educationally isolated.

426   Fry E. *An equal chance for disabled people* London Spastics Society 1986

The primary aim of this study was to establish whether disabled people experience discrimination in employment. Looks at discrimination in a systematic way by providing statistical evidence gained from a test using fictitious applications for a number of jobs. Evidence from this survey shows that disabled people experience considerable discrimination and are not given equal chances in the recruitment process.

427   Fuller A. and Saunders M. The paradox in open learning at work *Personnel Review* Vol 19 No 5 1990 29-33

A valuable case study is presented of the open learning schemes available to the employees of a major retailer. Principles of procedure for the management of open learning are offered.

428   Fullerton M. *Jobs for blacks* New Society Vol 76 20th June 1986 page 21

Reports on a course in Leeds which seeks to redress racial disadvantage in employment by providing training for black people in housing management. This also aims to help remedy discrimination in housing practices.

429   Fulton O. and Ellwood S. *Admissions in higher education* Sheffield Department of Employment 1989 25 pages

Based on interviews with Admissions Officers and other senior managers in a selection of higher education institutions and colleges of further education, this project maps the present pattern of admissions policies and practices and examines the rationales, constraints and incentives affecting them in order to assess the potential for an increase in the participation rate.

430   Fulton O. (Ed) *Access and institutional change* Milton Keynes SRHE/OU 1989 180 pages

This is a valuable book which explores three major themes: the processes of selection for, or exclusion from, higher education. The internal processes of higher education; and their effects on 'non traditional' students and the challenge of existing institutions to meet these new demands. Written by experts and practitioners, the book draws on a wide range of research and experience in access issues throughout higher education and beyond.

431   Furnham A. A question of competency *Personnel Management* Vol 22 No 6 June 1990 page 37

Managers are now being encouraged to list the competencies that employees need to operate successfully and which can be used in selection and promotion policies. The author argues competencies are just a list and often neglect other 'human abilities' which are clearly related.

432   Further education special needs teacher training working group *A special professionalism* London HMSO 1987 34 pages

These are valuable reports which examine the practical alternatives to LEAs, colleges and schools in seeking to offer adequate, effective and appropriate education and training to students with special needs. Part 1 addresses broad issues associated with organisation, planning, management and resources. Part II considers more specific curricular issues to do with curriculum design, delivery and support.

433   Further Education Staff College *Work based learning project* Bristol Further Education Staff College 1989 135 pages

A commentary on terms and definitions for work-based learning in vocational education and training.

434   Further Education Unit *Access to FE for black adults* London FEU/REPLAN 1989 4 pages
Report on a project carried out in Liverpool to provide vocational courses in an FE college aimed at the unemployed black community. Includes a series of recommendations for FE providers.

435   Further Education Unit *Access to further and higher education: a discussion document* London FEU 1987 16 pages
This paper attempts to clarify some of the issues surrounding access provision and

describes some of the support that has been developed and suggests an agenda for action.

436   Further Education Unit *Anti-racist strategies in college and community* London FEU 1989 9 pages
Summarises the lessons from a 3 year project aimed at combatting racism in higher education and the community. Includes sections and examples of courses on staff and curriculum development.

437   Further Education Unit *Assessment, quality and competence: staff training issues for NCVQ* London FEU 1986 49 pages
A handbook which deals with the issues surrounding the introduction of NVQs in further education. Provides information for those involved in assessment and negotiation in the new system. A description of the system is given and issues such as quality and competence are addressed.

438   Further Education Unit *Black perspectives on adult education: identifying the need* London FEU 1989 62 pages
Report on a project based in the Sheffield Adult Education Service looking at anti-racist strategies in curriculum development and ways of implementing institutional change.

439   Further Education Unit *Black students and access to higher education: summary of a feasibility study* London FEU 1987 11 pages
Questionnaires and interviews were used to investigate the experience of black students in

HE and to look at the opportunities for access. Includes a list of recommendations.

440   Further Education Unit *A college guide: meeting special educational needs* York Longman Group 1986 104 pages
This is a practical guide providing detailed background information and advice for those wanting to make better provision for students with a wide range of special needs. The book gives specialist advice about individual needs stemming from a range of physical impairments as well as learning, emotional and behavioural difficulties.

441   Further Education Unit *College marketing: a support pack* London FEU 1988 39 pages
A useful series of support materials including checklist and examples of documentation to be used in the development and implementation of a marketing strategy. Copyright on the materials has been waived.

442   Further Education Unit *Developing a marketing strategy for adult and continuing education* London FEU 1990 24 pages
Report of a pilot project to develop an educational marketing strategy within a local education authority which could then be applied in other authorities. The emphasis is on practical suggestions, cost effectiveness and the importance of market research. The report contains material from interviews with participant and non-participant groups.

443   Further Education Unit *Learning from Experience Trust embedding APL within learner centred assessment and guidance services.* Project 531(Stage 2) London FEU/LET 1990
This project is assisting three very different FE institutions to integrate the recognition and assessment of prior learning and achievement (APL/A) into mainstream curricular provision. Whilst the colleges are developing specific applications of APL/A to suit their particular circumstances there are common objectives, one of which is to develop coordinated learner-centred approaches to assessment and guidance.

444   Further Education Unit *Ethnic monitoring in further and higher education: an account of ILEA's initiative* London FEU 1989 42 pages

Report on the achievements of ILEA's policy of ethnic monitoring.

445   Further Education Unit *FE can really change your life: the experience of Afro-caribbean and Asian students in further education* London FEU 1987 36 pages

Report of a seminar organised by the FEU and the National Union of Students in which black students discussed their experiences of FE and suggested ways in which their needs could be met.

446   Further Education Unit *FE in black and white: staff development needs in a multicultural society* London FEU 1987 58 pages

A survey of four colleges looking at the staff development needs in relation to the participation of ethnic minorities.

447   Further Education Unit *Flexible learning opportunities* London FEU 1983 59 pages

One way for colleges to meet the demand for a wider range of learning opportunities for adults in Great Britain is to provide more flexibility within the further education system. Because the flexible learning approach is learner-centred, it requires a greater emphasis on negotiation, counselling, and guidance to help learners to identify and progress through the most appropriate learning programme to meet their individual needs.

448   Further Education Unit *Flexible learning opportunities and special educational needs* London FEU 1988 60 pages

This report arose from a recognition that the concept of flexible learning, with its emphasis on learner autonomy, can be of particular benefit to people with special learning needs. The project considers the extent of flexible learning opportunities in further and adult education and ways in which such opportunities could be extended.

449   Further Education Unit and Engineering Council *The key technologies: some implications for education and training* London FEU 1988 26 pages

This paper aims to explain the concept of key technologies which has important implications for all providers of education and training, especially in the formation and continuing education and training of engineers. The thrust

is all commercial and industrial employers need individuals with good technical, commercial and interpersonal skills who are able to keep up-to-date with changes in working practices and technology.

450   Further Education Unit *Marketing adult/continuing education* London FEU 1987 66 pages

This study aimed to examine public attitudes towards adult/ continuing education and to identify ways in which providers can market their services effectively. Six adult and continuing education colleges participated along with local employers and community organisations. The findings showed that the public view adult education as primarily a leisure based activity. Employers do not think it is relevant to their needs. Community groups see the providers as supporting their aims and roles. The college staff viewed marketing in narrow terms as promotion and publicity. The role of research, assessment and evaluation was less clearly defined. The report includes data on the findings and a series of recommendations.

451   Further Education Unit *Marketing FE: a feasibility study* London FEU 1985 133 pages

This study examines the way in which adult education is being marketed in five colleges through interviews and questionnaires with staff and local business and industry. Basic marketing principles were found to be widely understood but the mechanisms, skills and resources to back up the work was variable. In particular, a lack of any systematically applied strategy was noted. Recommendations were made including the need to develop a corporate identity, to target marketing and to develop closer links with local schools and business. The need to set up effective targeting and evaluation mechanisms was stressed.

452   Further Education Unit *National Vocational Qualifications: initial criteria and guidelines for staff development with specific reference to further and higher education* London FEU 1988 14 pages

A short handbook offering guidance to those involved in the financing, planning or running of staff development programmes relating to the implication of NVQs.

453 Further Education Unit *NVQs and learners with special needs: National Vocational Qualifications Number 3* London FEU 1990 7 pages

Reports on a project which explored the role of further education colleges in assessing the needs of adults with special needs and facilitating their access to NVQs. Includes a series of recommendations.

454 Further Education Unit *Opening doors: creating further education opportunities for the unemployed* London FEU 1986 72 pages

This report gives practical advice to unemployed people wishing to attend further education establishments while retaining their right to unemployment benefits. The report explores ways colleges can make provision for claimants through identification of needs, provision of guidance, and attention to specific needs of adults.

455 Further Education Unit *Opportunity 1992: college courses and the Single European Market.* London FEU 1989 7 pages

A bulletin which considers the effects that the European Single Market will have on education and training, in particular for those colleges selling customised, updating and similar courses to companies. PICKUP is discussed and three case studies are included.

456 Further Education Unit *Quality in NAFE* London FEU 1987 32 pages

Document which aims to give guidance on the achievement of quality in work related non-advanced further education. Attempts to define and construct criteria as a basis for applying quality measures to a wide range of aspects of further education such as course design, support services and evaluation. Concludes with a checklist.

457 Further Education Unit *Raising perceptual awareness in work with women and girls* London FEU 1986 69 pages

Describes strategies for counteracting early sex-role stereotyping and its effects in narrowing young women's subject opinions and career choices. Uses a 'personal construct' psychological approach.

458 Further Education Unit *Second chance to learn? A review of WEA 'second chance to learn' courses* London FEU 1988 66 pages

Describes a course, designed by the WEA, intended to fill a gap between informal discussion groups and access courses for higher education. Offers advice for designing and running such a course.

459 Further Education Unit *Special needs occasional paper no 5: A realistic goal? The integration of learners with special needs into adult education* York Longman Group 1987 38 pages

An important document for all those concerned with ensuring that adults with a range of disabilities are not excluded from the pattern of adult education. The report focuses on the integration of students with special needs into adult education, including mainstream courses. It has been written as the result of a project investigating activities within the Southwark Adult Education Institute and the adult education service in Inner London. It provides a detailed picture of current provision and points to general recommendations for community, peer and professional support. It highlights the need for student participation in planning, flexibility of provision, links with other service providers, a clear policy statement, staff development and the need for educational providers to raise their profile among people with disabilities.

460 Further Education Unit *Supporting adult learning: a curriculum strategy for the development of continuing education/training for adults. A discussion document* London FEU 1987 26 pages

Stresses the importance of curricular design and the recognition of a core of skills as a basis for learning. Written thematically the report includes sections on FEU, DES PICKUP, RESTART and training strategies for adults, the delivery of which are relevant to part-time recurrent nature of adult learning. Major national level initiatives and issues of coordination, guidance and the design of flexible modes of delivery are discussed.

461 Further Education Unit *Training for the future: how can trainees meet current and future needs of industry?* London FEU 1990 61 pages

Guidelines and models for the development of interdisciplinary assignments based on the concept of key technologies.

462 Further Education Unit *Vocational education and training: briefing notes for further education* London FEU 1990 32 pages

A pack containing information and three booklets aimed at staff who are implementing NVQs in further education based on the Administrative, Business and Commercial Training Group. The three booklets deal with learning programmes, assessment and recording systems and colleges in the workplace.

463 Gallacher J. *Part-time degree provision in Scotland -courses and students 1987/1988* Glasgow Glasgow College April 1990 129 pages

Provides a very useful overview of part-time degree provision in Scotland. Argues that the expansion of part-time degree provision will achieve the objective of involving greater numbers of adults in higher education. Illuminates areas where further research is needed.

464 Gallacher J. and Osborne M. Differing national models of Access provision: a comparison between Scotland and England *Journal of Access Studies* Vol 6 No 2 1991 147-164

This paper compares Access provision in Scotland and England to enable a better understanding of the two systems. It provides an initial analysis of the implications of these different models of access provision which will help develop an agenda for the future systematic evaluation of these models.

465 Gallagher A. Comparative value added as a performance indicator *Higher Education Review* Vol 23 No 3 1991 19-30

Discusses the use of performance indicators in the public sector of higher education. Argues that the necessity for standard measures which allow comparisons between institutions gives rise to oversimplified results. Describes a complex system of 'education value added' which attempts to more fully address the quality of education.

466 Gallagher P. The future for further education in Northern Ireland *In:*

Osborne R.D. et al (Ed) Education and policy in Northern Ireland Belfast Policy Research Institute 1987 245-256

Discusses the role of further education colleges in Northern Ireland and the ways that they can respond to changing demands. The problems faced by their clients are compounded in Northern Ireland by the weakened industrial base, its geographical isolation and political instability.

467 Galliers D. Racism and staff development in adult education *Adult Education* Vol 60 No 1 1987 28-33

The author gives examples of personal and institutional racism in adult education. In particular covert racism in institutional practices and procedures is examined. Two types of staff training are discussed, that providing multicultural information and that aimed at raising awareness of racism.

468 Garner A. Stepping out: a mature student's view of higher education *Journal of Access Studies* Vol 5 No 2 Autumn 1990 218-220

An interesting article which points out the conflicts a woman returning to study may face if she has a family. Concludes we need to recognise equality of opportunity as a right and not a privilege.

469 Garnett E. Careers guidance for women returners *Newscheck* Vol 7 No 6 April 1990 page 11

Discusses the computer-aided guidance system which is an expert system designed to give advice tailored to individual women's skills, needs, experiences and aspiration.

470 Garnier T. TECs and ex-offenders *Inside Out* Dec 1989 11-12

Tom Garnier, a board member of the Birmingham TEC, gives advice to rehabilitation bodies in their relations with TECs.

471 Garry A. and Cowan J. *Continuing professional development:a learner-centred strategy* London FEU/PICKUP 1986 56 pages

This report describes a project concerned with the continuing professional development of engineers. A learner-centred approach was taken to help the engineers continue their education. Identification of individual needs, peer-group learning and supportive tutoring were found to occupy a central role in this learner-centred approach. The report aims to give practical advice to all tutors who are interested in using such learner-centred strategies with adults.

472   Garry A. and Cowan J. *Learning from Experience* London FEU/PICKUP 1986 96 pages

This occasional paper is published as a companion volume to the above report - *Continuing Professional Development: a learner centred strategy.* It is intended as a practical guide for teachers in further and higher education who are involved in CPD and wish to use a strategy of participative workshops. The main message of both volumes is that in the provision of courses for the CPD of adults, it is essential to recognise and exploit their store of experiential learning.

473   Gartside P. Managing flexible college structures *Coombe Lodge Report* Vol 22 No 3 1990 175-277

This report describes the approach of one college to the task of developing its staff to enable them to respond to the demands of a changing education and training environment.

474   Gartside P. The national certificate in Scotland *Coombe Lodge Report* Vol 22 No 4 1990 277-376

Discusses the National Certificate modular system which emerged from the 16+ Action Plan in 1985, as a major element of vocational education and training in Scotland. This report is predominantly concerned with the views of students and concentrates in particular on the Action Plan objective of providing a wider range of choice for students.

475   Garvie I. Training access points: focus on women *Scottish Journal of Adult Education* Vol 8 No 3 Spring 1988 30-31

The authors offer a critical review of some trends in contemporary vocational education and training. Argue that training cannot and should not be separated from education. If the aim is flexibility and adaptability then much training depends on adequate levels of general education to enable men and women to take an active role in society. Highlights some of the initiatives resulting from the Government's report 'The New Training Initiative' (1981) and developments in experiential qualifications and also usefully documents those trends which

they believe do not form the basis of a continuing education.

476   Gaskell S.M. Education and culture: a perspective from higher education *Higher Education Quarterly* Vol 43 No 4 Autumn 1989 318-331

The classical cultural definition of higher education as an end in itself has encouraged an exclusive view, detached from the real world. This article illustrates how cultural expectations can be defined in relation to higher education today and offers some suggestions on issues which need to be addressed.

477   Gavine D.J. Special educational needs: fact or fiction? *Scottish Educational Review* Vol 17 No 1 May 1985 14-22

Argues that while the concept of special educational need as set forth in Scotland's 1981 Education Act may be useful in day-to-day decision-making, it is too vague and value-laden to sustain the extremely formal structure laid down in statute.

478   Geale J. Credit where its due *Pickup in Progress* Summer 1991 26-28

The author discusses the many benefits which may be accrued from accrediting short courses and in-company training.

479   Gellis P. Staff development for open learning *NASD Journal* No.22 January 1990 19-22

Buckinghamshire County Council's staff development programme for staff involved in Open Learning is reviewed in this article. The programme was based on the Certificate of Open Learning Delivery (COLD). Its success, problems and proposals for the second phase of staff development are discussed.

480   General Teaching Council for Scotland *Partnership in professional training:* Report of the conference held at Moray House College of Education 29th September 1989 Edinburgh The General Teaching Council for Scotland September 1989 19 pages

The message emanating from the seminars and papers presented at this conference is the need for attitudinal change towards partnership which should involve authorities in an open and collaborative venture. Three areas of professional training: initial, in-service training and staff development and accreditation of courses are discussed.

481   Gerver E. Access: some awkward challenges *Scottish Journal of Adult Education* Vol 9 No 4 Winter 1990 37-42
This paper appraises the current trends in adult access in Scotland. Considers the challenges created for education and government and makes a concrete proposal for one way ahead.

482   Gerver E. Steering group on adult access *Scottish Journal of Adult Education* Vol 9 No 1 Summer 1989 5-10
Reviews the activities of the Steering Group on adult access. The main issues are documented as educational guidance, basic education, schools and non-advanced further education.

483   Gerver E. and Hart L. *Strategic women: how do they manage in Scotland?* Aberdeen Aberdeen University Press 1991 203 pages
An excellent account of the professional and personal experiences of fifty senior women in Scotland, this book fills a gap in the literature on Scottish women in employment at senior levels. Tackles the barriers faced by women wanting to gain access to positions of seniority and notes a number of factors which the women appear to have in common and which have contributed to their success.

484   Gerver E. *Women's access to education and training and employment* - conference report 14 May 1988, University of Edinburgh Edinburgh 1990
This conference set out to evaluate the effectiveness of equal opportunity policies in redressing social inequality. Identifies those areas where women and girls still experience barriers to access.

485   Giles J. Second chance, second self *Gender and Education* Vol 2 No 3 1990 357-361
Giles using semi-biographical data, urges women to continue learning and reap the benefits of higher education but warns them to expect conflicts and disorientation if returning as mature students. Women's studies courses are encouraged by the author because they can provide both the space and academic framework in which to explore the ambiguities surrounding women's role in society.

486   Glascock S. In praise of older women *Management Today* Sept 1990 86-88
Discusses the changes companies are making in their recruitment policies to cope with demographic changes, in particular by recruiting women returners and older people. By way of example, those companies which are planning ahead and changing recruitment policy are illustrated.

487   Gleeson D. *The paradox of training: making progress out of crisis* Milton Keynes OU Press 1989 132 pages
This book maintains that a clearer understanding of the contradictions associated with government education and training reforms must be developed to enable a more coherent analysis of the alternatives needed in the future to secure a more comprehensive system of further education, training and work.

488   Glendinning C. Losing ground: social policy and disabled people in GB 1980-1990 *Disability, Handicap and Society* Vol 6 No 1 1991 3-19
Reviews the major themes of social policy in GB over the past decade and examines their impact on disabled people. Training and education and access to paid work are discussed in detail. The author notes that while training and further education opportunities have increased, the proportion of disabled young people aged 16-21 at home doing nothing is still unacceptably high. Discusses the Disabled Persons Employment Act and the persuasionist tactics preferred by government.

489   Glover D. *Enterprise in higher education: a briefing for employers* Cambridge CRAC 1990 16 pages
This is a succinct paper which usefully describes the objectives of the Enterprise in Higher Education Initiative. It has been prepared to help employers to determine their involvement in the Initiative.

490   Glucklich P. Women's management training in a ghetto? *Personnel Management* Vol 17 No 9 1985 39-43
Reviews the effectiveness of women's management development. Whilst the number of women managers has risen they are typically found in certain occupational sectors - retail, catering, personnel. The author concludes that the issues concerning the training of women managers cannot be

separated out from wider organisational issues. They should form part of a comprehensive and strategic approach to the management of equal opportunities.

491 **Goddard T. and Portwood D.** *PACE? Training Agency feasibility study into the formation of a staff development agency for continuing education and training in higher education* Sheffield Training Agency 1990

492 **Gold J. and Holden R. (Ed)** Enterprise in higher education: lighting the blue touchpaper *Education and Training* Vol 33 No 2 1991

The whole issue is devoted to papers examining the development of the Enterprise in Higher Education Initiative.

493 **Goodman L.M.** Evaluation of the further and higher education section of the Training Agency's AI applications to learning programme *Educational and Training Technology International* Vol 26 No 4 November 1989 322-334

This paper outlines the strategies, structures, tools, techniques and methods used for the further and higher education evaluation of artificial intelligence applications to learning in the education and training sectors.

494 **Gordon A. et al** Employer sponsorship of undergraduate engineers: a student perspective *Educational Studies* Vol 11 No 3 1985 189-202

The author suggests that since the mid 1980s many of those working in industry and government have seen sponsorship as one way for employers to develop the growing partnership between higher education and industry and to influence and increase the supply of new graduates in engineering subjects. This article considers the advantages and disadvantages, benefits and problems associated with employer sponsorship from a student perspective.

495 **Gordon P. et al** *Anti-racist resources: a guide for adult and community education* London Runnymede Trust 1988 91 pages

An annotated directory of anti-racist organisations and resources aimed at those working in adult and community education.

496 **Gorringe R.** Accreditation of prior learning achievements: developments in Britain and lessons from the USA *Coombe Lodge Report* Vol 20 1989 359 pages.

This detailed report describes the development in Britain of enabling people to use, in an educational or training context, evidence of their achievements drawn directly from their prior experience. The recurring theme is not the process of learning itself, which can be assessed or credited, but what has been achieved by it. A useful compendium term is accreditation of prior learning achievement of APLA. These issues are discussed in relation to NVQs.

497 **Gorringe R.** The work of NCVQ and its implications for further and higher education *NASD Journal* No 20 1988 4-13

Looks at the impact of NCVQ on further and higher education in terms of the changes in the work and organisation of further education colleges, colleges of higher education and Polytechnics. Provides a useful introduction to the subject, giving definitions of competence and the criteria which relate to NVQs.

498 **Goulbourn T.** A strategy for people with disabilities *TEC Director* Issue 5 Aug/Sept 1990 20-21

Reviews the approach used by the Barnsley and Doncaster TEC which has developed a strategy for people with disabilities aimed at integration rather than isolation within sheltered schemes. Shows specialist services such as the Rehabilitation Service and residential training and sheltered placements can all be brought to play to complement mainstream training and enterprise provision.

499 **Graham B.** *Messages from mature graduates: a report from the sub-committee on the employment and training of older graduates* Manchester Association of Graduate Advisory Services 1991 94 pages

The lack of research on mature graduate students outcomes makes this a timely and highly valuable report. The study explores the motivating factors which guided adults in their selection of degree courses and in their decisions after graduation. It is clear from the survey that employers continue to discriminate against older graduates because of preconceived, often negative, stereotypes. The author recommends the report be read by careers advisory staff, employers and mature students commencing their career search.

500 Graham F. and Kelcher M. Equipping manual workers with communication skills *Transition from Education through Employment* Jan 1989 17-19
Describes the work of Workbase, a trade union organisation which aims to give support to manual workers with communication skills. The emphasis is on flexibility to meet individual needs.

501 Graham P. et al *An equal chance? Or no chance?* London Spastics Society 1990 18 pages
Discusses the experiences of people with disabilities in employment and charts some of the discriminatory practices they must contend with.

502 Great Britain Standing Advisory Committee on Human Rights *Religious and political discrimination and equality of opportunity in Northern Ireland* HC 459 London HMSO 1990 135 pages
Annual report presented to the Secretary of State for Northern Ireland which reviews laws and institutions concerned with preventing religious discrimination. Includes sections on education and fair employment in which the Government's measures for ensuring equality of opportunity are given.

503 Green F. Sex discrimination in job-related training *British Journal of Industrial Relations* Vol 29 No 2 June 1991 295-303
Argues women and men have unequal chances of obtaining training. Presents data using the 1984 Labour Force Survey to support the hypothesis that women suffer discrimination over access to training.

504 Greenberg E.R. Some pointers on basic training techniques *Personnel* Vol 66 No 9 1989 22-26
Three experts in basic skills training give advice on giving job applicants and employees proficiency tests and the necessary training in reading, writing and numeracy.

505 Greenbury L. What do I want to do? *Women in Management Review* Vol 3 No 4 1988 202-206

This article discusses the problems faced by women going out to work for the first time or as returners. Concludes that support is necessary to increase the number of specialist women's career advisers to help those groups held back by old-fashioned notions and lack of financial resources.

506 Greenhalgh C. and Stewart M. The effects and determinants of training *Oxford Bulletin of Economics and Statistics* Vol 49 No 2 May 1987 171-190
The extent of vocational training taking place in the UK both on and off the job is documented, drawing on National Training Survey (NTS) data. The NTS shows that women receive significantly less full-time training than men and that this inequality is compounded in the case of married women by later periods of non-participation and part-time work.

507 Greig D. The lost domain in part-time FE *Education* Vol 174 No 23 1989 page 513
Reports on the issues raised at a NIACE conference on part-time adult study. The themes covered included the role of TECs, the 21 hour rule, funding and the use of performance indicators.

508 Griffiths M. et al *Enabled to work: support into employment for young people with disabilities: working together?* London Further Education Unit 1989 113 pages
Part of a series of studies carried out for the UK contribution to the OECD/CERI Disabled Action Programme. The study described in the first part of this two-part document identifies the kind of ongoing support which would be most beneficial to all those concerned with the employment of young people with disabilities. It is based on semi-structured interviews conducted with employers, representatives of preparation and placement agencies and people with disabilities. A number of useful recommendations are made as a result of the research findings. Part 2 consists of three separate papers offering a guide to vocational training initiatives and the employment of people with disabilities.

509 Grindrod R. The need for change: anti-racist initiatives in colleges of education *Multicultural Teaching* Vol 6 No 1 1987 28-31

A general discussion about racism in education in which the author defines racism and recognises that it manifests and perpetuates itself in many ways in education, through the distribution of power, discriminatory practices and personal prejudice. Discusses ways of combatting this at all levels.

510 **Groombridge J. (Ed)** *Learning for change* Leicester NIACE/REPLAN 1987 49 pages

Presents short summaries of the work of some of the National Institute's REPLAN projects. The projects highlight the importance of flexibility, variety and choice. Student participation and the need for building self confidence and the importance of support services which aid equality of access are also discussed.

511 **Guardian** Ticking 'demographic' time bomb as women await the back to work call *The Guardian* 4 Nov 1988

Reports on UK's poor childcare policy and reviews examples of lead companies who have recognised the importance of retaining women and the need for childcare facilities.

512 **Guy R.** Serving the needs of industry In: *Change and intervention: vocational education and training.* Raggatt and Unwin (Ed) London Falmer Press 1991 47-60

A detailed and interesting overview of the various initiatives devised in the 1980s to enhance links between education and job skills, for example, the New Training Initiative, NVQs, TVEI and WRNAFE. Offers some proposals for the future, notably the necessity of partnership between government, businesses and individuals.

513 **Guy R.F.** In-house training for information technology *Education for Information* Vol 7 No 1 March 1989 17-27

Training issues are discussed in detail and concentrate on who should provide training, who should receive it and the reasons for establishing in-house training programmes with the installation of library automation systems. A programme from the National Library of Scotland is described.

514 **Hackett G.** Learning skills to move off the bottom rungs *Times Educational*

Supplement No 3792 3rd March 1989 page A11

Report on a North East London Polytechnic course for black and Asian teachers to give them experience of educational management and help them achieve promotion.

515 **Hacking P.** Day training centre: credible alternative to custody *NASPO News* Vol 6 No 2 1986 15-16

Outlines the criteria which centres must fulfil to ensure credibility to those passing sentence and discusses how the centres approach the difficult issue of producing desirable changes in behaviour.

516 **Hagedorn J.** Down in the docks *Times Educational Supplement* No 3853 27th April 1990 page A33

Report on a training programme in Newham for Asian women with young children in literacy, childcare, new technology and office skills. Includes interviews with course members about how the courses have met their needs.

517 **Hale R. and Goodwin A.** *The enterprise competencies of undergraduates from different academic disciplines.* Conference paper series no. 62/89 Stirling Scottish Enterprise Foundation 1989 15 pages

This research concerns itself with a group of graduates from different disciplines to see what enterprising competencies and attitudes they display. Some interesting ideas emerge from the study. The authors conclude recruiters should consider mature candidates and those who hold alternative qualifications when looking for employees who show the entrepreneurial spirit needed for business.

518 **Hall D.** *Adult learning by choice: results of the CET Learning Links project* 1986 160 pages

A set of four case studies of the use of computerised databases on informal learning opportunities, set up in different and geographically separate host agencies. An eloquent illustration of the difficulties of establishing direct enquirer access to computerised information.

519 **Hall D.** Access to learning for adults. The CET learning links project *Adult Education* Vol 57 No 4 Mar 1985 325-328

The author looks at the problems of access to learning opportunities for adults and describes new developments under the CET Learning Links project which will tackle some of these by applying the new technology in information centres for adults.

520 Hall J.W. Distance education: reaching out to millions *Change* Vol 22 No 4 1989 page 48

Reports on the International Council for Distance Education's conference held in Norway 1988. Delegates shared many of their institutions' problems, the main ones being student drop out or attrition and the need for strong communication links with distance students. Concludes those that have developed effective telephone, mail and tutorial networks are more able to motivate their students and have established a better completion rate.

521 Hall V. NCVQ and further education *Coombe Lodge Reports* Vol 20 No 5 1987 283-327

The whole issue is devoted to tackling the questions posed by the Review of Vocational Qualifications and the ways in which staff in further and higher education must respond. Attempts to answer such questions as why change is needed and what competence really means. Provides a clear and concise introduction to the issues.

522 Hamilton M. and Stasinopoulos N. *Literacy numeracy and adults: evidence from the National Child Development Study* London ALBSU 1987 85 pages

Reports on the National Child Development Study - a study of people born in England, Scotland and Wales in one week in 1958. Explores issues relating to those within the group who have been identified as having problems with basic literacy and numeracy. Looks at the sorts of problems they encounter and if such problems relate to particular groups.

523 Hamilton R. *Budgets for adult education* Edinburgh SIACE 1988 43 pages

Identifies the sources and the extent of visible public expenditure on adult education in Scotland. Indicates some of the policy questions raised by exploring the question of budgets for adult education in Scotland.

524 Hammond M. and Collins R. *Self-directed learning: critical practice* London Kogan Page 1991 250 pages

Ideas of self-directed learning have received increasing attention over the past 20 years and are having an impact on education and training at all levels. The authors present a critical analysis of self-directed learning and consider aspects of self assessment, competency and education. This highly detailed, academic text will be useful for those considering implementing a self-directed learning system.

525 Hammond V. Management training for women *Journal of European Industrial Training* Vol 10 No 7 1986 15-22

Women have very often been bypassed for formal training and it is suggested here that employers need to check to see that they are including women in the training provisions for specialist and general management training courses. The article tends to favour separate training for women managers.

526 Hampton W. et al Adult education for the Afro-Caribbean community: a university community partnership *Adults Learning* Vol 1 No 2 1989 57-58

Reports on an initiative between Sheffield University and the Sheffield and District Afro-Caribbean Community Association which resulted in a certificate course in community studies for young black adults. Stresses the importance of community education for those who have had bad experience of the British school system and need to learn in a familiar environment.

527 Handy C. *The changing workforce: harnessing the female resource* London The Women's Educational Conference of 1989

528 Hanlow M. Women and the pursuit of excellence: Strathclyde's equal opportunity unit *Times Scottish Educational Supplement* No. 1233 June 1990 page 4

Strathclyde region has set up an Equal Opportunities Unit where a small team of lecturers are seeking to redress the balance in the gender war. The Unit promotes the findings of the report on Sex Equality in the Education Service. Recommends inservice training programmes for all teachers and lecturers within Strathclyde as well as key groups.

529   Hansard Society Commission Report *Women at the top* London The Hansard Society Commission 1990 114 pages
Documents how little change has been achieved in women's access to positions of power in Britain. For example, whilst the proportion of women studying in the universities increased from 35-42% between 1975 and 1988 the proportion of women in senior academic posts is derisory and has scarcely risen.

530   Hardill I. and Creen A.E. *An examination of women returners in Newcastle (Benwall and South Gosforth).* Report prepared for the Training Agency. Newcastle Centre for Urban and Regional Development Studies 1990 113 pages
This research outlines the changing labour market position for women; identifies factors which favour or inhibit labour market re-entry and posits policy recommendations relating to recruitment and retention of women returners. Concludes, the demand for further training on the part of women returners and the potential for training and career advice act as vital instruments in aiding labour market re-entry. Uses action research based on semi-structured interviews and group discussions.

531   Hardy D. *The UK 'PICKUP' programme updating the skills of adult workers in education and training in a changing employment market* part 2 No 1 European Bureau of Adult Education 1989 50-51
Presents a useful overview of the PICKUP programme to date. A strategy for future development is documented. Amongst the key areas discussed are the need to increase employers' investment in adult training and the development of training partnerships between higher education and employers. Whilst the importance of accessible information is recognised, most appropriately in the form of a national database of short courses, the emphasis throughout is on marketing and promotion rather than guidance.

532   Hardy D.I.B. Continuing education and pick-up *Educational and Training Technology International* Vol 26 No 1 February 1989 14-18

This review of PICKUP describes the range of activities carried out under that banner. The overall aim is to make training for working adults as much a part of the job of educational institutions as it is for school leavers.

533   Harris R.W. The CNAA, accreditation and quality assurance *Higher Education Review* Vol 22 No 3 1990 34-54
Describes in detail the role of the CNAA and the procedures involved in accreditation and the maintenance of quality in the non-university sector.

534   Harrison M.J. Access: the problem and potential *Higher Education Quarterly* Vol 44 No 3 Summer 1990 193-214
This article sketches the centrality of 'access' to government thinking but questions the compatibility of this ideological commitment with the current funding regime. Whilst focusing upon the success of 'Access courses' in promoting alternative, high quality routes to higher education, it indicates the depth of cultural and institutional change required if access and mass higher education are to become realities. Makes some pragmatic suggestions on how the widening of access can be achieved.

535   Hart L. *Women's perceived education and training needs* Edinburgh SIACE 1988
This research describes the perceived education and training needs of female participants at a 'Second Chance to Work' Conference which took place in June 1986. Participants were followed up, using a postal questionnaire, to assess the effectiveness of this event in providing relevant information and guidance.

536   Hart L. Recent research findings on women's education in Scotland *Scottish Journal of Adult Education* Vol 8 No 3 Spring 1988 5-9
This article tries to answer the questions women ask about why, where and how to study in Scotland.

537   Hart L. (Ed) *Second chance in Scotland: a women's guide to education and training* Edinburgh SIACE 1986 38 pages
This booklet tries to answer the questions women ask about why, where, what and how to study in Scotland.

538 Hartley D. Beyond collaboration: the management of professional development policy in Scotland 1979-1989 *Journal of Education For Teaching* Vol 15 No 3 1989 211-223

This paper is concerned with the Scottish Education Department's management of the professional development of teachers. Argues SED has dispensed with human relations management approaches to management development

539 Hartley D. Staff development in Scotland *British Journal of In-service Education* Vol 11 No 3 Spring 1985 133-137

540 Hartley D. (Ed) *Adult learning in Scotland: a review of research and policy* Edinburgh SIACE 1990

541 Hartley T.W. Interviews *Adult Education* Vol 59 No 1 June 1986 20-25

A useful account of an action research project with unemployed people in Sheffield to discover how adult educators could best serve their needs. Counselling and guidance proved to be very important and it is suggested that this sort of exercise could become an 'outreach' activity of a local counselling and guidance unit.

542 Hartress A. Valuing your experience: a project for women *Adult Education* Vol 59 No 2 Sep 1986 115-120

The author describes a short course for women returners, designed to help them evaluate their abilities and acquire the confidence needed to take informed decisions about their future. Although the course is short-term, it was found to be enabling in that it provided an initial impetus which participants can then build on. The course also showed that many women still do not know where to go for information about the opportunities available or how to go about getting help in assessing alternatives.

543 Hattersley A. *A flexible curriculum: thinking about management issues* Sheffield Department of Employment 1991 52 pages

544 Hawkridge D. et al *New information technology in the education of disabled children and adults* London Croom Helm 1985 268 pages

This book reviews the possibilities of using new information technology in the education of the disabled. Commencing with an assessment of the learning problems faced by disabled people, it goes on to look at the scope of new information technology and how it is actually being used for the education of students of all ages.

545 Hawthorn R. and Wood R. *Training issues in educational guidance for adults: a project report* Leicester UDACE 1988 46 pages

The report of a national project to identify and meet the training needs of guidance workers.

546 Hazelwood J. British standard BS5750 *TEC Director* Issue 6 1990 page 31

The chairman of Gloucester TEC reviews the work of the Training Agency on BS 5750 and discusses the benefits the use of the standard will bring to TECs.

547 Heaton A. Transferable credits *Times Higher Education Supplement* 20 October 1989 page 25

Outlines the work of JUPITER (Joint Universities and Polytechnics Industrial Technology Education Research) which is a consortium which provides industry with information on training courses.

548 Henderson D. Prison education *Times Educational Supplement Scotland* 11 September 1990 page 1

Reports on the main points raised in the Scottish Home and Health Department's Working Group report which registered serious concern over the lack of education and training facilities for prisoners. The working group calls for more formal links between education units and the local further education colleges to strengthen the educational input.

549 Hendy J. and Eady J. UK has worst maternity rights in western Europe *The Guardian* 8 May 1991

Illustrates the case of Dekker who fought a nine year legal battle through the Dutch courts and on to the European courts after being turned down for a training instructors job at a Dutch Youth Centre, despite the selection committee's recommendation that she was the best candidate. She did not hide the fact she was three months pregnant at this interview. The European Court concluded that using pregnancy as a reason for unfavourable dismissal has to be direct discrimination, on the basis of sex. Dekker's case and its implications have had little notice outside legal and academic circles.

550   Her Majesty's Inspectorate *Access courses to higher education: a report by HMI* London DES 1990 16 pages
A useful research survey which aimed to assess the quality of Access courses. The project covered well-established courses in Manchester, Sheffield and London. Fieldwork included class observation; examination of students' work; interviews with students and staff and exploration of issues surrounding continuity and progression with staff and former access course students.

551   Her Majesty's Inspectorate *Work based learning in further education: a review by HMI* London HMSO 1990 25 pages
This publication describes how students gain a broad knowledge and understanding of work through work-based learning which takes place in realistic settings in college.

552   Her Majesty's Inspectorate of Prisons for Scotland *Report on H.M. Prison Aberdeen* Edinburgh The Scottish Office 1990 55 pages

553   Hermann G.D. and Kenyon R.J. *Competency based vocational education: a case study: FEU/PICKUP project report* London FEU 1987 63 pages
Describes the background to and implementation of a competency based vocational education project in a catering college. Includes the reaction of students and staff to the project.

554   Heron G. Access, quality, community *Journal of Access Studies* Vol 1 No 2 1986 4-22
Reviews the history and politics surrounding the provision of Access courses for Black people.

555   Herron M. Helping them pick up the pieces *Voluntary Voice* No 8 London Aug 1986 page 6
Brief comment on the particularly severe resettlement problems of female ex-prisoners

and the work of the Women Prisoners Resource Centre in helping to overcome them. This was set up by NACRO to provide individual advice on employment, childcare, housing and other matters.

556   Hewitson-Ratcliffe C. (Ed) *Disability, employment and training - meeting the demographic challenge of the 1990s* London SKILL with ILEA 1990 37 pages
This publication records the work of the conference held in Autumn 1989 on the theme 'Employment and training for the disabled in the 1990s'. Part 1 records the voice of people with experiences to relate; Part 2 gives a broad, international vision of the future; Part 3 provides practical checklists and reference material.

557   Hewitt J. Case study: a retraining solution to skills shortages *Education and Training Technology International* Vol 14 No 2 1989 19-22
Describes a collaborative venture between Hatfield Polytechnic and a company in Hertfordshire which used retraining as a solution to its skills shortages problem in software engineering.

558   Higgins M.A. The student market *Higher Education Quarterly* Vol 45 No 1 1991 14-24
Discusses targets for the expansion of higher education in the face of declining numbers of school leavers. Argues that higher education institutions must target new groups, develop new approaches and market their services more aggressively if targets are to be achieved.

559   Highton J. The career development course *Scottish Journal of Adult Education* Vol 8 No 4 Autumn 1988 37-42
The career development course is designed for people in employment who want to review their current job situation, find out about options for change and decide on future strategy. This paper reviews the first course offered by Edinburgh University's Department of Extra Mural Studies (now Continuing Education) in October 1987.

560   Hillier Y. How do adult students learn about educational opportunities? *New Era in Education* Vol 71 No 1 April 1990 6-10

The author reviews the ways in which prospective adult learners gain information about educational opportunities. This report includes assessment of who does and does not use the information services which are available. She concludes with some recommendations to ensure that those for whom educational opportunities are available are able to find out about them. Makes useful differentiation between publicity and guidance.

561   Hitchcock G. Transferable skills: a Dip HE contribution to the debate *Journal of Further and Higher Education* Vol 11 No 3 1987 91-108

An informative paper which assesses the value of broadly-based social sciences diplomas and degree courses in terms of the general and transferable skills they give to students in preparation for employment. The author demonstrates the way in which one aspect of one course clearly provides students with the kinds of transferable skills which might prepare them for continuing degree study and/or professional training and employment. Concludes social science courses are capable of developing exactly those skills employers and industry are so keen for higher education to develop without damaging the integrity and academic basis of such a course.

562   Hitt M. Scotland's action plan for all *British Journal of Special Education* Vol 14 No 4 December 1987 162-165

This paper argues that Scotland's 'Action Plan' for students aged 16-18 which provides modular study programmes could be usefully adopted for students with special needs. These students in particular, could usefully benefit from the flexibility and potential for individualisation which are characteristic of the Action Plan.

563   Hodgkinson P. Crossing the academic/vocational divide: personal effectiveness and autonomy as an integrating theme in post 16 education *British Journal of Education Studies* Vol 37 No 4 November 1989 369-383

A critical evaluation of the academic-vocational divide. Argues that this is a result of both structural and institutional fragmentation. The author maintains that the split is historical rather than philosophical and in reality there are many similarities. For example, both want people to develop a full and active life. Many

students would like to choose a mixed academic/vocational course but at present this is extremely difficult.

564   Holmes B. Literacy and numeracy: what cause for concern *Employment Gazette* Vol 97 No 3 1989 133-139

Discusses the extent and nature of the adult literacy problem in Britain. Describes the state of current provision and the type of initiatives with which the Training Agency has been involved.

565   Holmes L. Competency approach to training *Training and Development* Vol 8 No 4 1990 17-23

Describes what is meant by the 'competencies' approach and explains why such an approach can be seriously flawed.

566   Hood N. Institutional strategy and environment: the case of the University of Strathclyde *International Journal of Institutional Management in Higher Education* Vol 10 No 1 March 1986 34-44

This article demonstrates how the University of Strathclyde responded to the contraction of government funding. Industry links and increased emphasis on efficiency are discussed.

567   Hood P. The transition to employment for people with disabilities: the role of further education *Training Officer* Vol 26 No 10 1990 292-293

Examines the issues surrounding the transition to employment for people with disabilities. Discusses the role that the further education sector can play in facilitating this transition.

568   Hopson B. Adult life and career counselling *British Journal of Guidance and Counselling* Vol 13 No 1 Jan 1985 49-59

The provision of life and career counselling for adults in the early 1970s is examined, distinguishing between counselling and other helping strategies. The author notes the definite shift from the provision of only information and advice to helping people to help themselves. Some speculation on future development are offered.

569   Horner D.J. Continuing professional development revisited *Adult Education* Vol 60 No 2 September 1987 133-137

An increasing number of professional groups now recognise the value of continuing professional development. This article examines the case for CPD programmes and sets out a logical approach.

570 **Horobin J. and Wilson V.** *Scottish handbook of adult and continuing education* Edinburgh SIACE 1989 72 pages
An invaluable reference source designed as a guide to public sector education and training opportunities for those with an interest in this area and particularly individuals and agencies who are called upon to provide advice to enquiring members of the public.

571 **Horobin J.C. et al** *Mature students in higher education* Edinburgh SIACE 1987

572 **Horrell S. et al** Gender and skills *Work, Employment and Society* Vol 4 No 2 June 1990 189-216
Levels of skill required in men's and women's jobs are compared based on interviews in Northampton. It is concluded that the main cleavage in the quality of skill level is between full-time and part-time jobs. The authors argue there is evidence to support the contention that women's and men's jobs involve different skills and perceptions of skills and job content are influenced by the status of the job.

573 **Horwitz C.** Total Quality Management: an approach for education *Educational Management and Administration* Vol 18 No 2 1990 55-58
Discusses why Total Quality Management has become so topical and examines its usefulness as a tool for improving the quality of education.

574 **Housee S. et al** Access to what? Black students' perceptions of their higher education experiences *Journal of Access Studies* Vol 5 No 2 1990 203-213
Reports on qualitative research which aims to discover the views of black students about the academic quality, social aspects and personal relevance of their experience of higher education.

575 **Howarth A.** Market forces in higher education *Higher Education Quarterly* Vol 45 No 1 1991 5-13
The author, a Government Minister, describes the different market sectors and the role of

market forces in higher education. Discusses the benefits of the shift to fees and student loans which the author argues will offer new opportunities and national benefits.

576 **Howe L.** *Being unemployed in Northern Ireland: an ethnographic study* Cambridge Cambridge University Press 1990 263 pages
This book provides a detailed anthropological study of social division and unemployment in Northern Ireland. The research was based on two council housing estates, one predominantly Catholic and the other Protestant. It discusses initiatives such as training schemes and counselling of the long term unemployed which have tried to improve their position in the labour market. Some comparisons are made between unemployment in Northern Ireland and in the rest of the UK.

577 **Hughes M. and Kennedy M.** *New futures: changing women's education* London, Routledge 1985 184 pages
Takes up the ideas and experiences of women in order to involve the adult educator in fresh ways of educational thinking, seeing and doing. The main section is a series of case studies of non-traditional women's educational initiatives and practices.

578 **Hull C.** Making the most of career breaks *Adults Learning* Vol 2 No 4 Dec 1990 105-106
This article asserts there is much to be gained by encouraging employees to value and utilise their career break learning. Posits a number of recommendations, and notes an important feature of any successful career break scheme is the attention paid to maintaining effective contact between the company and the employee during the career break.

579 **Hutchin T.** Case study: role and development of continuing education: the response in the East Midlands *Educational and Training Technology International* Vol 26 No 1 February 1989 31-35
This paper argues there is a need for a structured response from the traditional providers of training and education, whether they be vocationally based or academically based. This will involve a flexible approach to such provision comprising the traditional methods of formal courses and training and

more modern methods involving the use of open learning material, distance learning, and multi-media methods. Concludes training needs to be more closely linked to skill needs which implies a clear recognition of skills shortages. Uses examples of five institutions in the East Midlands.

580 **Hutchinson E.** *Women returning to learning* Cambridge NEC 1986 145 pages
Looks at the development of 'Fresh Horizons' and 'Fresh Start' courses for mature women in London and Richmond between 1976 and 1983, giving a statistical survey of the results of the questionnaire. Considers critically other 'return to learning' opportunities in higher, further and adult education.

581 **Hyatt J. and Parry-Crooke G.** *Barriers to work: a study of lone parents' training and employment needs* National Council for One Parent Families 1990 33 pages
Using documentary analysis this valuable report describes the acute barriers lone parents confront when wishing to enter the labour market. Recommends work expenses are disregarded from Family Credit so that lone parents are able to cover childcare expenses. Urges the government to treat lone parents as a priority issue.

582 **Imeson R. and Edwards R.** Embedding educational guidance in access to higher education *Journal of Access Studies* Vol 5 No 11 Spring 1990 60-71
This paper addresses in detail various models of educational guidance practice in access courses. The authors suggest that educational guidance could be formally integrated into courses through assessed and accredited modules and invite readers to regard educational guidance as fundamentally embedded within the access pedagogy rather than a 'bolt-on' activity. This follows the premise that learners need guidance prior to taking up access provision, while engaged in it and on exit. Recognising and accrediting experiential learning is at the heart of the access pedagogy.

583 **Imeson R.** Lightness of touch or a heavy hand: the cost of Access validation *Adults Learning* Vol 2 No 2 February 1991 176-177

Presents a critical discussion of the workings of access validation and looks with concern at the 'A-levelisation' of access.

584 **Inchley M.** Funding UK higher education: on the verge of expansion *Industry and Higher Education* Vol 4 No 4 1990 262-266
This article discusses how and why the UK higher education system will be expanded and examines how the funding gap will be filled by the public, industry and the students themselves.

585 **Incomes Data Survey** *Child care study* 472 IDS Dec 1990 28 pages
A useful study which examines the range of child care assistance which an employer might provide, from a workplace nursery to play schemes for school age children. The provision of a voucher scheme or a child care allowance is also considered. There are 27 detailed examples of company practice.

586 **Incomes Data Survey** *Employers failing to help women returners* IDS May 1990 29 pages
Looks at some of the findings of a survey carried out by the Institute of Manpower Studies which depicts how firms may retain women employees in order to counteract labour shortages.

587 **Incomes Data Survey** *Training and Enterprise Councils Study* 485 IDS July 1991 26 pages
A concise and recommended study which examines how TECs came to be established and their operation, including the membership of TEC Boards and funding arrangements. Discusses the TEC programmes, national relationships, local TEC initiatives and business and education links. Concludes with 5 case studies of individual TECs.

588 **Incomes Data Survey Report** *Training: the government returns to voluntarism* IDS Report No 536 Jan 1989 25-27
Discusses the White Paper *'Employment for the 1990s'* and argues that this is another part of the government's plan to devolve responsibility for the funding of training back to individual employers. The author claims that such a system will work no better now than it has in the past.

589 **Industry and Higher Education** *Times Higher Education Supplement* 28 June 1991 8 pages

A useful collection of articles which looks at the many aspects of collaboration and provides a comparative dimension. One article by Williams G. and Loder C. argues that a key feature of successful higher education-industry partnerships is a clear understanding by both of the proper functions of each.

590 **Inglis J.** 40 years on: where are we now? *Scottish Journal of Adult Education* Vol 9 No 2 Winter 1989 4-11

This review of the SIACE annual conference of 1988 presents a clear message that adult education should be about social and cultural change and the promotion of humane values. Concludes by stressing adult education in Scotland needs to be reanimated and to be seen as a major power tool for shaping a society fit to survive in the twenty-first century.

591 **Ingram P.** A new era in vocational training: NVQs and the implications for career guidance *Newscheck* Vol 7 No 6 April 1990 4-5

Discusses the importance of NVQs with regard to encouraging students to continue their education post school and provides a valuable update on the NVQ database and other recent developments.

592 **Innes S.** Opportunities for all? *Training Officer* Vol 26 No 10 Oct 1990

593 **Institute of Manpower Studies** *How many graduates in the 21st century - the choice is yours: access to higher education in the 1990s and beyond* IMS Paper No 155 1989 142 pages

This is a wide-ranging report which is concerned with the past, current and future supply of entrants to higher education. Includes projects on future participating groups: the working class, women returners, ethnic minorities, the disabled. Concludes that while there is a consensus on the need for expansion, targeted policies are urgently needed if this is to take place.

594 **Institute of Manpower Studies** *Women into management: issues influencing the entry of women into managerial jobs*

Brighton Manpower Studies, University of Sussex 1990

This is a paper commissioned in 1989 by NEDO and revised as Employment Brief No. 23 under the Co-operative Research Programme. It sets out some of the main issues which seem to influence the entry of women in the UK into management jobs.

595 **Institute of Personnel Management** *A partnership in learning* Leicester NIACE 1988 28 pages

Points to a rich source of untapped potential in solving employers' operational problems, namely the colleges of further and higher education. The IPM report describes examples of successful collaboration between employers and colleges which have led to tailor-made training provision. Concludes this was mutually beneficial and made effective use of resources which already existed.

596 **Institute of Personnel Management** *Work and the family* London IPM Jan 1990 71 pages

An excellent report which documents the results of the first major research project conducted on behalf of the IPM by Host Training and Consultancy Service which covers the whole field of care provision and its implications for employers. It analyses the extent to which they have already begun to consider the needs of employers with dependents, whether children, aged parents, ill and disabled relatives. Provides case studies of policies adopted by progressive organisations.

597 **Investors in People** *An initial briefing pack for TECs and LECs* Sheffield Employment Department Group 1990

A glossy briefing pack aimed at TEC and LEC personnel providing the context, framework and rationale behind the Investors in People scheme.

598 **Iphofen R.** Residential adult education *Adults Learning* special issue 1988-1989 10-11

Discusses and defends residential adult education in the wake of cuts in funding for Newbattle Abbey, the only long-term adult residential college in Scotland.

599 **Jack A.** Workshadowing in higher education: what, why and where next?

Industry and Higher Education Vol 3 No 4 December 1989 201-210

An interesting article on the value of workshadowing as a technique of careers education based in the workplace. Schools have begun to use it over the past few years but its role in HE has been badly neglected. This article analyses one exception - a scheme at Cambridge University. It stresses the benefits to participating companies as well as to students and organisers, and its particular value in HE. The problems encountered highlight the need to develop an effective implementation framework and to redefine what the notions of workshadowing should be.

600   Jackson C. *Careers counselling in organisations: the way forward* Brighton Institute of Manpower Studies 1990 64 pages

This report describes a range of possible career interventions which will harness the potential of all employees. Discusses issues involved with implementing individual career planning activities in organisations.

601   Jackson C. and Hirsch W. Women managers and career progression: the British experience *Women in Management Review and Abstracts* Vol 6 No 2 1991 12-16

This article considers the main reasons why women do not achieve promotion into management as readily as men. Argues, the trend towards defining management criteria more rigorously and assessing them less subjectively may be an important step towards promoting more women. Monitoring the retention and career progress of female employees is still undertaken only by a small minority of employers and is a powerful step in the change process.

602   Jameson B.J. and Raine R.L. A woman's perspective of a man's perspective of a women's place in work: a personal opinion *Management Services* Vol 34 No 5 May 1990 12-14

In the management and service sector, men and women should be allowed to achieve progression and promotion based upon their abilities alone. However, this equality, according to a survey by Incomes Data Services does not exist. Many women continue to be paid less than men for work of equal value and women are rarely encouraged to

advance from their initial occupation. The authors examine these issues and conclude employers must examine their recruitment and promotion opportunities in order to benefit from the increasing pool of able and intelligent women.

603   Janes F. (Ed) Managing flexible college structures: the current scene *Coombe Lodge Reports* Vol 21 No 2 1989 103-161

Based on a survey of FE college principals this issue examines the management structures and processes which enable a college to respond to changing circumstances. Discusses how further education colleges can develop flexibility in their response to changing demand and new clients.

604   Jeffcutt P. Education and training: beyond the great debate *British Journal of Education and Work* Vol 2 No 2 1988 51-59

Provides a historical analysis of education and training. The initiatives to date the author argues, have been regressive more than innovative. Discusses social change and the need for receptivity, ingenuity and guidelines as we work through the complex task of reframing our understandings of education and training.

605   Jeffries C. Trends in open learning *Training Tomorrow* May 1991 31-33

Surveys current trends in open learning and highlights some of the main issues for trainers.

606   Jenkins C. Striving for a degree of success *Times Educational Supplement* No. 3847 23rd March 1990 page A8

Report on a full time BEd course at Sheffield Polytechnic which targets black primary school teachers.

607   Jenkins T. Abilities not disabilities: a change of focus *Adults Learning* Vol 2 No 4 1990 page 116

Discusses 'Ideas in Motion', which is an autonomous group of severely disabled people who felt very strongly they wanted to ask education providers why they were being offered segregated and limited opportunities to become involved with education. The author worked with the group, and collected their statements which have been written up as a series of checklists which are now available as the 'Abilities not Disabilities' pack which clarifies the areas which need to be addressed if barriers to education and training are to be removed.

608 **Jenkins T.** All change: staff development and really equal opportunities *Adults Learning* Vol 1 No 4 1989 108-109

The focus of this article is women in staff development, and their role in the context of a form of staff development which is more about the evolution of the whole institution where the ethos of equality of opportunity is recognised at all levels.

609 **Jessop G.** *Accreditation of prior learning in the context of National Vocational Qualifications* London NCVQ 1990 21 pages

Based upon the main programme this is a summary of the National Programme sponsored by the Training Agency and NCVQ.

610 **Jessop G.** *Outcomes: NVQs and the emergent model of education and training* London Falmer Press 1991 198 pages

Discusses the origins of NVQs. Outlines a model for an outcome led as opposed to process based training system incorporating credit accumulation and transfer between academic and vocational routes. Brings together much of the material and analysis on this subject.

611 **Johnes G.** and **Taylor J.** Ethnic minorities in the graduate labour market *New Community* Vol 15 No 4 1989 527-536

Comparison of the work histories of white and ethnic minority graduates with reference to their family and educational background. Based on a sample from a CNAA national survey of nearly 8000 students who obtained a degree or diploma in 1980. The research found that the market status and salary of the two groups was not significantly different after 6 years. It concludes that although getting into higher education is more difficult black graduates do as least as well as white once established.

612 **Johnes J.** and **Taylor J.** Degree quality: an investigation into differences between UK universities *Higher Education* Vol 16 No 5 1987 581-602

Reports on a project in which the performance of different universities was measured by a comparison of degree results. Discusses the reasons for the different results and the usefulness of this way of measuring teaching quality.

613 **Johnson C.** Mature students: higher education institutions need to recognise the specific needs of mature students *Management in Education* Vol 3 No 4 Winter 1989 11-12

Reports on research carried out at the Polytechnic of East London into ways of increasing and improving its provision for mature students. The overall thrust, is that higher education institutions need to recognise the specific needs of mature students, whilst bearing in mind they are not a homogeneous group.

614 **Johnson E.** *The next decade: literacy at the crossroads* papers commissioned for international literacy year as a background to the conference 'The next decade : literacy at the crossroads' 7 September 1990 University of Stirling Edinburgh SIACE 1990

An interesting and valuable collection of papers hoping to provide a bench mark for the future provision of basic education.

615 **Johnston H.** SIACE's universal culture of learning *Times Scottish Educational Supplement* No. 1267 15 February 1991 page 17

Reviews the work of SIACE, before its recent demise. The article suggests SIACE had ambitious aims and had hoped to cooperate with other national organisations and make more use of the media to publicise its aims.

616 **Johnston I.** New challenges in training *Education and Training* Vol 31 No 3 1989 10-11

This article looks at the four challenges ahead: 1992, European competition, demographic changes and skills shortages. Training is important for future success and research shows that those companies relating training to business objectives get the best payback from training investment. Argues that the needs of the employer or trainee should determine training provision.

617 Johnston R. and Bailey R. *Mature students: perceptions and experiences of full-time and part-time higher education* Sheffield City Polytechnic PAVIC Publications 1985 200 pages

Report of a two-year study carried out at Sheffield City Polytechnic which confirms that mature students are drawn mainly from the professional, administrative and skilled groups in the community and which emphasises the need for pre-entry counselling and short preparatory courses and a preference for continual assessment.

618 Joint Working Group on Women and Computers *Women and computing in Scotland* - conference report of 14 June 1985 University of Strathclyde Glasgow University of Strathclyde 1986 30 pages

This report utilises the papers from the conference Women in Computing in Scotland and draws attention to the fact that women are significantly under-represented in learning about and working with computers and suggests possible solutions to the problem.

619 Jonathan R. The case for and against modularisation *Scottish Educational Review* Vol 19 No 2 November 1987 86-87

A useful discussion presenting both benefits and problems of modularisation as a form of curriculum organisation. Assesses the implications for the content of the curriculum, for the learning experience of students, for the professional development of teachers and educational institutions as well as for the wider society.

620 Jones A. and Field J. Attitudes to open learning: a survey of unemployed adults *Vocational Aspects of Education* Vol 41 No 108 April 1989 21-24

Reports on a survey of adults in basic training courses in England, the results of which, suggest that although many welcomed greater flexibility and wider access to institutions, they were realistic about their limitations to undertake distance learning and home study. Open learning modes may unintentionally raise new barriers to participation for the educationally disadvantaged.

621 Jones H. Sent down with a life sentence *Marketing Week* Vol 14 No 4 1991 page 26

The author severely criticises the poor quality of advertising for government training schemes and claims that the TECs will not solve long term economic decline.

622 Jones J. A positive approach to the employment of disabled workers *Personnel Management* July 1985 21-23

Jonathan Jones and Mike Pedler of Sheffield City Polytechnic's department of Management Studies offer some guidelines for positive action based on a recent survey of 56 employers in the Sheffield area. They conclude all firms should have a Policy on Disabled people which deals with conscious and unconscious discrimination.

623 Jones P. and Larden F. *Vocational guidance and counselling for adults in the UK, particularly the long term unemployed* CEDEFOP 1989 167 pages

This is a valuable inventory of vocational guidance and counselling provision for adults in the UK which includes model projects, useful addresses and bibliographies.

624 Jones P. Access courses into the 1990's *Adults Learning* Vol 1 No 5 January 1989 145-146

Discusses the development of alternative entry routes for mature applicants to higher education. The access course route has been one of the principal strands and, as a result of concern to ensure that students graduate, the DES has now agreed to create a national framework for the recognition of such courses.

625 Jones S. Opportunities and provision for students with physical disabilities in higher education *Educare* No 31 1988 38-40

The research described here was aimed at discovering the progress which has been made in government legislation to improve opportunities for people with disabilities and whether attempts to increase the proportion of students with physical disabilities in higher education have been successful. The writer argues that until a definition of physical disability is agreed upon, data will never reveal reliable information on the proportion of students with disabilities in higher education. General concluding remarks show some attempts at tackling structural barriers have been made but it is only through cultural change that total integration will succeed.

626   Jordinson R. Access to higher education in Scotland: an overview *Journal of Access Studies* Vol 5 No 1 1990 72-88

A most valuable overview on access to higher education in Scotland. The distinctive features of Scottish education are firstly presented. The author then usefully sets out the historical background and philosophies behind the concept of the Scottish Wider Access Programme (SWAP) and the introduction of SCOTVEC. The various consortia are then described and some reflections for future developments offered.

627   Keane P. (Ed) *Training information review: new developments in training and education* Watford Engineering Training Authority Information Centre 1991

A useful review which considers the latest developments in training policy and training material and training courses. Provides information on recent and forthcoming publications and articles on training topics.

628   Kearney A. and Diamond J. Access courses: a model for discussion *Journal of Access Studies* Vol 2 No 2 1987 33-43

Seeks to examine - by reference to current practice in a large community college - one model of access development. Places access provision within a specific context of institutional and curricular development. Concludes, a strategy for access courses based solely on entry to higher education, is neither tactically feasible nor philosophically tenable and the debate surrounding definition needs to be resolved.

629   Kearney A. and Diamond J. Access courses: a new orthodoxy? *Journal of Further and Higher Education* Vol 14 No 1 Spring 1990 128-138

Examines the implications of the moves to make pre-degree access courses part of 'mainstream' provision and to confer on them the status of being just another route into higher education.

630   Keegan D. *The foundations of distance education* Kent Croom Helm 1986 277 pages

A theoretically detailed review of the theories that underlie the evolution of distance education. Argues distance education is a necessary component of most national educational systems.

631   Keen S. A sense of greater strength: women and post compulsory education *Vocational Aspect of Education* Vol 42 No 3 April 1990 13-16

This article explores a number of pertinent questions: why are there more female than male adult students? Are the traditional attitudes of colleges toward women changing? Answers are provided by looking at some women's experiences at polytechnics.

632   Kelati B. *The learning needs of refugees in North London University wishing to enter higher education* London ALFA (North London Open College Network) 1989

Identifies some of the problems which stop refugees from entering higher education and suggests policies for overcoming them. Contains a list of North London community groups and contacts.

633   Kells H.R. The nature of the university-industry alliance and its limits *Higher Education Policy* Vol 2 No 2 June 1989 9-12

Presents an overview of the motivations and possible benefits of university-industry linkages. Importantly, some perspectives for policy-makers are drawn out. Most of the analysis is drawn from experiences in the USA but European examples and literature are illustrated.

634   Kelly J. Adult education's role in providing women-friendly training and work opportunities *Adult Education* Vol 61 No 1 1988 20-24

This is an overview of the author's study of a women's training project. Women only training offers students the opportunity to benefit from the support of others going through similar phases. The author concludes adult educators must consult with women returners to identify their needs and develop suitable courses.

635 **Kelly M.** Learning support in colleges of further education *Journal of Further and Higher Education in Scotland* Winter 1990 page 11

Reports on Strathclyde Region's new commitment to comprehensive learning support mechanisms. Learning support is viewed as an essential element in the delivery of an effective curriculum. This paper aims to set out a framework which can be used as a starting point and tailored to suit the requirement of students at particular colleges. The Advice Shop is deemed a crucial feature of such a strategy.

636 **Kelman M.D.** Experience of a disabled student *Journal for Further and Higher Education in Scotland* Vol 15 Winter 1990 page 10

The author, who is severely deaf, but continued with her nursing studies, reflects on the benefits she gained from being able to use a device called a pressure zone microphone which enabled her to listen to conversation around the room and contribute to discussion. Stresses the strong support from lecturers and fellow students and recommends this type of aid to be made available to other severely deaf students.

637 **Kettle M. and Massie B.** *Employers guide to disabilities* Woodhead-Faulkner 1986 144 pages

One of the few books tackling the employer's role in dealing with disability and rehabilitation and is therefore a valuable reference tool, especially for employment advisers and personnel managers. The case studies describing certain individual's employment problems and how they were solved are excellent.

638 **Kidd J.M.** *Assessment in action* Leicester UDACE 1989 62 pages

This manual is addressed to all those involved in the educational guidance of adults. In particular, it is aimed at those who work with adults on a day-to-day basis, helping them to make decisions about learning opportunities and draws upon evidence from visits to a range of guidance agencies and educational institutions. Includes practical training and an information resources sheet.

639 **Killeen J.** Adults' vocational mobility intentions: the roles of ages, sex and labour market position *British Journal of Guidance and Counselling* Vol 17 No 1 Jan 1989 76-93

The demand for vocational guidance by adults has been shown to be negatively related to occupational commitment. Thus in coming to understand the causes of occupational commitment, we are simultaneously able to form an appreciation of a major source of demand for vocational guidance. Three possible predictors are examined: age, sex and labour market position. Of these, labour market position is the best predictor. The implications for guidance are outlined.

640 **Killeen J.** Vocational guidance for adults: a study of demand *British Journal of Guidance and Counselling* Vol 14 No 3 1986 225-239

A sample study was conducted of economically active adults and of non-employed adults who intended to return to work. It demonstrated considerable uncertainty concerning the existence of adult vocational guidance and substantial public support for guidance provision. This strong demand emanates from those in employment as well as those seeking work. Adults wish to match, through guidance, the human resource and 'capital' at their disposal to available options.

641 **King H.** Student fee levels in adult education *Adult Education* Vol 58 No 3 1985 258-261

Examines the relationship between fees and uptake of adult education courses in one college. Argues that increases in price above the inflation rate have a negative effect on uptake.

642 **King M.M.** Entry qualifications and performances of mature age chemistry students in higher education *CORE* Vol 13 No 2 1989 1-31

This paper presents data obtained from a research study carried out in British universities and polytechnics which looked at the experiences of students who had spent a minimum of five years in employment before returning to higher education. One of the key areas of research concerned the 'routes of entry' into higher education taken by this sample and the degree of compatibility between their initial entry qualifications, the mode of study by which these were achieved and what they found in their first years of degree level programmes.

643 **Kinsey J.** Teaching marketing at a distance *Management Education and Development* Vol 17 Part 4 1986 324-335
This paper discusses some evidence resulting from two years of teaching marketing at a distance.

644 **Kirby D.** Encouraging the enterprising undergraduate *Education and Training* Vol 31 No 4 1989 9-10
Explores the objectives of the TA Enterprise in Higher Education Initiative and examines how they are being interpreted and implemented in Durham University.

645 **Kirkland G.** 'Tis distance lends enchantment..' *Media in Education and Development* Vol 15 No 4 December 1982 162-164
Discusses a two-year distance education course in educational technology developed at Jordanhill College. Includes students' learning activities and some of the benefits and problems associated with this form of education.

646 **Kirkup G.** *CAREERWISE: a fresh start in technology - women tell their stories* Milton Keynes Open University 1986
A booklet written for the Women into Science and Engineering (WISE) group and funded jointly by the Technology Faculty and the Equal Opportunities Commission. Contains case studies of 9 women students whose OU courses helped them to find satisfying careers in technical environments. Careers advice incorporates suggestions for juggling the dual commitments of professional and family responsibilities.

647 **Kirkwood A.** Enabling new students to examine their expectations of distance learning *Education and Training Technology International* Vol 26 No 1 1989
Pre-course counselling is invaluable for those about to embark on distance education courses. Several institutions provide assistance by means of materials in which a student-centred approach is adopted, some examples are discussed here.

648 **Kirkwood G. and Kirkwood C.** *Living adult education: Freire in Scotland* Open University Press 1989 155 pages
This book describes how the Gorgie Dalry Adult Learning project (ALP) came to be created and sustained as a systematic attempt to implement Freire's ideas in Scotland. Useful for all involved in adult, continuing and community education.

649 **Kitchen P.** Higher education/industry interface *Journal of Further and Higher Education* Vol 12 No 3 August 1988 47-53
Describes research which has developed the view that industrialists and academics see the need for higher education institutions to use the marketing concept with specific reference to the needs of the industrial sector.

650 **Knapper A.J.C. and Cropley A. J.** *Lifelong learning and higher education* 2nd edition Kogan Page 1991 224 pages
This book which interleaves theory and practice attempts to show how colleges and universities might respond to the pressing need for lifelong learning whereby people are encouraged to take the initiative for their own education and are motivated to continue to learn through organisational structures and teaching methods.

651 **Knasel E. and Rossetti A.** *Further education and employment training: a quality response* Leicester NIACE/REPLAN 1989 53 pages
Drawing on the experiences of a number of institutions this handbook is aimed at senior and middle managers in further education and supports them in responding to the issues raised by Employment Training. It describes good practice and suggests ways in which institutions can implement a quality response to the needs of those on Employment Training.

652 **Knight L.** A concerted response to employers' training needs *Transition* October 1987 16-17
An interesting article in which the author argues that colleges of FE and HE have a better chance of providing the kind of training industry requires if they collaborate rather than compete. Four different types of consortia are illustrated and the benefits accrued are discussed.

653 **Knight L. and Harris S.** *Training for small and medium companies* London FEU/PICKUP 1991 33 pages.

This document is the report of an interesting FEU/PICKUP project relating to training needs analysis. The aims of the project were to research, design and pilot training courses and their delivery methods to meet the particular needs of small and medium enterprises in the engineering sector more effectively than courses currently available. Describes how these aims were realised and how they were developed.

654 **Knox A.B.** Reducing barriers to participation in continuing education *Lifelong Learning* Vol 1 No 5 Feb/March 1987 7-9

This is a useful article which sets out a strategy for increasing participation in continuing education. The article stresses the need for institutions to assess reasons and deterrents and amongst other things stresses the need for educational counselling as a part of the programme to reduce barriers such as lack of confidence and inability to recognise programme relevance.

655 **Korving M.** *The Kogan Page mature student's handbook 1991/2* London Kogan Page 1991 428 pages

A highly detailed and practical handbook aimed at mature students wishing to enter higher education.

656 **Korving M.** *Making a comeback: a women's guide to returning to work after a break* London Business Books 1991 133 pages

A practical guide to returning to work after a break.

657 **Kotler P.** *Strategic marketing for nonprofit organizations* 4th Ed Englewood Cliffs N.J. Prentice-Hall 1991 644 pages

A much cited standard work on the theories, principles and structures involved in marketing.

658 **Kremer J.** *Women and work in Northern Ireland 1983-1988: a bibliography* Belfast Queens University 1988 6 pages

A short bibliography of about 150 entries dealing with many aspects of women in the labour market in Northern Ireland published between 1983 and 1988.

659 **Krukita T.** Excellence, equality and educational reform: the myth of South Asian achievement levels *New Community* Vol 16 No 3 1990 349-368

Provides a critical analysis of the literature and research on the schooling of South Asian pupils which has largely assumed that they do as well as white pupils. The author investigated the schooling of a sample of South Asian graduates and concluded that if the process by which qualifications are obtained rather than the qualifications themselves are assessed the schooling of South Asian pupils can be viewed as highly unsatisfactory.

660 **Kuh D. et al** Work for disabled people *Disability, Handicap and Society* Vol 3 No 1 1988 3-26

This paper presents results from a population based action research study in East Devon of the needs of 383 young people aged 16-25 years with a whole range of impairments and disabilities and 152 able-bodied controls. Results show training and further education opportunities have increased but do not appear to be leading to long-term employment. The disabled need many more opportunities to progress out of static or unstable occupations and we need to move away from the 'should be grateful for any job' syndrome.

661 **Labour Market Quarterly Report** Special Feature - Women returners to the labour market *Labour Market Quarterly Report* August 1990 14-16

This special feature considers the definitions of Women Returners; the size of the group; factors which prevent women returning to work and factors which would enable women to remain in work or facilitate their return.

662 **Labour Market Quarterly Report** Survey of employers funding of training in Britain *Labour Market Quarterly Report* Nov 1989 13-14

Relates to the Training Agencies major survey of training. Describes the models used and the problems of assessing funding. Presents estimates of employers funding of training for 1986/87.

663 **Labour Research** Do companies really care for children? *Labour Research* Vol 79 No 2 Feb 1990 7-9

Reports on a recent survey of top UK firms which shows that while many are introducing flexible work arrangements there are as yet only a handful of workplace nurseries.

664 **Laid G.H.** *A trade union case for partnership: the UK Amalgamated Engineering Union* Industry and Higher Education September 1989 161-166

The AEU welcomes all positive training initiatives and is set to seize the opportunities that the 1990s will present. The new policies of training to standards are more flexible than time-served apprenticeships. Argues for increased dialogue between management and workforce.

665 **Lambert P.** The mature student, formal assessment and entry into higher education *Journal of Access Studies* Vol 2 No 2 1987 66-77

A useful paper concerned with the nature of mature students' learning experience and modes of formal assessment. Concludes closer links between further, higher and adult education in course planning and development is essential if higher education is to learn from the pre-degree course experience of the mature student.

666 **Lambert P.** Women into educational management *Adults Learning* Vol 1 No 4 Dec 1989 106-107

Women are under-represented in management generally as well as educational management. Improving the situation requires equal opportunity policy and practice, training and staff development, and women's appreciation of their own management skills and knowledge.

667 **Lancaster B.** Changing job needs: commutable counselling *Industrial Management and Data Systems* Issue 6 1989 8-10

A survey of top business and industry managers in the UK, discussed in this article, revealed a need for career transition counselling services. The survey, confirmed that this brings benefits to companies by enabling them to move people more readily or by retraining managers to undertake new roles.

668 **Landon J. et al** *Multicultural resources and development unit* Edinburgh Moray House College of Education 1983 - onwards

The Unit collates and produces resources in the area of multicultural and anti-racist education to support college, regional and other initiatives within the field.

669 **Lane D.** Redundancy counselling for those still in employment *Journal of Managerial Psychology* Vol 3 No 4 1988 13-15

This article discusses a study conducted with 50 senior and middle managers in private and public sector organisations that had recently undertaken a major restructuring. Key managers who did not have access to external counselling services felt ill-equipped to meet the stress and some left without careers advice.

670 **Lavender P.** Theme with variations: social policy, community care and adult education *Adults Learning* Vol 1 No 6 1990 172-174

Major policy developments underlie the move towards community care. The author looks at the background to these developments and sketches 3 scenarios for joint care planning for adults with special education needs.

671 **Lavender P.** Theme with variation: 2 *Adults Learning* Vol 1 No 7 March 1990 185-187

This article concludes the review of care in the community and its implications for adult continuing education.

672 **Law Society Gazette** Ethnic minority students face tougher time getting into profession *Law Society Gazette* Vol 87 No 17 1990 4-5

A study of the data on ethnic minority entry into law points to racial discrimination and entrenched attitudes in many law firms. Graduates from polytechnics are deemed 'less employable' and ethnic minorities lack a 'suitable' background. Concludes that new recruitment criteria are needed.

673 **Leadbeater C.** Too far from campus *Financial Times* August 29 1991 page 12

The author studies the Prince of Wales' latest strictures on UK industry and the launch of the initiative 'Partners in Innovation'.

674 **Learning from Experience Trust: Newsletter** *Academic validation of companies in-house training* London LET June 1990 page 3

A brief overview of a pilot project carried out by LET to test the feasibility of granting academic credit for companies in-house training. The study found that there was a wide range of high quality training courses being carried out and all the participants had some in-house training meriting academic credit. Credit-rating of in-company courses is a powerful way of strengthening links between the world of work and post school education and a more substantial study is under way.

675 **Lea-Wilson F.** TECs and ex-offenders *TEC Director* Issue 5 Aug/Sep 1990 21-22

This valuable article considers the importance of re-integrating ex-offenders into the job market and argues employers should consider carefully the nature of an individual's offence and whether or not it is relevant to the job for which they have applied. Also discusses the work of NACRO Employment Training and some of the initiatives TECs are taking to develop the potential of ex-offenders.

676 **Leeds S. and Scott M.** Equal opportunities: rhetoric or action *Gender and Education* Vol 2 No 3 1990 333-343

This is an excellent paper which questions whether the equal opportunities legislation of the 1970s and the announcements made by many higher education institutions to be equal opportunity institutions have had any more than a marginal effect on the power structures and day-to-day running of institutions. It proposes that a positive action programme should be adopted to increase the proportion of women lecturers in higher education. It draws on the experience of equal opportunities initiatives in a number of higher education institutions and emphasises the importance of understanding resistance to change and concludes it is important not to become disillusioned with lack of progress in attitudinal change.

677 **Leicester M. and Field J.** Anti-racist post-initial education: reform after the act *New Community* Vol 16 No 3 1990 417-423

Examines the implications for racial equality in further education, adult and community education under the 1988 ERA. It views the provisions of the act as largely inequable through its emphasis on delegation and performance measures. However, the authors do see scope for anti-racist progression through the withdrawal of state control.

678 **Lengrand P.** *Area of learning basic to lifelong education* Hamburg, Germany UNESCO Institute for Education 1986 251 pages

Presents nine papers by experts from various countries who are known internationally for their outstanding contributions to the problems of learning as a basis for lifelong education.

679 **Levy D.** Ethnic minority enterprise *TEC Director* Issue 10 1991 20-21

Discusses the need for fair access for ethnic minorities to education and training opportunities and the role that TECs have to play in ensuring this.

680 **Levy M.** The role of core skills in work-based learning *Transition* Oct 1988 17-19

The move towards work-based learning rather than formal classroom teaching and towards recognition of people's competence in a job in place of their ability to pass tests puts new pressures on trainees supervisors and trainers. How do you prove someone can do a job? What skills does a task really involve? Some answers to these questions are being provided by the Work Based Learning Project which has drawn up guidance for the Employment Training Programme.

681 **Lewis J.** Breaking through the creche barrier *Management Today* Feb 1989 104-106

Argues that inflexibility of working arrangements in the majority of British organisations and the lack of suitable childcare facilities are barriers to women. Although companies pay lip-service to equal opportunity, the risk that a female manager will become pregnant and decide not to return to work limits opportunity for women.

682 **Lewis J.K. and Thomas K.** Occupational change and career development amongst graduate engineers and scientists *British Journal of Guidance and Counselling* Vol 15 1987 182-186

Occupational change is discussed. The writers suggest, drawing on evidence from interviews, people who find occupational change difficult can be helped towards flexibility through counselling techniques based on construct theory and/or the humanistic idea of potential for self-actualisation. Concludes counselling can be overtly directed towards re-framing and re-constructing life narratives.

683 **Lewis R. and Robinson G.** *Marketing PICKUP* Wigan Wigan Tech 1985
Reports on the results of a DES PICKUP programme giving step by step guidance on the marketing of training to the professions, industry and commerce.

684 **Lewis R.** Quality in education and training *OLS News* No 33 1990 1-4

685 **Lewis R.** The recognition of access courses to higher education: a perspective from CNAA *Journal of Access Studies* Vol 4 No 1/2 1988 15-24
Looks at the benefits and problems of a national scheme for the validation of Access courses. Discusses the CNAA's role in establishing such a system and maintaining academic quality.

686 **Lewis R.** What is 'quality' in corporate open learning and how do we measure it *Open Learning* Vol 4 No 3 1989 9-13
Examines the concept of quality in the context of organisations who use open learning to improve their business performance. Discusses why organisations choose open learning and suggests models which can ensure that quality is maintained and monitored.

687 **Lilley A. and Newton S.** Mentorship: supporting the adult learner: an investigation of the working of a mentorship scheme *Journal of Further and Higher Education* Vol 14 No 3 Autumn 1990 71-82
Focuses on the role of mentors and their relationship with the adult learner. Explores the demands made upon adult learners and examines the contribution which a mentorship system makes to meeting them.

688 **Limage L.J.** Prospects for adult literacy in a period of economic austerity *Comparative Education* Vol 24 No 1 1988 61-73

Examines the impact of economic recession and recent changes in legislation on the provision of support for adults with literacy problems.

689 **Linklater P. (Ed)** *Education and the world of work: positive partnerships* Surrey SRHE 1987 220 pages
A selection of papers following the theme of cooperative education. Those with an interest in sandwich degrees will benefit most from this book.

690 **Little A.** Planning the education-employment link: a brief guide to methods *International Journal of Educational Development* Vol 6 No 2 1986 85-92

691 **Littlefield D.** Tapping new sources of recruitment *Industrial Society* Dec 1990 28-29
Describes a scheme of pre-recruitment training courses aimed at getting ethnic minorities and women into the workforce thereby alleviating recruitment problems.

692 **Locke M. and Johnson C.** Institutional provision for mature students in higher education *New Era in Education* Vol 70 No 3 Dec 1989 66-69
The authors report on research they have conducted into the needs of mature students in a higher education institution in London. Based on action research with a selected number of mature students who were asked about their experiences and views of the polytechnic and factors of motivation. Concludes their findings suggest ways in which provision for these students might be improved, both in terms of academic provision in courses and in terms of non-academic support.

693 **Lockman P.** *Replan focus on special needs* No 3 Leicester NIACE/REPLAN 1989

694 **Loder C.** Links between industry and higher education in: *Training and Competitiveness* Kogan Page London 1991 186-200
An informative article which seeks to identify both good practices and barriers to successful collaboration and suggests areas that offer the best prospects for future business and higher

education partnerships. Some of the constraints on meeting the needs of industry are poor communication, lack of guidance on training needs, reluctance to view students as clients and marketing.

695   **Loder C.J. (Ed)** *Quality assurance and accountability in higher education* London Kogan Page 1990 112 pages
Seven essays on issues such as the role of the CNAA, external examiners, appraisal and a higher education inspectorate which are drawn together through the themes of quality and accountability. These themes are seen to be central to higher education debate in the coming years. Contains an extensive bibliography.

696   **Lones J.** Higher education: the changing needs of students with physical disabilities *Educare* No 39 March 1991 3-6
A valuable article which suggests that higher education establishments, the DES and Social Services Departments need to recognise the changing population and needs of the more severely disabled degree study applicants. Illuminates the practical barriers facing potential students and offers recommendations on how these may be effectively tackled.

697   **Long D.G.** *Learner managed learning: the key to lifelong learning and development* London Kogan Page 1990 176 pages
An interesting and in depth appraisal of the issues involved in developing learner managed learning.

698   **Lothian Adult Guidance Development Team** *Lothian Adult Resource Guide* Lothian 1990 66 pages
This guide is intended for advisers in adult guidance. The information on each organisation includes an address, telephone number and contact name (where appropriate). A brief outline of the organisation's adult provision is also given.

699   **Lothian Region Adult Guidance Network Libraries and Information Subgroup** *Libraries and adult education working group* Edinburgh Lothian Adult Guidance Unit 1991
A discussion document on current provision for the adult learner in Scottish public libraries.

Argues that public libraries can take an active and essential part in continuing education.

700   **Lovett T.** Community education and community division in Northern Ireland *Convergence* Vol 23 No 2 1990 25-34
Discusses the role of two colleges in Northern Ireland in providing non-sectarian programmes of community education in an attempt to promote social change and understanding and challenge stereotypes.

701   **Lowden K.** *Employers and adult training: attitudes and practices* Edinburgh Scottish Council for Research into Education 1989
Explores issues arising from the skills gap in industry and business and employers' attitudes towards retraining adults to fill these gaps. Concentrates on the extent of adult training; the factors employers saw as affecting training and employers' view of what training was and who should be responsible for it.

702   **Lowe P.** Improving employment opportunities for disabled people *Careers Journal* Summer 1989 24-26
This article is concerned with the social and occupational integration of disabled people. Sets out some of the principles which should be taken into account if this group of people is to be given an equal chance to gain employment.

703   **Lucas S. and Ward P.** Mature students at Lancaster University *Adult Education* Vol 58 No 2 Sept 1985 151-157
Reports on mature student progress at one university and provides an optimistic picture of their success. It is clear from this small-scale survey that mature students can be well-motivated, qualified and prepared and can make a challenging, positive and refreshing contribution to higher education.

704   **Lucas S.** Open college and the transition to university *Journal of Access Studies* Vol 5 No 1 Spring 1990 35-46
Results of the survey undertaken in 1987 which examines the extent to which open college courses seem to provide an adequate preparation for degree level, from both institutional and student viewpoint. The evidence gathered, both in terms of actual results and in questionnaire exercises, serves to

confirm the appropriateness of the open college.

705 **Lyon E.** Unequal opportunities: black minorities and access to higher education *Journal of Further and Higher Education* Vol 12 No 3 1988 21-37

Reports on research undertaken at South Bank Polytechnic which provides information on the patterns of enrolment of ethnic minority groups. Minority group students differed from others in terms of subject choice, the importance of further education, they were likely to be older and live in the locality. Access courses were shown to be particularly significant for Caribbean students. The policy implications of the findings are examined and the author calls for a more coherent and centralised approach to the problem.

706 **Mabey C.** Factors influencing the effectiveness of training and development *Training and Management Development Methods* Vol 3 No 1 1989 1-5

Discusses the factors needed to produce quality training. These include the support of senior management, the involvement of all staff and good design and delivery.

707 **McAleer J. and McAleavy G.** Accreditation of prior learning: implications for trainers and managers of colleges of further education *International Journal of Educational Management* Vol 4 No 4 1990 18-21

Gives an account of a pilot scheme on APL carried out in Northern Ireland. The scheme looked at the possibility of accrediting the skills of instructors in community workshops for the unemployed. The instructors were interviewed to assess their previous experience and their needs with regard to formal certificates. The authors note the lack of any certification for trades learned in the past.

708 **McCall R.W.** Continuing professional development: can universities earn profits? *Industry and Higher Education* Vol 3 No 4 December 1988 135-144

The author agrees universities can profit from offering continuing professional development (CPD) but suggests there are several inhibitors limiting success and makes some recommendations on how to overcome these. Notably, senior officers responsible for CPD must have self confidence and courage to initiate fundamental changes in academic staff attitudes.

709 **McCann J.** TECs and ethnic minorities: conference report *TEC Director* Issue 10 1991 12-13

Reports on a conference held at Warwick University on TECs and ethnic minorities. The key themes included the need for equal opportunities to be a fundamental part of TEC policy, the avoidance of tokenism and short term responses and the importance of monitoring activity.

710 **McCartney J.R. and McIlheney C.J.** Day release in Northern Ireland *Journal of Further and higher Education* Vol 11 No 3 1987 120-129

Reports on a project designed to examine the value of day release and evening courses to employers and employees in Northern Ireland. Attempts to assess the standing of such courses in further education colleges. Looks at how colleges can respond to changing demand such as those implemented in new employment training schemes.

711 **McClean S.D.** Marketing and the college *Journal of Further Education and Higher Education in Scotland* May 1985 18-21

Seeks to present a case in favour of marketing concepts and practices in further education while recognising that there are restrictions and opposing attitudes affecting the future of colleges.

712 **McClure C.** Equalising access *Local Government Chronicle* 9 February 1990 20-21

Review of Avon County Council's policy of positive action for the employment of disabled people.

713 **McCormack V. and O'Hara J.** *Enduring inequality and religious discrimination in employment in Northern Ireland* London National Council for Civil Liberties 1990 82 pages

714 **McCrae J.** Enterprise in higher education: reflections of a practitioner *Scottish Journal of Adult Education* Vol 9 No 4 Winter 1990 29-37

Some useful reflections on the EHE initiative from someone who has been involved in the first year of implementation of two EHE programmes. Suggests EHE should be viewed as an opportunity to improve the quality of higher education.

715   MacDonald C. et al *Providing for adults: the views and policies of providers of education and training* Edinburgh Scottish Council For Research in Education 1989 36 pages

A study of 32 public and 25 private randomly selected providers of adult education in Scotland focused on their policies toward adult participants and the extent to which the organisations cater for adults. Providers clearly regard the teaching of adult students positively and recognise the many obstacles and barriers such students face. Recommendations to alleviate these are provided. The report concludes it is crucial that the government help convince individuals, providers and employers that adult training and education is valuable and important.

716   Mace J. and Yarnit M. (Ed) *Time off to learn: paid educational leave and low-paid workers* London Methuen and Co Ltd 1987 179 pages

This is both a readable and informative collection which addresses itself to paid leave for those in the non professional sector. Combines analysis with narrative, political argument with first person account and takes a thematic approach to include the attitudes of government, trade unions, women, ethnic minorities and the unemployed.

717   Mace J. and Yarnit M. Now or never: women, time and education In: Mace J. and Yarnit M. (Ed) *Paid educational leave and low paid workers: time off to learn* 1987 Methuen 21-36

Women who work in low paid, part-time jobs are frequently denied paid educational leave. The author argues women need time and space for education and training to be deemed legitimate. Draws on discussion with some women who have benefited from paid educational leave.

718   McElroy A.R. Resourcing and supporting open and distance learning: some educational and managerial

models *Learning Resources Journal* Vol 4 No 3 October 1988 100-112

Examines the implications of providing library resources and support for open and distance learning based on Napier Polytechnic library's experience both as the central library service and as a provider of directed private study through their own distance learning programme in library and information science.

719   McEvedy I. Who's killing whom *Management Today* April 1990 92-94

This article draws on data from a recent CBI report which concluded that while 64% of women not in the workforce are interested in working, 79% are prevented from doing so because they have young children at home. However, the burden of childcare is placed on the employee. Concludes those companies that have invested in childcare will prosper in the coming labour shortage.

720   McGivney V. *Childcare: a guide to organisations, publications, research and campaigns concerned with day care provision and facilities for young children* REPLAN/NIACE 1990 31 pages

A practical booklet covering many aspects of childcare provision, including key contacts for professional advice, useful publications and sources of information.

721   McGivney V. and Bateson B. Childcare: the continuing debate *Adults Learning* Vol 2 No 7 Mar 1991 203-204

A succinct and informative review depicting the continuing lack of childcare facilities which reinforces the barriers facing women trying to gain access to education, training and employment. Argues a cultural attitude change is needed which will combat the ambivalence of women's role in society. A number of recommendations is advanced which suggests how providers can remove the barriers caused by lack of childcare.

722   McGivney V. Come in, the door is open *Education* Vol 78 No 9 August 1991 167-168

Reports on the NIACE project on making colleges more attractive to adult learners.

723   McGivney V. *Education's for other people: access to education for non participant adults* Leicester NIACE 1990 210 pages

This book presents the results of qualitative research which investigated the characteristics of those who do not voluntarily take part in education after leaving school and suggests strategies for opening up educational opportunities to non-participants. These include the urgent need for accessible support, advice and guidance systems.

724   McGivney V. (Ed) *Opening colleges to adult learners* Leicester NIACE/TEED 1991 159 pages

This report analyses the issues that affect adult learners returning to education, highlighting examples of innovative practice in the provision for adults within further education and shows how educational opportunities for adults can most effectively be improved. The conclusions posited for effective provision support earlier studies: institutional flexibility, a strategic staff development strategy, marketing, a student centred approach and curriculum design and delivery tailored to identified needs. There is a particularly useful section on equal opportunities.

725   MacGregor K. More ethnic poly applicants *Times Educational Supplement* No 3839 26th Jan 1990 page 3

Reports on the figures released by the Polytechnic Admissions system on the breakdown of ethnic minority applicants.

726   McIlroy J. Continuing education: do the universities mean business? *Studies in Higher Education* Vol 14 No 3 1989 331-345

This paper briefly reviews the current involvement of universities in continuing education and then goes on to examine recent developments in liberal education and professional and vocational education. Argues existing provision is handicapped by competing conceptions of purpose, lack of resources and organisational fragmentation. Concludes a greater degree of strategic thinking and unified philosophy is needed for progression.

727   McIlroy J. The funding of adult and continuing education in Britain: the acid test *International Journal of Lifelong Education* Vol 8 No 4 1989 345-353

Discusses the background and implications of the 1987 decision to abolish special funding arrangements for adult and continuing education in universities. Examines the financial difficulties faced by extramural departments in some universities.

728   McIlroy J. A turning point in university adult and continuing education *Adult Education* Vol 61 No 1 1988 7-14

Surveys the work of university extra mural departments in adult education. Considers the implications for these departments now that the funding has been shifted from the DES to the UFC.

729   MacIntosh M. Second time pupils: the return of women to school In: S.M. Paterson and J. Fewell *Girls in their prime* Edinburgh Scottish Academic Press 1990 54-70

This paper is an account of why women go back to school for a second time. Based on conversational analysis with members of a Women's Group who come together weekly to share experiences and explore ideas. The main benefits from such an experience are shown to be increased confidence and personal development. A valuable paper for anyone hoping to return to study of any form.

730   McKail C.R. *An evaluation of a living skills training programme for adults with a mental handicap* Aberdeen University of Aberdeen, Department of Education 1990

A case study which investigates the effects of a training programme comprising self help, social, academic and interpersonal skills provided at a college of further education for adults with a mental handicap who have been in hospital care for many years. Clearly demonstrates they had the capacity and motivation to learn and respond to training.

731   Mackenzie M.L. Education, management and industry *Management in Education* Vol 4 No 2 Summer 1990 12-13

A brief overview which explores the management implications of the developing relationship between education and training in Scotland.

732   McKeown A. Industry's needs versus the further education curriculum *Journal of Further and Higher Education* Vol 9 No 3 Autumn 1985 81-86

Reviews a research project, the objective of which, was to assess how far the further education curriculum meets the needs of industry. The report raises a number of issues which are documented by the writer, for example, the need for liaison with employers, feedback from former students, staff development and industrial input into courses. It is suggested that a framework be set up whereby senior full-time staff, employers and employees and examining bodies would negotiate, forecast and plan courses and evaluate existing ones.

733   McKinlay A. *Employment of mature graduates* Edinburgh SIACE 1989

734   McKinlay A. *Women in computing in Scottish higher education* Edinburgh SIACE 1989
A report on why women are not well represented in computing and related occupations and some of the initiatives being launched which may encourage them into this field.

735   McLaghlin J. ESL for the unemployed *ELT Journal* Vol 39 No 2 1985 88-95

736   McLaughlin E. In search of the female breadwinner: gender and unemployment in Derry city In Donnan H. and McFarlane (Ed) *Social anthropology and public policy in Northern Ireland* Aldershot Avebury 1989 47-66
Reports on research carried out in Derry in Northern Ireland in which 540 women were interviewed about their experience of employment and unemployment.

737   McLaughlin J. Information paper 21: the Scottish vocational education council *Scottish Educational Review* Vol 20 No 1 May 1988 52-58

738   McLean A. Leisure management education *Scottish Journal of Physical Education* Vol 18 No 1-2 19-20
This article highlights some of the developments in leisure management education and training which have occurred in further and higher education establishments in Scotland. It is particularly concerned with management education at advanced level. The author considers how one college is

responding to an increasing demand from employers within the leisure industry considers SCOTVEC developments at HNC/HND level.

739   MacLean C. et al *Adult basic education provision in Scotland* Edinburgh Critical Skills Development 1991
The study aims to produce a cost-benefit appraisal of a number of different ways of providing basic education in Scotland and to identify in particular those elements which contribute to effective service delivery.

740   McNair S. A national credit framework *Adults Learning* Vol 2 No 9 1991 251-2
Calls for a coherent national framework for recognising the achievement of adults. Argues that the work of agencies such as NCVQ, UDACE and Open College Network has brought such a system closer to becoming a reality.

741   McNay I. Continuing education: will the trans-binary initiative survive and suffice *Higher Education Quarterly* Vol 41 No 1 January 1987 73-91
A review of lost opportunities suggests that higher education, employers, professional bodies and the government must develop a serious commitment to continuing education. Present provision lacks a coherent framework. The potential of the joint NAB/UGC initiative as a force for development is considered.

742   MacPherson I. *Attracting new students to adult education: the learners' point of view* Edinburgh SIACE 1989 55 pages
This report is based on a case study of an adult education centre in Glasgow. Using the views of students at the selected centre, the author considers, in some depth, the issues involved in attracting low participant groups within the adult population back into education. The main focus of the report is upon what students from such groups consider to be appropriate provision. The model of appropriate provision which emerged, whilst recognising the survey was on a small scale, should be helpful as a role model for other projects seeking to attract low participant groups.

743 McRae D. and Lakey J. *Women into engineering and science: employers' policies and practices* London Policy Studies Institute 1990

This is a new report which examines how ten major British firms aim to attract more women into technical careers as scientists and engineers. Their policies fall into two categories: liaison with schools to encourage girls to choose subjects which later allow them to take up technical careers and sponsorship of women graduates; and the retention of qualified women employees through the introduction of career breaks, extended maternity leave and part-time working arrangements. Based on in-depth interviews with both management and employees, the report concludes that companies should provide more childcare provision and remove remaining barriers to training and promotion.

744 MacRae J. *More ladders than snakes* REPLAN/DES Review Issue 5 Oct 1989 31 pages

This review is about how adults move into and through education and on to other things. Case studies are portrayed whereby adults actually speak about their own experiences. Guidance and staff empathy are perceived as crucial by those interviewed.

745 McVicar M. Competitive tendering in higher education *International Journal of Educational Management* Vol 4 No 1 1990 19-21

A useful article which clearly describes the mechanisms and assesses the impact of the PCFC and the Education Reform Act on English polytechnics.

746 McWhirter L. et al Transition from school to work: cohort evidence **In: Osborne R.D. et al (Ed)** *Education and policy in Northern Ireland* Belfast Policy Research Institute 1987 167-190

Based on a study of nearly 3000 young people in Northern Ireland in the three years after compulsory education. This research looks at the decisions made by the young people about their transition from school to work and the factors which influence their decisions. The decisions made at this time are seen to be crucial particularly in an environment where employment opportunities are limited.

747 McWhirter L. et al Transition from school to work: cohort evidence from Northern Ireland on post-compulsory school activities and influencing factors *Irish Educational Studies* Vol 7 No 2 1988 131-147

Paper which examines the transition from education to the labour market of young people in Northern Ireland. Part of its aim is to investigate the factors which influence those decisions made after the age of 18. Concludes that academic attainment does not by itself redress the social and religious inequalities which seem to exist in Northern Ireland.

748 Magee S.R. and Alexander D.J. Training and education in continuing education *International Journal of Lifelong Education* Vol 5 No 3 July-September 1986 173-185

The authors offer a critical review of some trends in contemporary vocational education and training. Argue that training cannot and should not be separated from education. If the aim is flexibility and adaptability then much training depends on adequate levels of general education to enable men and women to take an active role in society. Highlights some of the initiatives resulting from the Government's report 'The New Training Initiative' (1981) and developments in experiential qualifications and also usefully documents those trends which they believe do not form the basis of a continuing education.

749 Maguire M. *Employer's view of work related further education* Labour market studies University of Leicester 1990

This study documents the results from 202 interviews with employers. There are some interesting conclusions made. For example, whilst there had been an increase in employers' use of external training provision, this in reality was often partial or dated, which would point to the need for up-to-date and coherent information and guidance.

750 Mann S. Why open learning can be a turn off *Personnel Management* Vol 20 No 1 January 1988 41-43

The thrust of this article is trainers must be certain that the individual student chooses the most appropriate material and provide proper support if open learning is to be successful. No single form of training suits every person. Reports on a study on open and distance learning for managers and draws out the main factors which appear to have an impact on the individual's commitment to open learning.

751   Manpower Services Commission *The funding of vocational education and training: a consultation document* Sheffield MSC 1987 34 pages
Report prepared by Deloitte Haskins and Sells Management Consultancy Division based on a mapping study of the funding of vocational education and training.

752   Manpower Services Commission *Training for enterprise scheme: guide for training providers* Sheffield Employment Department 1988
The purpose of this guide is to help training providers arrange and deliver the Business Enterprise Programme.

753   Mansell J. Delivering vocational education and training *Coombe Lodge Report* Vol 17 No 10 1985 595-600
Illustrates the changing context of further education, new strategies of curriculum development and new elements of the language delivery. Rather than relying on fixed courses and patterns of provision existing competence, however gained, should be taken into account thus optimising the autonomy of the learner.

754   Manson-Smith D. (Ed) *Paying for Training* 1990/91 4th Edition Glasgow The Planning Exchange 1990 172 pages
Guide aimed at employers, training providers and their advisors giving details of the financial assistance available for adult training. Gives guidance on the schemes and directs users to sources of further information.

755   Mant J. and Winner A. A second chance to learn science *Adults Learning* Vol 2 No 6 February 1991
A valuable article which looks at courses designed specifically for adults who wish to enter into science but have no formal qualifications. The 'second chance' approach can be effective in building confidence in people's ability to learn in the science area. Concludes that careful measures are needed to attract non-standard adult students onto this kind of course. These include networking, use of personal contacts and the provision of progression routes. The science course depicted

here is a success story, it enabled students to see science as accessible and enjoyable. The author asserts it is possible to provide such courses with access to laboratories on limited resources.

756   Marker W. The open door: how the OU has helped teacher education come of age in Scotland *Times Scottish Educational Supplement* No. 1217 2 March 1990 page 4
Reports on the immense contribution of the Open University to the post experience education of Scottish teachers. The Open University in Scotland provides a wide range of opportunities quite unmatched by that of any other agency and has used distance learning to reach teachers the colleges and universities could not.

757   Marker W.B. Staff development: the Scottish scene *British Journal of In-service Education* Vol 15 No 2 Summer 1989 68-72
An account of the importance given to staff development in Scotland.

758   Markula M. Continuing education for increased competitiveness *Industry and Higher Education* Vol 4 No 1 March 1990 2-3

759   Marsh L.R. Survey feedback and policy formulation: equal opportunities and promotion in Strathclyde *Scottish Educational Review* Vol 21 No 1 May 1989 26-35
This book is the outcome of interviews with forty nine departments in higher education institutions covering six academic disciplines. The author wished to illustrate how far there has been a shift from knowledge for its own sake towards the acquisition of knowledge and skills instrumental to economic and social objectives. Whilst the majority of academic staff recognised the relevance of academic experience to graduate employment and the importance of developing general enabling skills, it became clear that there was wide variation in opinion across disciplines in relation to curriculum changes and the involvement of outsiders.

760   Marshall J. Less equal than others *Times Higher Education Supplement* No 754 17 April 1987 pages i-ii

The author describes the tactics some women must adopt to avoid 'hostile cultures'. Many women in management feel they must imitate the male model to fit in with an existing culture, whilst others decided to draw on their identities as women in developing as managers and thus contribute to a changing world of employment for men and women.

761 **Martin V.** Adult education in the shopping centre *Adult Education* Vol 59 No 1 1986 14-19
Describes a mutually beneficial venture in which Brighton's adult education service collaborated with W.H.Smiths in using their premises for publicity, enrolment and meeting tutors.

762 **Mason R.** *Flexible learning case studies - project B of the Scottish open learning federation* Scottish Open Learning Consortium/Training Agency 1990
The aim of this project was to gather information about present flexible learning developments in post-sixteen computing. Case studies of good practice in the delivery and management of flexible learning are valuable. The project highlights areas needing further materials development.

763 **Mason R.** Flexistudy at Borders College: a case study *Learning Resources Journal* Vol 6 No 3 October 1990 72-75
This article describes the way flexible learning operates at Borders College and its resource implications. The problems posed to existing systems, the allocation of tutor time and the need for accountability are discussed. The qualifications involved are SCE O and H grades, O Level and SCOTVEC. There is a staffed open learning unit where enquiries and information needs are dealt with. Tutor's guidance notes for flexistudy are included in the appendix.

764 **Mason R.** The logic of non-standard entry: mature students and higher education *Journal of Further and Higher Education* Vol 11 No 3 1987 51-59
A valuable paper which briefly summarises the history of non standard entry since the second world war and then looks at some of the current developments surrounding the access movement.

765 **Massey A. and Goldsmith M.J.F.** Breaking down the barriers to higher education *British Journal of Education and Work* Vol 1 No 3 1987 187-199
An excellent paper which explores the barriers to higher education. Considers the reasons why change is necessary, developments in Access and some of the projects currently taking place.

766 **Mathews D.** Evaluating occupational standards *Competence and Assessment* No 10 1990 10-13
Examines the aims of a national system of occupational standards and discusses the positive economic and social outcomes which may result. Calls for careful monitoring of the system to discover whether potential benefits are becoming realities.

767 **Mawditt R.** In partnership for profit: academic intentions and opportunities *Industry and Higher Education* Vol 2 No 2 June 1988 80-84
This article discusses ways for universities to take advantage of opportunities for collaborative projects with particular reference to the University of Bath which has experienced many benefits from liaison.

768 **Maycell K. and Smart D.** *Visual impairment training reviewed* National Foundation for Educational Research 1989 11 pages
This pamphlet summarizes the key issues of the report *'Beyond Vision: training for work with visually impaired people'*. This involves a study of the training provided for workers who are visually impaired and the work carried out by them.

769 **Megson C.** The merits of marketing *Education* Vol 172 No 17 1987 page 382
Discusses the possible advisory role of an LEA in the planning and analysis of a college marketing strategy. Describes how this role has developed in Gloucestershire.

770 **Michaels R.** Entry route for mature students: variety and quality assessed *Journal of Access Studies* Vol 1 No 1 1986 57-71
Highlights some of the more recent initiatives which have developed in order to introduce flexible entry into higher education.

771 **Miliband D.** *Learning by right* London Institute of Public Policy Research 1990 24 pages

Whilst most recent training policy proposals concentrate on the level of training expenditure, this report argues for the spread of education and training throughout the workforce. In the long term, it argues for a 'symbolic promise' to all adults of three years' post-compulsory education and training. For the present, it puts forward the case for a statutory annual entitlement to five days paid educational leave. The report examines the partnership of individual, government and employer that would be necessary to make this entitlement a reality, and sets out the priorities for the introduction of the scheme.

772 **Miller C.** Assessment in the workplace: quality issues *Competence and Assessment* No 9 1989 15-16

Discusses the stages involved in the implementation and the costs of quality assurance in relation to work based learning.

773 **Miller J. and Dower A.** *Improving quality in further education: a guide for teachers in course teams* Ware Consultants at Work 1989 38 pages

A practical handbook aimed at teachers involved in setting up quality control systems and course evaluation in further education through a process of collecting and analysing information and basing decisions upon it.

774 **Miller J. and Inniss S.** *Managing quality improvements in further education: a guide for middle managers* Ware Consultants at Work 1990 39 pages

A project commissioned by the Work-related Further Education Development Fund which aims to support the work of managers involved in implementing quality measures in further education.

775 **Miller J. and Inniss S.** *The strategic management of a quality further education service: a working paper for LEA officers and college principles* Ware Consultants at Work 1990 57 pages

Document resulting from a project based on three diverse LEAs which aimed to identify the components of Strategic Quality Management in relation to the further education sector. Examines the way quality can be defined and measured and the role of different staff in working towards quality.

776 **Miller R.L.** *Higher education and labour market entry: the different experiences of Northern Ireland Protestants and Catholics* Belfast Policy Research Institute 1990 39 pages

Reports on research based on the 1979 cohort of higher education entrants from Northern Ireland. A number of issues are addressed including the characteristics, experience and economic activity of the participants. The movement of students between Northern Ireland and Great Britain is also discussed.

777 **Millins K.** Access and quality control: the Lindop onslaught *Journal of Access Studies* Vol 1 No 2 1986 68-71

Severely criticises the report of the Lindop Committee (DES 1985) which warned institutions of the 'possible dangers' of Access courses. The author argues that such statements are based on assumption rather than fact.

778 **Millins K.** Quality control of access studies to higher education: the role of the moderator *Journal of Access Studies* Vol 1 No 1 1986 52-56

Examines the mechanisms which exist for controlling the quality of Access courses and in particular the role of the moderator in the system.

779 **Millins K. (Ed)** *Access to higher education: courses directory* Milton Keynes ECCTIS, CNAA, FAST 1989 140 pages

Lists the 583 Access courses aimed at facilitating access into higher education. Shows the diversity in structure, hours, content, student body and relations with higher education inherent in such courses.

780 **Milne K.** A black stair to yuppidom *New Society* Vol 81 No 1283 1987 page 24

Describes a course at Central London Polytechnic in the Ethnic Minority Development Unit providing training for black and Asian people aiming to set up in business.

781 **Milton C.** Staying power: Scottish teenagers in higher education *Times*

Scottish Educational Supplement No. 3898 15 March 1991 page 27

An excellent overview of the Scottish higher education system which will be of help to those with little awareness of Scottish education. Considers some of the cultural, institutional and historical factors which may account for why 24% of Scottish teenagers go onto higher education and 90% to institutions in their own country.

782   **Mitchell H.** Improved access to higher education *Bulletin of Educational Development and Research* No 32 Summer 1986 6-9

This article focuses on the approaches adopted by Newcastle-upon-Tyne Polytechnic in meeting the continuing education and training needs of the community. Background information to the introduction of a number of initiatives are outlined.

783   **Mitchell H. and Tallentyre F.** Widening access to higher education *Education and Training* Vol 30 No 5 1988 11-14

Discusses access to higher education in the UK up to 1995, including the increased opportunities and assistance available for those over 18. The falling number of school leavers over this period has led to greater awareness of the educational needs of the over-18s.

784   **Mitchell L.** Assessment at work *Scottish Education Review* Vol 18 No 2 1986 93-99

Discusses competence in the workplace and highlights those issues which need to be addressed before full scale implementation of assessment systems is possible.

785   **Mokades J.** REPLAN and education for black unemployed people: a personal view *Multicultural Teaching* Vol 6 No 1 1987 page 45

Argues that REPLAN lacks the particular expertise needed to deal with the ethnic minority unemployed. Calls for a co-ordinated approach to the collection and dissemination of information about the training on offer. Describes the formation of the Forum for the Advancement of Education and Training for the Black Unemployed (FAETBU).

786   **Molloy S. and Singh R.** Caught behind by convention: how institutions

are failing to embrace fully ethnic minorities *Times Higher Education Supplement* No 968 24th May 1991 page 14

Reviews evidence on routes of access and participation and progress of black and ethnic minority students in higher education. Argues that the evidence available masks a great deal of variation in terms of ethnic groups, subjects and institutions.

787   **Molyneux F. et al** *Learning for life: politics and progress in recurrent education* Croom Helm 1988 320 pages

This is a collection of papers covering all facets of continuing education and represents the Association for Recurrent Education's policy of continuing to press the argument for political decisions which will signal the conclusive shift in thought and attitude away from the outmoded apprenticeship view of education.

788   **Monds F. and Van-Barneveld D.** Training for technology entrepreneurs *European Journal of Engineering Education* Vol 13 No 4 1988 447-454

Describes graduate training programmes in Northern Ireland and Holland which aim to help graduate technologists make the transition between full time education and entrepreneurial activity.

789   **Moore A.** How they modelled modules in Scotland *Transition* April 1988 24-25

Andrew Moore, formerly of the Scottish Vocational Education Council explains the Scottish Action Plan. Points to the growing interest on the part of adult and community education in offering national certificate modules for adults. Many adults returning to work after a break have found the modular system particularly suitable for part-time study and for sampling different vocational areas. Issues of quality and assessment are discussed.

790   **Moore K.M.** Women's access and opportunity in higher education: towards the 21st century *Comparative Education* Vol 23 No 1 1987 23-24

A detailed survey of women's access and opportunity in higher education which carefully documents the constraints and barriers faced by women and how these may be eliminated.

791 Moore P.G. Marketing higher education *Higher Education Quarterly* Vol 43 No 2 Spring 1989 108-124

The paper explores the development of marketing in higher education since 1945 citing the formation of UCCA and the Robbins report as significant events. Stresses the need for higher education institutions to have a strategic plan in which marketing is a key component. Argues that education and training must be viewed as a long term investment rather than a consumer good.

792 More M. Provision for life *Education* Vol 172 No 16 14 October 1988 366-367

Describes how one school responded to the threat of falling numbers by delivery of continuing education for the whole community.

793 Moreton T. *The case for unequal opportunities for disabled people in higher education* Leeds University of Leeds 1990 27 pages

794 Morphy L. *Career change* Hobsons 1986 158 pages

A useful book which describes the problems and some solutions facing women and men who want to change their career direction.

795 Morrell J. *The employment of people with disabilities: research into the policies and practices of employers* Research Paper No 77 IFF Research Ltd 1990 36 pages

This paper suggests there was substantial good will towards employing people with disabilities. In practice this was tempered by the perception that employing people with disabilities may present the employer with problems. The degree of awareness and understanding of the Quota scheme among employers was relatively low.

796 Morris I. Memo to the MSC - we do not pat hedgehogs: need to fund the growth of open learning *Times Educational Supplement Scotland* No 1120 22 April 1988 page 2

Reviews the benefits of open learning as an education and training method and why there is a strong need to fund its growth.

797 Morris J. *Women in computing* Computer Weekly Pubs. 1989 124 pages

The author provides a valuable insight into the experiences faced by women in the computing industry. Considers whether the current education system is preventing more women from entering technological posts and whether some dead-end jobs are reserved just for women. Contains much practical advice, further reading and addresses.

798 Morris M. Operation enterprise *Education* Vol 173 No 8 February 1989 192-193

Discusses the rise of education for enterprise throughout the European community and in the UK in particular.

799 Morrow N.C. and Hargie O.D.W. Communication as a focus in the continuing education of pharmacists *Studies in Higher Education* Vol 11 No 3 1986 279-288

The authors stress the need for the development of interpersonal and communication skills through continuing education for pharmacists. A training course in Northern Ireland is described and the need for similar courses in other professions is discussed.

800 Mowat I. and Uttenthal B. Transcript of an interview at Palmont young offenders institution *Journal of Further Education and Higher Education in Scotland* Vol 13 May 1989 12-19

An interesting article which describes the education available for offenders. On offer are adult basic education and a range of SCOTVEC modules and leisure activities including group work. Contrasts the Scottish prison system with that of England and Wales.

801 Muller D. and Funnell P. *Delivering quality in vocational education* London Kogan Page 1991 180 pages

A detailed account of developments in vocational education and training including TECs and national vocational qualifications.

802 Mumford A. Learning in action *Personnel Management* July 1991 34-37

Discusses action learning which is reported to be a useful management education and training strategy. Action learning asks managers to focus primarily on their own life experiences rather than hypothetical case studies. Managers should be able to relate theory against the reality of organisations.

803   **Munn P. and Tett L.** *Adult education: provision, guidance and progression* Edinburgh SCRE in association with SCEC Completion date November 1993

The research comprises four inter-related studies which provide a broad-based national picture of opportunities for progression. It presents detailed information on adults' experiences and on the operation of particular guidance systems.

804   **Munn P. and MacDonald C.** *Adult participation in education and training* Edinburgh Scottish Council for Research in Education 1988 59 pages

A useful and interesting survey of 2000 adults in Scotland which looks at their attitude towards participation in education and training. Identifies a number of important and subsidiary reasons for non-participation. Looks at attitudes among particular groups such as women and social classes.

805   **Munn P.** *Evaluation of Scottish wider access programme* (SWAP) Edinburgh Scottish Council for Research in Education completion date August 1992

The aim of the project is to explore the experience of students on access courses and particularly those moving from access courses into higher education in order to identify any problems encountered and suggest possible remedial measures.

806   **Munn P. and McDonald C.** *Mature in students: student teachers* Edinburgh Scottish Council for Research into Education completion date August 1992

The research will consider why there are not more mature entrants to secondary teaching and what can be done to attract them. Will utilise results from survey findings.

807   **Munn P. et al** *The needs of mature entrants with special reference to science and technology* Edinburgh Scottish Council for Research in Education December 1991

The research focuses on the identification and effectiveness of innovative approaches in supporting the needs of mature students in

higher and further education and on ways of attracting potential adult returners back into education and training. The case studies concentrate on engineering, electronics, mathematics and science, where there has traditionally been difficulty in attracting mature students.

808   **Munn P. et al** *Opportunities for mature students* Edinburgh Scottish Council for Research in Education 1990

This research explored the pattern of uptake by mature students of educational opportunities in Scotland. It investigated the factors which affect adults' participation or non-participation in such opportunities. Perceptions of adult 'returners' to education and training, 'potential returners' and providing institutions and employers are usefully highlighted.

809   **Munn P. et al.** *Part-time adult educators and training: a study of needs and provision* Edinburgh Scottish Council for Research in Education 1989 46 pages

This report depicts research on the training needs of adult educators. Using qualitative research methods the interviewee groups came from inner city, rural and mixed areas of a large town with rural hinterland and included 21 part time adult educators and 11 immediate employers or trainers. The training needs fall into four broad categories: an introduction to the setting in which one is operating; the development of key basic skills necessary to perform the job of part-time adult educator; refresher courses and specialist courses such as counselling and computers. The results will be of value for those developing training courses for adult educators.

810   **Munn P. et al** *Part-time community development workers and training: a study of needs and provision* Edinburgh Scottish Council for Research in Education 1989 46 pages

The study reported here canvassed the views of part-time Scottish community education workers, their employers and their trainers about training needs and how adequately those needs were being met. The study found that training and refresher courses were valued but there were some worries about training standards and delivery. Part-time training was considered successful when it involved practical activities relevant to the work places and when the work was performed alongside experienced staff. On-the-job training is perceived as highly effective and desirable by part-time workers. Questions of policy, information, support services and modularisation are clearly discussed.

811   Munn P. and Hamilton D. *Part-time youth workers and training: a study of needs and provision* Edinburgh Scottish Community Education Council 1989 47 pages

This report examines survey responses by Scottish part-time youth workers, their employers and trainers about programme training needs. The study, drawing on interview data, focuses on the characteristics and roles of part-time staff, their level of satisfaction with existing training, and their attitudes toward a modular training system. Training was considered successful when it involved practical, relevant work alongside experienced staff. Residential weekends were favoured; distance learning was not. Main training access problems were seen to be caused by a lack of full-time staff and inadequate budgets. The document recommends that organisations more clearly identify goals and needs, and make training as relevant to the needs as possible. On-the-job training with experienced trainers is also encouraged.

812   Munns R. and Furnborough P. Meeting the training needs of the ethnic minority unemployed *Adult Education* Vol 59 No 3 1986 244-249

Describes Training for Change, a scheme aimed at providing redundant Asian textile workers in Lancashire with retraining for other local industry. The scheme integrated training with basic education.

813   Munro N. LECs enter the battle of the budgets: local enterprise companies in Scotland *Times Scottish Educational Supplement* No. 1272 22 March 1991 page 4

Written ten days before the launch of LECs, this is an informative report which charts the prospects for LECs and looks at some of the training proposals.

814   Murgatroyd S. *Counselling and helping* London Methuen 1985 176 pages

This is a valuable book for anyone involved in counselling and guidance work. Gives examples of the basic forms of helping, giving information, coaching, advocacy, providing feedback and counselling.

815   Murphy B. BS 5750 and training: the gathering storm *Transition* Vol 91 No 4 1991 page 4

The author who is the director of BACIE argues against the application of the standard kite mark to training in Britain.

816   Murphy D. Training for quality *Training Officer* Vol 27 No 2 1991 43-45

Argues that the notion of quality is becoming of central concern to many organisations and is the focus of much of the training undertaken. Describes what a large multinational company is doing in this area.

817   Murphy P. Northern Ireland: out of the doll's house: women's opportunities women's rights In: Poster C. and Kruger A. (Ed) *Community education in the western world* London Routledge 1989

The author notes the poor training and employment opportunities for women in Northern Ireland. A number of new training initiatives for women and their positive outcomes are discussed.

818   Murphy P. Time for women in information technology in Northern Ireland *Adults Learning* Vol 1 No 4 1989 113-115

Describes the introduction of a women's only certificate in information technology at the University of Ulster which tries to meet the particular needs of women. The article notes the relative under representation of women on employment training schemes in Northern Ireland.

819   Murray A. Access to further and higher education: an FEU perspective *Journal of Access Studies* Vol 2 No 1 1987 42-53

Draws on the FEU discussion document '*Access to Further and Higher Education*'(1987) and highlights achievements and future needs as well as offering clearer definitions and agreed criteria for Access courses. The long term objective remains that of raising the consistently low proportions of non-traditional students in higher education.

820   **Nash T.** *Director* Vol 42 No 8 March 1989 50-53
Discussion of skills shortages and management strategies. Following the government and IPM, the author concludes that the increasing age of the workforce will make training the most important way of ensuring its efficiency.

821   **Nash T.** The great no-win situation *Director* Vol 43 No 12 June 1990 38-42
Discusses the barriers faced by women wishing to return to work and argues many working women have found it difficult to return to work after having children, primarily because of employers' negative attitudes and the lack of adequate policies and facilities for working mothers. Many working mothers share the view that the male domination of senior management means that most companies fail to comprehend the dilemma faced by working mothers. Although there are strong forces for change, the image of a woman who combines a career and a family is still that of superwoman. Statutory measures are needed, not forthcoming as yet.

822   **National Advisory Board** *Transferable, personal skills in employment: the contribution of higher education* London NAB 1986 11 pages

823   **National Association for the Care and Resettlement of Offenders** *Bridging the gap: report of a working party on the transition from education in penal establishments to education in the community* London NACRO 1981 53 pages
This is an extremely useful text for all involved in developing and carrying out policy on prison education. Discusses the improvements that could be made to help prisoners make the change from the separately administered education system in prison to the wider one outside it. Advisory services which assist prisons with the information about continuing educational possibilities and sources of financial assistance are strongly recommended.

824   **National Association for the Care and Resettlement of Offenders** *Education and training for offenders* London NACRO 1989

This report is aimed at policy makers and practitioners in the education, training and criminal justice fields, and outlines the important contribution that education and training can make to the prevention of crime and the resettlement of offenders. It sets out a practical framework for future developments and makes specific recommendations to central and local government, probation services and voluntary organisations.

825   **National Association for the Care and Resettlement of Offenders** *Employment training and offenders: a report of a one-day conference for managers of probation services and managers of the prison service* London NACRO 1988
A report of a conference sponsored by ACOP, the Apex Trust and NACRO which focused on the importance of employment in resettling offenders and preventing crime and the potential role of the new Employment Training programme.

826   **National Association for the Care and Resettlement of Offenders** *Employment training for disadvantaged people into the 1990s* London NACRO 1989
A report of a conference organised by NACRO and the Training Agency in July 1989 to consider the potential of disadvantaged people to the labour market and to identify the processes by which this can be drawn out and people equipped with the skills needed.

827   **National Association for the Care and Resettlement of Offenders** *Equal opportunities for ex-offenders: a guide for employers, managing agents and managers of MSC employment and training schemes* London NACRO 1987
Suggests how employers can have a fair and rational employment policy towards previous offenders, and contains guidance on good practice in the treatment of employees who offend.

828   **National Association for the Care and Resettlement of Offenders** *Facing the problem: a report on alternatives to unemployment for offenders* London NACRO June 1987 20 pages
The central argument of this report is that the challenge of resettling people who have had convictions is hugely enhanced if the individual has either a job or the chance of

training leading to a job, or further education opportunity. This is a thoroughly practical paper about the issues of unemployment and resettlement.

829   National Association for the Care and Resettlement of Offenders *Training for change* London NACRO 1989
A report based on a survey of the experiences of 800 NACRO Employment Training trainees which indicates that while trainees are finding ET worthwhile, higher levels of funding are necessary.

830   National Association of Guidance Services for Adults *Special edition Bath conference report* London National Association of Guidance Services for Adults Spring 1990 page 18
Addresses the issues surrounding TEC Advisory Services (TECAS) which are designed to develop the foundations for information and guidance agencies. It is suggested that TECs should ensure that existing providers of information and advice know what each other can offer; providers are committed to referral and potential clients are aware of such facilities.

831   National Association of Teachers in Further and Higher Education *Handicap, disability and special learning needs: a guide to good practice in further and higher education* London College Hill Press 1985 24 pages
These are valuable reports which examine the practical alternatives to LEAs, colleges and schools in seeking to offer adequate, effective and appropriate education and training to students with special needs. Part 1 addresses broad issues associated with organisation, planning, management and resources. Part II considers more specific curricular issues to do with curriculum design, delivery and support.

832   National Council for Vocational Qualifications *Accreditation procedures* London NVCQ 1988 23 pages
A detailed guide to national vocational qualifications and accreditation.

833   National Council for Vocational Qualifications *Criteria for National Vocational Qualifications* London NCVQ 1991 9 pages

A useful booklet which briefly sets out the criteria which are used by the NCVQ in deciding whether a qualification can be accepted as part of the NVQ framework.

834   National Council for Vocational Qualifications *General National Vocational Qualifications: proposals for the new qualifications* London NCVQ 1991 41 pages
A consultation paper which sets out the proposed criteria for general NVQs. Models are presented on the form such qualifications might take at levels 2 and 3.

835   National Council for Vocational Qualifications *National Vocational Qualifications: What it means for colleges. What's in it for employers. What they mean for you* London NCVQ 1988 23 pages
Provides three brochures aimed at employers, colleges and potential employees which explain the NVQ system.

836   National Council for Vocational Qualifications *NVQ framework: progress to date* London NCVQ 1990
Describes the work of the NCVQ and the progress made to date towards implementing a national framework for vocational qualifications.

837   National Council for Vocational Qualifications *The National Vocational Qualifications: the NVQ criteria and related guidance* London NCVQ 1988 24 pages

838   National Council for Voluntary Organisations *Making training accessible* London NCVQ June 1991 43 pages
Report of the Special Training Needs Task Force, established by NCVO. The key findings are clearly summarized and the proposals made are intended to encourage voluntary organisations and TECs to be more effective locally in promoting, planning and providing for special training needs.

839   National Economic Development Office and Royal Institute of Public Administration *Women managers: the untapped resource* London NEDO 1990 88 pages

Examines the reasons why women are under-represented in management jobs and suggests measures employers can take to remedy this situation. It is based on a research survey commissioned from the Institute of Manpower Studies by the National Economic Development Office in collaboration with the Royal Institute of Public Administration.

840   **National Educational Guidance Initiative (NEGI)** *Policy and practice in educational guidance for adults in England and Wales* First Annual Review London NEGI 1988-89

This review places the present position on educational guidance for adults and summarises activities leading to the setting up of the NEGI. It discusses the impact of significant funding, together with changes in the education and training system following the Education Reform Act and the White Paper *'Training for the 1990s'* which are likely to contribute to the emergence of policies and clearer organisational structures for the provision of educational guidance.

841   **National Extension College** *The A-Z of open learning* Cambridge NEC 1990 137 pages

This book represents a lengthy attempt to identify a consensus as to what open learning is and what its proliferating terminology means.

842   **National Extension College** *Return to Work and Return to the Office* Cambridge NEC 1990

Written by women returners who have themselves experienced similar worries and concerns, these valuable packs are designed for use in group counselling sessions and as a training resource on a range of access courses, return to work programmes, employment training or job search schemes.

843   **National Institute for Careers Education and Counselling** *Guidance in open learning* Occasional Paper 2 Cambridge NICEC 1984

Looks at guidance services, and where information can be gained with detailed descriptions on the public library and careers services. Illustrates the necessity for guidance when delivering options for open tech projects.

844   **National Institute for Careers Education and Counselling** *Investigation of guidance in the Enterprise in Higher Education initiative* Cambridge NICEC

This project is investigating ways for institutions involved in enterprise in higher education to improve guidance to students in making use of their enterprise competencies in planning their future careers.

845   **National Institute of Adult Continuing Education** *Adults in higher education: a policy discussion paper* Leicester NIACE May 1989 29 pages

This paper seeks to identify the main policy issues concerning adults in higher education in the 1990s and indicates ways in which NIACE can support the development of policy in this area.

846   **National Institute of Adult Continuing Education and REPLAN** *Assessment of prior learning and achievement: a study guide and resource pack to support staff development* Leicester NIACE 1991

This pack is designed to help meet an identified gap in training provision. Aims to illustrate and encourage good practice in APL/A, and is in open learning form for use as a flexible resource. Copying rights have been waived for the purchaser who uses the pack solely within their own organisation.

847   **National Institute of Adult Continuing Education** *Learning throughout life: a policy discussion paper on continuing education* Leicester NIACE 1990 43 pages

This important policy paper, produced by a working group of NIACE's Executive Committee, addresses the wider policy issues of adults' needs for lifelong learning, and the means of providing for these.

848   **National Institute of Adult Continuing Education** *Partnership in action* Leicester NIACE 1988 28 pages

Highlights examples of some of the changes which have occurred in the North-east as a result of educational agencies and individuals working together in sharing resources and expertise and a genuine desire to help the unemployed.

849 National Institute of Adult Continuing Education *People, learning and jobs* Leicester NIACE 1990 3 pages

This paper sets out a context and programme for the education and training of adults in the 1990s, building on the success and experience of the DES REPLAN programme, it briefly considers the economic, demographic and structural changes which have shaped the progress and development of the REPLAN programme and how that programme can be transformed to help more and more individuals use education and training to realise their own potential in the labour market.

850 National Institute of Adult Continuing Education *Second chances* Leicester Careers and Occupational Information Centre 1990/1991 497 pages

The national guide to adult education and training opportunities.

851 National Institute of Adult Continuing Education *Understanding competence: a development paper* Leicester NIACE 1989 40 pages

Discusses the concept of competence in relation to education and training. Argues that the work of the NCVQ on vocational qualifications will have an impact on non-vocational and higher education. However, the issues of personal effectiveness, transferability and potential have not been adequately addressed. Discusses alternative competence models in use in the USA.

852 National Institute of Adult Continuing Education *Valuing volunteers - the accreditation of voluntary training and experience* Leicester NIACE REPLAN NACAB 1990 84 pages

This handbook is the outcome of a research project which explored options for the accreditation of structured training in a voluntary organisation, using the National Association of Citizens Advice Bureau as a case study. Among the options explored were the feasibility of accrediting NACAB training within the NCVQ framework; the potential for recognising and acknowledging NACAB training by examining and validating bodies; joining with other organisations to form a Lead Industry Body.

853 National Union of Students *Grant us a living* London NUS 1985 29 pages

Aims to provoke discussion and aid the development of NUS policy on student financial support. Summarises the threats to provision of support and identifies the principles which should underpin the system such as financial support not determining access.

854 Neale K. and Normie G. (Ed) *Strategies for education within prison regimes: comparative approaches* OU & Home Office Prison Dept 1985 100 pages

This is a set of conference papers delivered by a wide variety of practitioners and academics from several countries looking at a number of aspects on the subject of prison education and covering organisation, structures, policies, research and post initial education.

855 Neane P. Given the ability *Community Care* 21 March 1991 14-15

An interesting review of Abilities Ltd, a company set up by Henry Llewellyn providing franchise for people with disabilities to become self employed. People with disabilities are trained in tachograph analysis, when someone completes their training, funding is sought for their own equipment so they may become self-employed. This company has been extremely successful but unfortunately there are problems in seeking funding for those over 30 years of age.

856 Nelson P. *Advice and guidance to adults in Scotland: training and vocational education* Edinburgh SIACE 1988

A detailed appraisal of the importance given to training and educational advice and guidance for adults in Scotland. Illuminates good practice models.

857 Newby T. Personnel training and corporate strategy: the marketing approach *Training Officer* Vol 24 No 4 1988 364-366

Argues that the marketing of training must aim primarily to meet the needs of the client rather than those of the training provider.

858 Newnham A. *Employment, unemployment and black people* London Runnymede Trust 1986 30 pages

Based on the findings of national surveys this pamphlet aims to bring together information about employment and unemployment among black people in Britain. It examines the position of black people in the economy and looks at occupational distribution and wage levels. The author offers explanations for and proposals to reduce high black unemployment levels.

859   **Newscheck** The older graduate: over 30?, over the hill?, overlooked? *Newscheck* Vol 7 No 6 April 1990 page 10

Negative and inaccurate stereotypes of the older graduate continue to prevail. Reports employers often perceive the older graduate as someone who will not be able to fit into the existing career structure.

860   **Newscheck** Open University studies can yield bonus for jobs *Newscheck with Careers Service Bulletin* Vol 1 No 11 June 1991 4-5

Reports on how Open University studies can enhance career prospects. A high proportion of students believe that such study has a good effect on their careers. The benefits of the Open Business school which has proved an increasingly popular way to study is also discussed.

861   **Nicholson B.** What industry needs from higher education *Education and Training* Vol 30 No 4 1988 14-15

Reviews the dissatisfactions felt by industry towards higher education and argues that better links could be made if HE projects a positive image of what industry is really like, raises its level of understanding of what actually goes on in industry, presses for more secondment into business and widens access. Key link between learning environment and real world through project-based work requiring placements in industry.

862   **Nicholson D.** Turning burglars into businessmen? *Probation Journal* Vol 32 No 3 Sep 1985 100-102

Following disillusionment with existing community service opportunities and post community service MSC schemes and their lack of ability to help offenders towards full time legal employment; a group of community service officers in the Manchester area have developed a new agency - Manchester In To

Work Training which aims to promote legal self-employment and other economic self reliance initiatives amongst ex-offenders. The paper describes how this agency works to help potential entrepreneurs to legitimise some of their activities in the black economy.

863   **Nicol I.** Adults, opportunities, schools and SWAP *Scottish Journal of Adult Education* Vol 9 No 1 Summer 1989 13-18

Discusses the part secondary schools can play in delivering continuing education for people of all ages and suggests an expansion and investment in non-recreational areas could prove effective in providing pre-entry qualifications for higher education.

864   **Nicolson B.** Second class workers with first class brains *Times Education Supplement* No 3718 2 Oct 1987 page 14

This article covers the controversial issue of making traditionally, male orientated subjects compulsory for girls at school, which, together with better careers guidance may encourage women into non-traditional areas of work. Also asserts the need for employers to open their eyes to the possibility of giving existing staff, including women, the skills they require through training.

865   **Niven S.** Information paper 16: Further education in Scotland *Scottish Educational Review* Vol 17 No 2 November 1985 128-31

Traces the history and development of the post secondary vocational and technical educational system in Scotland since 1956. Summarizes organisational structure, courses of study, entrance requirements, and services.

866   **Niven S.** Staff development in further education in Scotland: towards comprehensive provision *British Journal of In-service Education* Vol 13 No 3 Autumn 1987 117-122

Assesses the need for a comprehensive scheme for the continuing professional development of academic staff within the further education sector in Scotland. In order to facilitate this, a specialist training unit was set up known as the School of Further Education at Jordanhill College of Education. The unit is a national centre, which provides initial and post initial training for further education teachers and is also engaged in research and development work.

867   Norfolk D. The female potential *Chief Executive* Feb 1988 page 50
Argues that few female executives are allowed to achieve their full potential. A psychological frame of reference is used and the author believes women have different abilities or qualities which can benefit a work organisation, whilst this notion is disputable, the author nevertheless points out that companies can lose valuable female executives if their talents are not used to full potential.

868   Northern Ireland Council for Continuing Education *Adult basic education in Northern Ireland* Belfast Northern Ireland Council for Continuing Education 1985
Report of a working group of the council which defined needs and advised on future policy for adult basic education in Northern Ireland. The report calls for improvements in structures, communications and resources.

869   Northern Ireland Council for Continuing Education *Guidance for adult learners* Belfast Northern Ireland Council for Continuing Education 1987
Report of the working party of the Council which looked at the development of an accessible and comprehensive system of guidance and counselling for adults including those with special educational needs.

870   Oakeshott M. *Educational guidance and curriculum change* London FEU UDACE 1990 128 pages

871   Oakeshott M. *Educational guidance for adults: identifying competencies* London FEU/UDACE 1991 63 pages
This project drafts a set of competence statements for educational guidance work with adults. As one of the first attempts to do this, the report is of particular value and should be read by all interested in guidance and quality.

872   Oates T. *Work-based learning and modular accreditation: an analysis and a methodology for a development project* Bristol Further Education Staff College 1987 198 pages

873   Ollerearnshaw S. Action on equal opportunities in inner cities: the need for a policy commitment *New Community* Vol 15 No 1 1988 31-46
Argues for a co-ordinated policy on equal opportunities for young ethnic minority persons to take account of employment, vocational training and business enterprise. Such a policy must encompass effective monitoring systems and ethnic minorities must be involved in all stages as advisors.

874   Open Learning Directory *Open Learning Directory 1991* London Pergamon and the Employment Department Group 1991 592 pages
An essential resource for flexible and cost effective training. Comprehensive and user friendly.

875   Osborne R. D. et al Graduates: geographical mobility and incomes *In: Osborne R.D. et al (Ed) Education and policy in Northern Ireland* Belfast Policy Research Institute 1987 231-244
Reports on a large scale study of the initial labour market experience of Northern Ireland graduates. The research was undertaken by a postal survey. The issue of the flow of undergraduates out of Northern Ireland without a compensating influx from the rest of the UK. Some assessment of the social characteristics of undergraduates is made and their mobility and incomes are assessed.

876   Osborne R.D. *Religion and educational qualifications in Northern Ireland* Belfast Fair Employment Agency 1985 92 pages
Updates earlier research which compared the performance of Catholics and Protestants in O and A Level examinations and related educational attainment of social background. Provides useful background information on the education system in Northern Ireland. Also gives some information on the destination of young people and patterns of employment after school.

877   Osborne R.D. and Cormack R.J. *Religion, occupations and employment 1971-1981* Belfast Fair Employment Agency 1987 110 pages
Attempts to assess the extent to which patterns of Catholic and Protestant employment have changed over the past 20 years. The paper

makes some evaluation of the importance of educational qualifications in determining occupational access and achievement.

878   Osborne R.D. and Cormack R.J. Higher Education and fair employment in Northern Ireland *Higher Education Quarterly* Vol 44 No 4 1990 325-343

Considers the employment profiles of Northern Ireland's two universities in terms of equality of opportunity in the employment of Catholics and Protestants.

879   Osborne R.D. and Cormack R.J. Unemployment and religion in Northern Ireland *The Economic and Social Review* Vol 17 No 3 1986 215-225

Paper which examines data on the employment status of Protestants and Catholics in Northern Ireland. The rates of unemployment for the two groups are compared and reasons for the differences are briefly discussed including the differences in educational attainment.

880   Osborne R.D. et al *Education and policy in Northern Ireland* Belfast Policy Research Institute 1987 309 pages

An excellent collection of essays which provides information and analysis on many aspects of education and education policy in Northern Ireland.

881   Osborne R.D. et al Class, sex, religion and destination: participation and higher education in Northern Ireland *Studies in Higher Education* Vol 9 No 2 1984 123-137

The characteristics of college entrants in Northern Ireland in 1973 and 1979 were analysed in terms of class, sex, religion and destination. The findings were then related to aspects of public policy. Those groups most affected by public policy, particularly in terms of the movement of students into and out of Northern Ireland, were identified.

882   Osborne R.D. et al Trends in higher education participation in Northern Ireland *Economic and Social Review* Vol 19 No 4 1988 119-301

Discusses the causes and effects of changes in the patterns of participation in higher education of Northern Irish students in recent years.

883   Osbourne M. Access courses in mathematics, science and technology: current and planned provision *Journal of Access Studies* Vol 3 No 1 1988 75-80

Presents the results of a survey of current and planned Access courses in maths, science and technology. The Access listings and descriptions are offered as an indication of pattern and progress in what is a difficult and important area of Access work.

884   Otter S. *Understanding competence* London NIACE 189 36 pages

A development paper which explores the notion of competence and the way it has been interpreted by the NCVQ. The implications of a system where the emphasis is on outcomes is considered in relation to adult learners. Issues which the NCVQ model does not encompass are addressed and other techniques for defining competence are discussed.

885   Otter S. *Understanding learning outcomes* London UDACE 1989 24 pages

A paper describing the implications and potential benefits of an outcomes led approach to the education and training of adults.

886   Paddison L. The targeted approach to recruitment *Personnel Management* Vol 22 No 11 Nov 1990 54-58

Describes the movement to attract ethnic minorities and other neglected groups to meet skills shortages. Argues that it will require a complete reorientation in personnel practices if such groups are to be recruited and retained.

887   Paine N. (Ed) *Open learning in transition: an agenda for action* London Kogan Page 1989 383 pages

This book is essential reading for anyone involved in producing or delivering open learning systems or interested in their use. Presented, are 29 specially-commissioned papers which offer informed analysis of current open learning initiatives in the UK.

888   Parker J. and Donovan B. *Adult numeracy and training pack* Edinburgh Scottish Community Education Council 1987

Presented as 11 modules in a loose leaf ring binder, this pack is written to help the prospective tutor in providing one-to-one numeracy tuition on a basic level to adults who are reasonably at home with counting. Offers a mix of concepts and can be used either individually or as part of group tutor training courses. Selection of material is the result of much 'grassroots' research with students in the Lothian region.

889   Parker S. et al Managing equality in access *Higher Education Quarterly* Vol 44 No 4 1990 360-371

Argues that the management of the equality of access must have a place in the strategic plans of a higher education institution. Such a system must incorporate elements of monitoring and evaluation if equality and quality are to be maintained.

890   Parry G. and Wake C. (Ed) *Access and alternative futures for higher education* London Hodder and Stoughton 1990 228 pages

The nineties are likely to see real changes in the character and objectives of higher education. This excellent volume examines the issues surrounding the widening of access to increase participation of non standard students.

891   Parry G. and Davies P. *Framing Access* London Unit for the Development of Adult Continuing Education 1991 24 pages

An interim report on the evaluation of Access courses established by Authorised Validating Agencies under the aegis of the Access Courses Recognition Group.

892   Parry G. and Davies P. *Wider access and the professional engineering institutions* London CNAA & British Petroleum 1990

893   Parry G. From patronage to partnership *Journal of Access Studies* Vol 1 No 1 1986 43-53

The author considers partnership and Access. In forging links with a wide range of local colleges and institutes it has the potential to open up much more of higher education to a different kind of student as well as to new ways of working.

894   Parry G. and Davies P. Paper and people: evaluating the national framework for the recognition of access courses *Adults Learning* Vol 2 No 6 1991 174-175

Provides a summary of the initial findings of an independent report on the national framework for the recognition of Access courses.

895   Parry G. (Ed) *Engineering futures: new audiences and arrangements for engineering higher education* London Engineering Council 1990 76 pages

This valuable report summarizes the major recommendations of the conference 'Wider Entry to Engineering Higher Education', held at the RSA, 17 January, 1990. It discusses programmes and proposals to extend participation, improve retention and broaden curricula in engineering higher education.

896   Parsons D. and Berry-Lound D. Planning for many happier returns *Transition* Mar/Apr 1989 16-17

Considers issues of demographic change, the growing numbers of women returners in the workforce and their training needs.

897   Paterson R.W.K. Adult education and the individual *International Journal of Lifelong Education* Vol 6 No 2 1987 111-124

Although thinking and planning in adult education is centred on groups and types of potential students, practice is concerned with concrete individuals. Category-based provision in terms of class, race or gender ignores the individuality of real people.

898   Patrick F. Attracting the non-participant *Scottish Journal of Adult Education* Vol 9 No 2 Winter 1989 12-15

This paper is concerned with those people who do not take up any form of further education and describes a campaign in Scotland known as the 'What's APL Doc', designed to emphasise local, personal contact and follow through strategy. Discusses the role of the community/adult education worker who should, the author argues, be encouraged to engage with the non-participant rather than set out to attract the non-participant.

899   Paulet R. Working while learning *Vocational Aspect of Education* Vol 39 No 103 August 1987 65-67

900   Payne F.G. Management and professional development: who needs

it? *Management Accounting* Vol 68 No 5
May 1990 50-55
Argues management and professional
development is vital if members of the
Chartered Institute of Management
Accountants are to realize benefits, from
progressive development to maturity of their
management and professional competencies.

901   **Payne J.** *Adult off-the-job skills training:
       an evaluation study* Sheffield Training
       Agency 1990 111 pages
An important study which assesses the impact
of adult training on the lives of those who
have experienced it. It describes the
employment history of the 785 participants and
reports on their experience of training, the
qualifications obtained and their subsequent
progress in the labour market. The report then
uses statistical models to assess whether such
training had made a difference to the success
of the participants in the labour market.

902   **Payne J.** *Women training and the skills
       shortage: the case for public investment*
       London PSI 1991 190 pages
This book explores the wide range of
circumstances which prompts women to seek
training, their personal gains, and the impact
on their employment and earnings. Looks
particularly at the experiences of women
returners and of women who have taken low
skill jobs because of domestic constraints.
Women's progress is compared with that of
male trainees. Stresses the need for public
investment in high quality training.

903   **Payne J.** Educational guidance services
       and the provision of adult education
       International Journal of Lifelong Education
       Vol 4 No 1 1985 35-54
This is an excellent paper which emphasises
the central role of advocacy in pressing for
institutional and curricular change. It
concludes that such change must include a
critique of the ideology of needs, access and
provision. Educational guidance must be
concerned as much with the transformation of
institutions and what counts as knowledge in
our society as with the amelioration of
individual needs.

904   **Peach L.** Access concepts and access
       courses *Journal of Access Studies* Vol 4
       No 1/2 1989 4-14

An excellent overview of the underlying
ideologies of Access courses and the notion of
accessibility. The author argues access needs to
be approached in a broad way and not
narrowly focus on access courses alone.
Usefully discusses the importance of staff
development in relation to access.

905   **Peaker A. and Vincent J.** *Arts in
       prisons: towards a sense of achievement*
       Arts Council Dec 1990 246 pages
This is a valuable and detailed account on the
role of arts in prisons. The research categorises
the different forms of arts activities and offers
insights on how they are designed and
implemented, evaluates the outcomes of a
selected number of arts programmes, offers
advice on the development of training
resources for those working in the field.
Extensive bibliographical details given.

906   **Pearn M. and Downs S.** Developing
       skilled learners: a strategy for coping
       with new technology *Media in
       Education and Development* Vol 21 No 1
       Jan 1988 7-12
By way of two case studies, this article
explores the technique used to enhance the
development of learning skills, called
Developing Skilled Learners. The effects of
change generated by new technology are
discussed and the emphasis on learning
processes rather than training methods is
explained.

907   **Pearson C.** The view from the modular
       bridge: vocational education in
       Scotland *Times Educational Supplement
       Scotland* No 1151 25 November 1988
       page 2
An excellent paper which considers the factors
which have led to mature student participation
in higher education being placed high on the
agenda of OECD countries; outlines some
international patterns in relation to adult
involvement in higher education; considers
individual motivations and barriers faced by
mature students. Finally, the author explores a
number of innovations which have developed
to promote access and illustrates this with an
example of a recently developed credit
accumulation scheme at one particular
polytechnic.

908   **Pearson R.** Doubling student numbers:
       what are the prospects *Higher*

Education Quarterly Vol 44 No 3 1990
215-229
An interesting article which gives an overview of a number of issues. It looks at the feasibility of doubling the numbers of first degree students in the UK and charts the probable pattern of change in the coming decade. Considers changing higher education policy and looks at the likely changes in the supply and demand of graduates in the 1990s.

909   **Pearson R.W.** Creating flexible careers: some observations on a 'bridge' programme for unemployed professionals *British Journal of Guidance and Counselling* Vol 16 No 3 September 1987 182-196
Redundancy among qualified people is a continuing problem. Those affected can be helped by group programmes providing both career guidance and training in job-getting skills. An important factor in re-employment is the ability to change occupation in mid-career which is often dependent on confidence. Confidence building by means of social support is suggested as the primary objective and particular competence of group programmes.

910   **Peck D. and Little R.** Gap in the jigsaw *Times Educational Supplement* 25 July 1986 page 4
The authors argue that adults in search of education or training need personal counselling to help them find their place in the picture. Some interesting points are raised in relation to strengthening coordination between the careers service, library service and educational guidance services for adults.

911   **Pelissier C. and Smith R.** Student centred continuing education: a county strategy for access *Journal of Further and Higher Education* Vol 12 No 2 Summer 1988 64-71
Describes the Essex County Access Programme which emphasises flexible student centred education for adults. Looks specifically at access courses which by-pass the traditional qualifications at 'O' and 'A' level.

912   **Pell C.** Forward planning is the way through the funding jungle *Transition* Jan 1989 10-13
A detailed and useful article which looks at the funding of training in Britain and argues that

despite the large sums of money involved forward and coherent planning of training is not undertaken by employers. Argues that effective training must be part of an overall business plan.

913   **Perry R.** The role of participants in training *Scottish Journal of Adult Education* Vol 8 No 1 Spring 1987 21-26
Discusses community education and social work training. Raises questions about the planning, management and delivery of training generally.

914   **Personnel Management** Education industry links: sandwich courses hit by recession *Personnel Management* August 1991 page 51
Reports the economic recession and the rapid increase in the number of sandwich degrees has caused a shortage of work placements for students. It may also appear sandwich courses have become victims of their own success.

915   **Personnel Management** Education industry links *Personnel Management* July 1991 page 49
Reports on an industrial placement programme for up to 500 UK teachers which aims to strengthen school/industry links across the economic community. The organisations they visited were varied and placements either included workshadowing, attending training courses or carrying out research assignments.

916   **Personnel Management** News *Personnel Management* May 1991 3-5
This paper addresses in detail various models of educational guidance practice in access courses. The authors suggest that educational guidance could be formally integrated into courses through assessed and accredited modules and invite readers to regard educational guidance as fundamentally embedded within the access pedagogy rather than a 'bolt-on' activity. This follows the premise that learners need guidance prior to taking up access provision, while engaged in it and on exit. Recognising and accrediting experiential learning is at the heart of the access pedagogy.

917   **Personnel Management** Voluntary sector cuts hitting 'valuable' ex-offenders pool *Personnel Management* May 1991 page 11

Reports on the cuts forced on voluntary organisations providing Government funded training for ex-offenders.

918   **Pettigrew A.M. et al** *Training and human resource management in small and medium sized enterprises: a critical review of the literature and a model for future research* R & D Paper No. 56 Sheffield Employment Dept March 1990 77 pages

Looks at human resource training needs of the small firm. Reviews relevant literature published in this area. Highlights important research questions for the future.

919   **Picard W.** Town and gown versus the 'golden triangle' future of the Scottish universities *Times Educational Supplement Scotland* No 1114 11 March 1988 page 2

Review of the close links between Scottish universities and the community. Suggests universities which remain community-based are in a good position to raise private finance through involvement with the business of the community.

920   **PICKUP Directory** *National Training Directory* London Macmillan 1991

The Directory provides valuable information about what training is available, where, from and for whom. Particularly valuable for those wishing to update skills.

921   **PICKUP in Progress** *Keeping the customer satisfied* London DES Spring 1991 31 pages

This issue includes up to date news on employee development, links and quality.

922   **PICKUP in Progress** *Women set for time of their lives PICKUP in Progress* London DES Spring 1990

This article discusses women who wish to become leaders and the barriers faced by them. Suggests more employers now recognise the need for better careers development for women. In east Lancashire for example, a survey showed strong industry backing for positive action to encourage women to train. Also illustrates successful examples of 'women only' management course.

923   **Pike A.** Hiring of ex-offenders urged *Financial Times* 28 June 1991 page 9

Reports on the recently launched Offender Employment Charter organised by the Apex Trust. Reviews the results of recent studies by Apex, which shows that only about 10% of those 100,000 people discharged from prison each year have jobs to go to, and many employers are reluctant to employ former prisoners. According to the survey more than 40% of private-sector employers had never heard of the Rehabilitation of Offenders Act.

924   **Pilley C. (Ed)** *Women and computing in Scotland: a conference report* Edinburgh Scottish Institute of Adult and Continuing Education 1985 44 pages

A useful collection of papers focusing on the under-representation of women in computing. Also gives brief workshop reports on work training and education.

925   **Pitts D.** To be young, British and black *Black Enterprise* Vol 20 No 5 Dec 1989 86-98

Describes the growth of small black businesses in Britain. Argues that the key to successful black business is access to training and information.

926   **Plant P.** *Transnational vocational guidance and training for young people and adults* Berlin CEDEFOP 1990 62 pages

A report which clearly documents the importance of vocational guidance and training European-wide.

927   **Platt S.** Workshop closures *New Society* 11 April 1986

Looks at the effects of prison workshop closures and argues that if nothing is put in their place, then most prisoners will have nothing to do for most part of their sentence.

928   **Platt, Baroness of Writtle** Equal opportunities *Education Today* Vol 37 No 4 1987 4-8

A Presidential Address to the EOC which highlights some of the developments in equal opportunity such as WISE, and discusses the need for positive action by employers in developing career break schemes with clear paths of keeping in touch.

929   **Policy Studies Institute Report** *Britain in 2010* London PSI 1991 364 pages

A valuable interdisciplinary study which forecasts some of the likely socio-economic and political changes in Britain. The chapter on employment covers the changing structure of the labour market and the shift towards high-level occupations. Concludes those who work in unskilled, manual jobs are in danger of being alienated if not given adequate education and training.

930   **Pollitt C.** Measuring university performance: never mind the quality, never mind the width *Higher Education Quarterly* Vol 44 No 1 1990 60-81
Sets performance indicators in the context of wider changes facing universities. Criticises some indicators for their narrowness and their failure to address teaching and issues of quality. Compares the British system to practice in the USA.

931   **Pollitt C.** The politics of performance assessment: lessons for higher education? *Studies in Higher Education* Vol 12 No 1 1987
Discusses the different types of performance assessment schemes which have been applied within public sector higher education. Argues that those which emphasise economy and efficiency have received greater political and organisational support. Assesses the effects of such schemes on other kinds of objective such as effectiveness.

932   **Polytechnic of North London:** Project Officer: Ann Bridgwood *Women into science and technology* London
This forthcoming research project aims to identify specific learning and support mechanisms needed to provide a positive learning environment for women into science and technology. Structural change in the ways courses are managed and monitored, curriculum change and staff development are among the possible areas for consideration.

933   **Polytechnics and Colleges Funding Council** *Funding choices: methods of funding higher education in polytechnics and colleges* London PCFC 1989
A consultation document setting out the PCFC's aims and objectives and explaining the funding methodology. The aims include elements of widening access, meeting national needs, links with industry, value for money and accountability for public resources.

934   **Polytechnics and Colleges Funding Council** *Widening participation in higher education* London PCFC 1990 8 pages
Sets out the aims of the PCFC on widening the participation of non-traditional students in higher education. Asks for information from public sector higher education institutions on how they intend to achieve these aims.

935   **Port J. and Burke J.** Business planning for HE institutions Higher Education Quarterly Vol 43 No 2 Spring 1989 125-141
A very practical article which argues that business planning is as necessary to higher education as traditional academic strengths. It points out the advantages of business planning and suggests how such plans should be implemented.

936   **Portwood D.** *Outreach and Inreach: colleges and unemployment groups* London FEU/REPLAN 1988 43 pages
This report examines the setting for outreach in terms of individuals' experience of unemployment and provides colleges with guidance, information, insights and techniques for developing work with unemployed adults. It also indicates to unemployed groups how they may more adequately use, influence and contribute to educational services.

937   **Povall M.** Overcoming barriers to women's advancement in European organisations *Women in Management Review* 1990 9-31
Barriers to women's progress, both attitudinal and structural are examined, with examples from banking and other industries. Considers how a 'positive action' strategy can break down barriers.

938   **Powell B.** *Performance indicators and the education of adults* London UDACE 1989
A paper which provides an overview of the issues involved in the use of performance measurement in the education of adults.

939   **Powell B.** Will continuing education continue? *Education* Vol 175 No 4 1990 page 88
Reports on the disappointing response of LEAs to the 1988 Education Reform Act which gave adult education a firmer statutory basis.

Suggests that many LEAs neglect adult education in their strategic planning.

940 **Pratt J.** Abolishing the public sector in British higher education *New Era in Education* Vol 70 No 1 1989 11-13

Reviews the implications of the changes in the financing of public sector higher education with particular reference to the increase of central control.

941 **Pratt J.** Funding higher education *Higher Education Review* Vol 23 No 1 1990 3-6

Discusses the problems surrounding the necessary expansion of higher education with inadequate funding. Considers the problems associated with treating higher education as a product within a market.

942 **Pritchard D.R.** The 16 plus action plan in Scotland *Education in Chemistry* Vol 26 No 3 May 1989 83-84

This article describes how a major new educational initiative affected the SCOTVEC Certificate in Chemistry and the reaction of the students and staff. Notes former students are beginning to return to take extra modules as they develop in their jobs or change them.

943 **Purcell D.** Counselling Open University students in prison in Ireland *Open Learning* Vol 3 No 2 1988 49-51

In 1988 one in thirty prisoners in Ireland were studying for an open university degree. The article discusses some of the problems prisoners face such as isolation and lack of contact with tutors. The important role of the OU counsellor in these circumstances is described.

944 **Purdey M.** Models, aspirations and progression: REPLAN development work with black women *Adults Learning* Vol 1 No 4 1989 116-118

Describes a 2 year REPLAN project in Southall to develop courses to meet the training and educational needs of Asian women. Priority was given to careful planning to ensure the courses met their specific requirements eg language and study skills, domestic commitments and after guidance and support.

945 **Pursaill J.** *National vocational qualifications and further education: a*
commentary on progress London FEU 1989 39 pages

Describes the process of developing NVQs and discusses the issues to be faced by colleges, employers and students. Describes the progress to date in a number of employment sectors.

946 **Pursaill J.** *Flexible access to vocational qualifications* Leicester REPLAN NIACE 1990 58 pages

Starts with the premise that access to many vocational qualifications is still not easy for non-traditional learners. This report is a snapshot of current issues and practice and also an agenda for future action. It shows how colleges can offer a more flexible service which begins to remove the barriers. 5 case studies illustrate how colleges are making access to NVQs more flexible for new groups of learners in further education.

947 **Pyke N.** Dewsbury authority funds ethnic minority PGCE *Times Educational Supplement* No 3874 28th Sept 1990 page 11

Report on Kirklees LEA which has devised a PGCE for ethnic minority candidates as a way of increasing the numbers of ethnic minority teachers.

948 **Quassim A.** Severe disruption to training services? *Marketing Weekly* Vol 13 No 47 1991 18-19

Discusses the 12M Department of Employment advertising campaign for TECS and the National Training Awards and criticises DE for cutting training programmes. Points out the danger of such training schemes failing to live up to the advertising campaign.

949 **Raban B.** Special education aspects of PGCE courses in university departments of education: a survey report *Journal of Further and Higher Education* Vol 13 No 2 Summer 1989 49-61

The research findings reported here investigated further the special education input to PGCE (secondary) courses in university departments. The departments were surveyed by post and a number were visited and staff and students interviewed. Conclusions demonstrate the wide variation in provision and highlight the main implications.

950 **Race P. and Portwood D.** CATs bring education and training together *Educational Training Technology International* Vol 27 No 4 Nov 1990

This paper presents a review of developments in Credit Accumulation and Transfer Schemes (CATs), drawing attention to the ways in which such schemes bring education and training providers together. The authors examine current trends in education and training in Britain which aim to meet the changing needs of the labour market. They point out several common threads in contemporary developments in education and training but conclude there is an urgent need for various 'piecemeal' initiatives to be linked in a coherent way.

951 **Rae L.** Quality training on a low budget *Training Officer* Vol 26 No 7-8 1990 203-205

Offers advice to those planning and carrying out training on how to achieve the best results working within a small budget.

952 **Raggatt P.** Quality assurance and NVQs In: *Change and intervention: vocational education and training* Raggatt P. and Unwin L. (Ed) London Falmer Press 1991 61-81

Considers the reforms introduced through NVQs in terms of quality assurance. The tensions between policy and practice are examined. The problems of administering a national system through local centres and the resulting inconsistency is discussed.

953 **Ramsay R.** Tapping the talent of disabled workers *Personnel Management* January 1985 page 3

Here the past president of IPM urges personnel in positions of influence in both private and public sector organisations to help more unemployed disabled people to find employment and highlights some of the important and practical steps employers can take in achieving this goal.

954 **Rapp N.** Basic skills at work *Employment Gazette* June 1991 347-350

Reports on the Basic Skills at Work Programme launched in January 1991 which will support local initiatives on literacy and numeracy training. Discusses the need for such a scheme and describes the important role TECs will play within it.

955 **Rathbone Society** *Investing in potential* Manchester The Rathbone Society 1991

The report of a conference held on Training Credits for people with special needs on 21 February 1991.

956 **Rathbone Society and National Bureau for Students with Disabilities** *Taking Special Action* Manchester The Rathbone Society 1990 44 pages

This is a report of a conference on TECs and people with special needs held on 26 November 1990. Addresses the value of training and employment to people with special needs, equal opportunities and action for the future.

957 **Rathbone Society** *TECs and people with special training needs: a discussion document* Manchester The Rathbone Society May 1991 6 pages

A discussion document which aims to clarify issues of concern and assist the debate on TEC funding and structure for the training of disadvantaged people.

958 **Record D.** Employer sponsorship: helping women back into the job market *Adults Learning* Vol 2 No 7 Mar 1991 211-212

Discusses an employer-sponsored course for women returning to secretarial work. The aim of the scheme is to enable returners to get back into employment through a supported programme of training. An important feature of the course is the strong identification and support network that develops between members of the group.

959 **Recruitment and Development Report** BS 5750: the quality standard *Recruitment and Development Report* No 486 Apr 1991 page 16

Explains how the British quality assurance standard BS 5750 can be successfully applied to training.

960 **Redpath B. and Robus N.** *Mature students incomings and outgoings* London HMSO 1989 99 pages

DES commissioned research which looked at the financial circumstances of 1000 mature students in 60 institutions.

961 **Rees P.** Definitely an opportunity *Training Tomorrow* July 1991 18-20

Discusses the implementation of BS 5750 from the point of view of training tutors. Describes the largely positive effects it has had on the organisation.

962　**REPLAN and NIACE** *Building a guidance service: a guide for practitioners* Leicester REPLAN/NIACE 1987 28 pages
A short and practical introductory guide presented in checklist format.

963　**REPLAN and NIACE** *Education from everyday living* Leicester NIACE 1988 141 pages
Reports on the views of 76 unwaged adults who have undertaken community based adult education courses in Leeds and Bradford. Looks at the needs of those participating, the way they heard about them and what the outcomes of the courses were.

964　**REPLAN and NIACE** *Educational guidance for unemployed adults* Leicester REPLAN/NIACE 1989 26 pages
This handbook is specifically concerned with aspects of educational guidance designed to meet the needs of unemployed people. It asserts the importance of educational guidance in enabling unemployed adults to make use of educational provision which should provide the opportunity to acquire new skills, updating existing skills, change direction, achieve qualifications and improve self-confidence. The thrust is that adults should be encouraged to see education as a realistic option.

965　**REPLAN and NIACE** *Educational guidance with black communities* REPLAN/NIACE 1990 60 pages
This is a practical guide which will prove useful to many organisations who seek to provide good quality guidance and genuine educational and training opportunities to black communities. A number of recommendations are posited including a commitment to finding ways of actively promoting anti-racist practices within existing and developing guidance services.

966　**REPLAN** *Educational guidance: new responses for inner city areas* Leicester REPLAN 1989 28 pages
Summarises the work of a project which aimed to develop the provision of educational guidance for the unemployed with particular reference to ethnic minorities in inner cities.

967　**REPLAN and NIACE** *Exploring the needs of unwaged adults* Leicester NIACE 1987 80 pages
Reports on a two year project which aimed to investigate the needs of unwaged adults through outreach and guidance strategies. Discusses some of the educational initiatives designed to meet these needs.

968　**REPLAN** *Performance indicators in educational opportunities for unemployed adults* Leicester NIACE/REPLAN 1989 27 pages
A briefing document which discusses the development and use of performance indicators in educational work with unemployed adults. It considers which measures of success are appropriate and offers advice to colleges on planning and monitoring the services they offer.

969　**REPLAN** *Working with women* REPLAN No 3 NIACE Summer 1989
This bulletin is for all those interested in learning opportunities for unwaged women. This issue is based on the theme 'evaluating change'. Excellent articles on open learning, changing labour market, employment training and access courses are featured.

970　**REPLAN** Briefing *Work experience in adult training* Leicester NIACE May 1991 27 pages
Considers the extent to which experiences of work are being integrated into whole learning programmes within adult training. Concludes effective learning from planned experiences at work makes considerable demands on learners, trainers and employers. The many benefits include contribution to wider access, by broadening the training and employment possibilities for adults who for a variety of reasons have gained little from the formal educational system.

971　**Report of the Equal Opportunities Team** *Equal opportunities* Milton Keynes Open University 1990

972　**Rethinking the three R's: basic communication skills in the workplace** *Recruitment and Development Report* No 10 Oct 1990 2-6

Looks at a basic skills training programme run by Workbase Training for manual workers in the NHS.

973   Rhodes P. Adult training and assessment *Training Tomorrow* Sept 1991 29-30
Argues that assessment is the key to the efficient use of training resources but questions some of the methods that are being applied and the advice being offered to some TECs on this issue.

974   Rhys S. Study skills and personal development *Open Learning* Vol 3 No 2 June 1988 40-42
The principal theme underlying this article is that both study skills and personal development are as much the concern of those who facilitate the development of skills in studying as they are of those who seek to learn how to study more effectively.

975   Richards M. Women forced off the shop floor *Times Higher Educational Supplement* No 776 18th Sept 1987 page 5
Drawing on a recent survey by Young Women's Christian Association it is revealed that many firms avoid male shop-floor hostility by sponsoring young women to go on to higher education which will take them into more senior supervisory levels as graduates, usually away from the shop floor. Supports special single-sex supervisory skills courses to equip them before entering management in male dominated environments.

976   Richardson P. and Hartshorn C. *Training for enterprise start up: the gender dimension:* conference paper series no 37/89 1989 22 pages
Explores in some depth the issues surrounding training for women and the efforts necessary to ensure that the training is appropriate and of high quality. The benefits of gender-specific business start-up training and the work of the Women's Enterprise Unit are discussed.

977   Richardson S.A. et al Job histories in open employment of a population of young adults with mental retardation *American Journal of Mental Retardation* Vol 92 No 6 May 1988 483-91
Documents the job histories of 154 Scottish mentally retarded adults. The analysis found that no one with an IQ less than 50 had been in open employment. Half of those with IQs above 50 and who received adult education had some open employment.

978   Rivis V. *Delivering educational guidance for adults* London UDACE 1989
This is a practical handbook for policy makers, managers and practitioners, and for those developing local educational guidance services and networks.

979   Rivis V. Educational guidance for adults: an overview of principles and practice in the European Community *Adults Learning* Vol 2 No 3 Nov 1990 78-80
This is a valuable paper which charts the history, current and future position of educational and vocational guidance for adults in member states of the European Community. Changes which may emanate from the creation of the Single European Market in 1992 are also explored.

980   Rivis V. Educational guidance for adults: meeting individual 'needs' or an agent for change? *Journal of Community Education* Vol 6 No 4 1988 17-19
An informative review of educational guidance for adults which stresses the continuing and growing necessity of good quality, independent educational guidance. Argues, EGSA to survive, must move away from an individualistic (client pathology) model of educational guidance towards a radical and dynamic model whereby adults learning together become a catalyst for social change.

981   Rivis V. *Present developments in educational guidance for adults* In: National Association of Educational Guidance Services for Adults. Bath conference report Spring 1990
The thrust of this article is the need for EGSA to convince central government, employers and educators and training providers that they need a well-developed system of independent educational guidance just as much as the adult learners.

982   Roberton E. Women in enterprise *Scottish Journal of Adult Education* Vol 8 No 3 Spring 1988 24-28

Presents a snapshot of two research projects which encourage women into enterprise. Discusses single sex training in enterprise skills for women as an effective method of encouraging and enabling more women to take up business.

983   Roberts A. and Cooke M. Skills shortages and adult industrial training: the contribution of pen learning *Industrial and Commercial Training* Vol 20 No 5 Sept/Oct 1989 21-26
Qualifications of British managers are dramatically lower than those of competing countries. The author argues companies that want to gain maximum economic benefit from investment in new technology must also invest in developing skills which can be provided through open learning programmes.

984   Roberts H. Don't brush us underneath the carpet: a training scheme for women blue collar workers in local authorities *Women and Training News* No 23 Summer 1986 page 4
Report on a pilot course in Bradford for cleaners leading to a Trade Certificate, with the aims of improving job satisfaction and opening up pathways to other career grades in local authority. A training pack has been produced.

985   Robinson A. and Long G. Marketing FE: products or people? *NATFHE Journal* Vol 12 No 2 1987 19-22
Concentrates on the role of staff in the marketing of further education. Argues that a successful strategy depends on the involvement and commitment of staff at all levels. Provides model showing staff input at all stages of the process.

986   Robinson A. and Long G. Substance v trappings in the marketing of non advanced FE *Journal of Further and Higher Education* Vol 12 No 1 1988 42-53
Criticises institutions which have adopted traditional marketing priorities of manufacturing industry in an attempt to appear market oriented. Argues that concentration on external factors (product, price, place, promotion) to the exclusion of internal factors such as personnel, processes and physical facilities, results in an ineffective marketing strategy.

987   Robinson B. *Continuing education and training for higher education staff* Nottingham Nottingham Polytechnic October 1989
The Polytechnic Association for Continuing Education set out to explore the potential level of support amongst higher education institutions, industry and voluntary agencies for the establishment of a national staff development agency for continuing education and training, to serve higher education establishments across the sector. Areas of staff development identified as most important were credit accumulation and transfer, modularisation, working with employers, adult access and learning.

988   Robinson J. Papers of the Association of Recurrent Education *Opportunities for lifelong learning in the 1990s - an optimistic view of information technology* Sheffield Association of Recurrent Education 1983 42 pages
This is a valuable, if slightly dated collection which argues for the enlargement of 5 basic principles: freedom of learning, freedom of time, freedom of place, freedom of choice and freedom of action, if the concept of lifelong learning is to be fruitful.

989   Rocks P.D. Attitudes to participation in education of adult prisoners in HMP Maze (Compounds) and HMP Belfast *International Journal of Lifelong Education* Vol 4 No 1 1985 69-82
Attempts to assess the effects of prisoners' attitudes to participation in education in two very different prison environments. The article examines the effects of factors such as family, previous school experiences and reason for participation/non-participation. Concludes that a positive attitude is a pre-requisite of participation.

990   Roizen J. and Jepson M. *Degrees for jobs: employer expectations of higher education* Guildford SRHE and NFER - Nelson 1985 190 pages
Based on interview analysis this book highlights the central role of 'enabling skills' or 'transferable skills' and the responsibility of higher education to develop them. Good oral and written communication skills, problem analysis and solution, numeracy, leadership and team working, adaptability, understanding of business and technology are among those

most frequently mentioned. Considerable criticism of the lack of contact between education and industry is apparent and the author emphasises the need for extended dialogue between suppliers and users of the products of higher education.

991   Rosa P. *The nature, diversity and complexity of 'training needs' and response to training in small firms.* Conference paper series no. 72/90 Stirling Scottish Enterprise Foundation 1990 35 pages

The paper evaluates the response to training provision in small firms. Demonstrates that the identification of training needs and response to training is a complex process which differs widely in small firms. Argues we may be able to account for such diversity through the analysis of rationalities associated with differing business organisations.

992   Rosa P. et al *The training needs of managers in central region: results from a local collaborative project:* report Series No. 41/89 Stirling Scottish Enterprise Foundation 1989 77 pages

A valuable and accessible study which examines the managerial training needs of firms in central region arising from changes in the industrial base. Among the key points highlighted is the need for organisations involved with training to develop a combined marketing strategy to combat the overall lack of awareness which exists towards training ,particularly among small business owners.

993   Roweth B. Continuing education in science and technology: a survey of part-time postgraduate students and their employers *Studies in Higher Education* Vol 12 No 1 1987 65-85

This paper presents some descriptive statistics about part-time postgraduates in science and technology. The study indicates that there is effective demand for continuing study in these subjects and also that students taking such courses are highly work-oriented. Employer response emphasises the value of combining study with work and the beneficial effect of this arrangement. Describes the costs and funding of such part-time post graduate study.

994   Royal Society of Arts *Access to higher education:* Papers presented to the Conference on Access to Higher

Education held at the Royal Society on 14 June 1988 London RSA 1988

995   Royal Society of Arts *Raising the standard: Wider access to higher education* London RSA 1988 12 pages

Short report on why the aim of raising the standard of expectation of higher education is both worthy and necessary.

996   Rudd E. Students and social class *Higher Education* Vol 12 No 1 1987 99-106

Reports on a postal survey of undergraduates entering British universities in 1986 which aimed to investigate the link between university admissions and social class.

997   Rural Focus Rural Work and Women *Rural focus* Winter 1990/Spring 1991 3-5

Whole issue is devoted to women who live in rural areas. The leading article discusses the additional barriers faced by such women who wish to return to work, notably sparsity of population, distance and isolation. In other articles various initiatives are discussed which are helping women to overcome such barriers and gain access to wider job opportunities. Case studies depicting the success of some women living in rural areas are informative.

998   Salmon M. A radical approach to HE funding *Transition* Nov 1986 page 3

Argues for a radical approach to public sector funding of higher education rather than tinkering with the existing mechanism. The author believes that the present system does not allow the flexibility needed to meet the needs of the economy.

999   Sanders C. No access? *New Statesman and Society* 17th March 1989 18-19

Discusses the need for Access courses but claims that the government's policies make it difficult to gain financial support for students to do such courses.

1000   Sanders C. Unlocking the dread: ethnic minorities in higher education *Times Higher Education Supplement* No 696 31st May 1991 page 14

Discusses the ways in which two different higher education institutions with very different student intakes are trying to widen the social and ethnic base of their intake and to implement equal opportunities policies.

1001 Schuller T. Small A access and the structure of higher education *Adults Learning* Vol 2 No 4 1990 97-98
Discusses a number of issues relating to the structure of higher education which affect the participation of adults. Argues that increasing demand from school leavers makes the future of adults in higher education uncertain.

1002 Schuller T. et al Continuing education and the redrawing of boundaries *Higher Education Quarterly* Vol 42 No 4 Autumn 1988 335-352
A valuable article discussing credit accumulation and transfer schemes (CATs), PICKUP and consortium ventures. As the author shows, CATs and related ventures, are reaching beyond the established boundaries of higher education.

1003 Scott M.G. *Scottish enterprise foundation: conference papers series No 23/88* Stirling University of Stirling 1988 10 pages

1004 Scott P. Higher education and the media *Higher Education Quarterly* Vol 41 No 3 1987 241-256
The author examines what he sees as misunderstanding and ignorance between higher education and the media. Argues that this leads to a distorted portrayal of higher education which in turn influences the making of higher education policy.

1005 Scott P. U and non-U: non-traditional students in higher education *Journal of Access Studies* Vol 1 No 2 1986 53-61
Traces the development of the current concern with quality in higher education. Argues against increased access for non-traditional students being seen as a threat to quality.

1006 Scottish Adult Basic Education Unit *The 16+ action plan: implications for the ethnic minority communities* - reports of a seminar held 30 April 1985, SCET, Glasgow
Discusses 16+ modules in relation to heterogeneous ethnic minority communities. By identifying the general needs, suggests how the modules may be adapted.

1007 Scottish Committee on Open Learning *National guidelines on open learning - public draft* Edinburgh Scottish Committee on Open Learning 1990 64 pages
A useful publication setting out national guidelines on open learning developed by the Scottish committee on open learning. Provides summary and recommendations, national structures, elements of open learning, funding implications and some interesting case studies.

1008 Scottish Community Education Council *A picture of adult basic education in Scotland 1989-1990* Edinburgh Scottish Community Education Council 1990 36 pages
This document is an analysis of data on adult basic education provision in the Community Education Service (CES) and some voluntary organisations and further education colleges which has been gathered in response to a questionnaire. Much more detailed information has been gathered from CES providers than FE providers and therefore the analysis of this information has more divisions.

1009 Scottish Education Department *Fast forward with further education* Scottish Education Department 1990 32 pages
A concise and informative policy document looking at further education colleges' role in contributing to the country's enterprise activity and economic vigour. Usefully describes the functions of LECs, Scottish Enterprise, PICKUP Scotland Initiative, SCOTVEC, issues of access, flexibility and quality assurance.

1010 Scottish Office *Access and opportunity* Edinburgh HMSO May 1991 32 pages
This White Paper considers the need for a change in culture towards education and training so that participation becomes the norm and lasts a lifetime. Sets out the framework for change which includes education and industry working together to enable people to develop the skills employers require. It is set within the context of the Government's overall national policies for training.

1011 Scottish Office *Scottish enterprise: a new approach to training and enterprise creation* Cmnd 534 Edinburgh HMSO December 1989

1012 Scottish Office Home and Health Department *Prisons in Scotland Report for 1989/90* Edinburgh HMSO April 1991 38 pages

This is a general report on conditions for staff and prisoners in Scottish prisons. The education and vocational training needs of prisoners are given a high priority. The training and development needs of prison staff are clearly valued from the amount of attention and resources devoted to it.

1013 Scottish Open Learning Consortium *Flexible learning case studies* Edinburgh Scottish Open Learning Consortium 1990 165 pages

A selection of case studies illustrating good practice in the management and delivery of flexible learning within an emphasis on computing.

1014 Searle P. and Stibbs A. The under representation of ethnic minority students in post graduate teacher training *New Community* Vol 15 No 2 1989 253-260

Article looks at the under representation of ethnic minorities in teaching through an examination of application forms. Relates the findings to the subject choice and level (primary or secondary) of different ethnic groups.

1015 Shaffer A. et al Barriers to progress in anti-racism *NATFHE Journal* No 3 1986 20-22

Article argues that racism is pervasive throughout further education. Suggests measures to combat this and describes the role of NATFHE in implementing an anti-racist strategy.

1016 Shanks D. The master of education degree in Scotland: Information paper 20. *Scottish Educational Review* Vol 19 No 2 November 1987 122-25

A historical review of the Master of Education degree and how this adapted to the changing needs of students over the years by placing greater emphasis on independent research and learning.

1017 Sharp N.L. *Adult access to higher education in Scotland - barriers to progress* Glasgow Policy Analysis Research Unit 1 986 33 pages

This paper examines some of the central issues surrounding adult access to higher education with illustration drawn from Scotland generally and West Central Scotland in particular.

1018 Sharp N.L. Higher education in Scotland: barriers to adult Access *Journal for Further Education and Higher Education in Scotland* Vol 11 May 1987 28-41

Identifies the barriers to higher education in Scotland which are similar to those in England and Wales, although access and bridging courses are less developed in Scotland. No equivalent of open college networks.

1019 Sharples S. Women into management *Retail and Distribution Management* Vol 14 No 12 Mar/Apr 1986 18-21

Describes a unique management development course designed solely for women run by the Co-operative College (Loughborough). This programme was a response to the paucity of women in responsible management positions in retailing. Women's role in society is one distinguishing feature of the course and the case studies used throughout the 5 day course have been specially chosen for their relevance to women at work. Feedback obtained by Tina Lee, who devised the course, indicates that the programme has boosted the confidence of women and offered them an involvement in a new challenge.

1020 Sheen A. Recognising the skills and potential of women returners *Women in Management Review and Abstracts* Vol 5 No 3 1990 5-7

While running a home and raising a family, a woman may have developed organisational and interpersonal skills which can be adapted to the workplace. Ways in which these skills can be recognised and built upon for the benefit of employers and returners are examined. NATWEST Bank is used as a model example of how experiential learning can be assessed by recruit personnel.

1021 Sheen P.A. Cost and cost effectiveness within a college *Coombe Lodge Reports* Vol 18 No 1 1985 25-38

Looks at the role of management systems in making the most effective and efficient use of resources within a further education college.

1022   Shephard E. Special education: a regional perspective *Educational Media International* Vol 25 No 2 June 1988 115-117

Reports on the introduction of microcomputing in schools providing education for pupils with moderate learning difficulties and stresses the need for in-service training for educators.

1023   Silver M. The costs of learning from experience with respect to the firm *Personnel Review* Vol 16 No 1 1987 15-18

The costs of learning from experience are evaluated from an economics perspective. Argues learning from experience for new technologies/skills is a form of specific training. Firms will bear the costs of specific training if they expect a reasonable rate of return from the trained employee.

1024   Simmons S. (Ed) *Directory of specialist career officers for the handicapped* London National Bureau for Handicapped Students 1985 24 pages

The specialist careers service offers advice on the range of special and integrated courses for disabled people as well as advising on all aspects of employment and training generally. This Directory provides a useful guide to addresses and contact names.

1025   Simpson G. Education partnership: the key to lifelong learning *TEC Director* Issue 8 Feb/March 1991 22-23

A review of the Rover Group Education Partnership Programme. This scheme supports schools in delivering the work-related curriculum and effectively promotes lifelong learning by encouraging the link between learning and earning.

1026   Simpson R.G. and Umbach B.T. Identifying and providing vocational services for adults with specific learning disabilities *Journal of Rehabilitation* Vol 55 Spring 1989 49-55

Presented here is a model for identifying specific learning disabilities in adults and recommendations for services that address the needs of this population. In particular, focus on vocational guidance and counselling and importantly stress that persons with learning disabilities are a diverse group of people who have unique needs which should always be considered by counsellors and tutors.

1027   Sims A. and Pilkington R. *Effects of 'Actively Seeking Work' on 21 hour study* London Central and West London Open College 1990 20 pages

A short pamphlet giving practical advice to those attempting to study under the restrictions of the 21 hour rule and in particular the 'actively seeking work' obligation. Calls for a review of this policy.

1028   Sims A. and Goddard T. *The struggle to study: financial implications for adults studying in London* London Open College Networks 1990

Research report on the financial difficulties faced by adults in education and training. The research uncovered particular problems caused by social security legislation such as the 21-Hour Rule. Uncertainties over the fee structures and the discretionary awards system also caused problems.

1029   Singh R. Education for black and ethnic minority adults: towards a national agenda *Adults Learning* Vol 3 No 1 1991 13-14

Argues for the needs of ethnic minorities to become a central theme in debates about continuing education and training. Identifies key issues in recent white papers which relate to black and ethnic minority adults.

1030   Singh R. Ethnic minority experience in higher education *Higher Education Quarterly* Vol 44 No 4 1990 344-359

Reviews research on the participation rate of ethnic minorities in higher education. Discusses the issues influencing participation and those factors acting as barriers. Describes a research project based on five higher education institutions in the north of England which looks at the performance of ethnic minority students. Suggests that further research is urgently needed in this area.

1031   Siraj-Blatchford I. Access to what? Black students' perceptions of initial teacher education *Journal of Access Studies* Vol 5 No 2 1990 177-187

Addresses the problem of the supply of ethnic minority teachers. Reports on research which focuses on the forms of racism and discrimination which students on initial teacher training courses experienced.

1032 **Skills and Enterprise Briefing** *Further education: does it work for employers?* Issue 2/91 August 1991 4 pages
This Briefing appraises a survey on 'Employers' Views of Work-related Further Education' which was carried out in 1990 to investigate employers' views of local college further education provision and its responsiveness to their needs and how this provision could be improved upon.

1033 **Skills and Enterprise Briefing** *What do employers want from education?* Issue 3/91 August 1991 5 pages
This Briefing reviews a study in the Thames Valley linked to studies in France and Germany. Aimed to find out what employers were looking for in 16-18 year old recruits.

1034 **Sloman M.** On-the-job training: a costly poor relation *Personnel Management* Vol 21 No 2 February 1989 38-41
Training delivered on the job accounted for half the total training (1986-1987). This method according to the author, is not widely recognised, recorded or researched. Discusses National Training Award winners and a set of basic rules for good on-the-job training.

1035 **Slone P.J.** Flexible manpower resourcing: a local labour market survey *Journal of Management Studies* Vol 26 No 2 March 1989 129-150
This is a valuable article which appraises the rise of the enterprise movement in the 1980s and the establishment and performance of TECs. The concept of enterprise as used on enterprise courses is examined. A number of crucial issues in relation to TECs (the need for a national plan for education, training and employment, the commitment of employers etc) are discussed and constructive suggestions made.

1036 **Slowey M.** Adult students: the new mission for higher education? *Higher Education Quarterly* Vol 42 No 4 1988 301-316
An excellent paper which considers the factors which have led to mature student participation in higher education being placed high on the agenda of OECD countries; outlines some international patterns in relation to adult involvement in higher education; considers individual motivations and barriers faced by

mature students. Finally, the author explores a number of innovations which have developed to promote access and illustrates this with an example of a recently developed credit accumulation scheme at one particular polytechnic.

1037 **Slowey M.** Adults in higher education: the situation in the UK *In Schutz H.E. (Ed) Adults in higher education: policies and practice in Great Britain and North America.* Stockholm Almquist & Wiksell International 1987 21-75
An excellent paper concerning the policies and practice of institutions of higher education; characteristics of mature students; continuing education programmes and the financing of educational courses.

1038 **Sluckin A. and Hanna B.** Educational needs in the psychiatric setting *Adults Learning* Vol 2 No 9 May 1991 253-255
This research study, carried out for Norwich Health Authority, looks at hospital and community provision for mentally ill adults. The authors conclude their results have helped to convince adult educators in the field of their worth, highlighted the validity of an educational model of therapy and has helped to promote greater contact between health and education management. Concludes the report can be seen as part of a changing perspective on how to address the needs of psychiatric patients.

1039 **Smith A.** *Quality assured: Labour's proposals for safeguarding and enhancing quality in higher education* London Labour Party 1991 21 pages
Presents Labour Party policy explaining how the higher education system is to be developed and extended while high quality is maintained.

1040 **Smith A.** et al High impact on-the-job training *Industrial and Commercial Training* Vol 18 No 3 May-June 1986 22-25
Discusses on-the-job training and contends this can be simple and cost effective if approached systematically. Instruction should be geared to the trainee's prior knowledge/skill and then rate of progress. Practice should begin immediately after training and feedback should be frequent.

1041 Smith D.J. *Equality and inequality in Northern Ireland: Part 1: employment and unemployment* London PSI 1987 256 pages

Part of a large scale research project undertaken by the PSI to review the coverage and effectiveness of laws and institutions involved in securing equality of opportunity and freedom from discrimination in Northern Ireland. This section examines patterns of employment and unemployment among Catholics and Protestants.

1042 Smith D.J. Policy research: employment discrimination in Northern Ireland *Policy Studies* Vol 9 No 1 1988 41-59

Reports on research undertaken by the PSI which aimed to show how far there is inequality in the distribution of jobs and housing between Catholics and Protestants in Northern Ireland.

1043 Smith D.M. and Saunders M.R. *Other routes: part-time higher education policy* Buckingham SRHE/OU Press 1991 106 pages

An excellent study on the theme of widening access to educational opportunities by expanding the provision of part-time degree study. Interleaving theory with empirical work, the authors explore the current structure and funding of part-time degree study and also consider the development of credit accumulation and transfer schemes, distance learning and performance indicators.

1044 Smith D.M. and Saunders M.R. Part-time higher education: prospects and practices *Higher Education Review* Vol 20 No 3 1988 7-25

The study presented here is a response to a perceived gap in research on part-time degree study at a national level. Based on statistical observations from a national survey of part-time degree level courses. The main conclusions are that part-time students are not a homogeneous group but have diverse needs. Part-time routes continue to be marginal and planning for mature students is predominantly for those going full-time.

1045 Smith E. *Skill needs in Britain 1990* London IFF Research Ltd 1990

A detailed assessment of the British labour market situation which depicts areas of skills shortages and how these may be tackled.

1046 Smith J. *The role of vocational adult education in promoting the successful employment of women: a British perspective* 1987 32 pages

In vocational training today, educators are finding that women entering the labour market have many common problems including a lack of appropriate education, a lack of employment and mobility of opportunity, and a lack of self confidence to pursue successful careers. Successful programmes for women should address all of these areas. Both bridging and vocational programmes offered by a variety of sponsors are described.

1047 Smith P. Strategic developments in higher education *Studies in the Education of Adults* Vol 22 No 1 1990 94-106

Focuses on the role of strategic planning and the marketing function within the structure of the higher education institutions.

1048 Smith P.A. Training and Enterprise Councils: the shattered illusion *Training Officer* Vol 26 No 11 1990 318-321

Reviews the development of TECs to date concluding that until conflicts over funding and accountability are resolved there will be inconsistency in delivery and goals.

1049 Smith R. Equal opportunities in management education and training *Open Learning* Vol 2 No 3 September 1987 36-39

An informative article addressing the barriers to access and promotion in management facing women. Cites examples of distance taught management education programmes and concludes the major barrier is organisational and changes are needed to corporate consciences to encourage women's participation in management education and training and stresses courses should not promote solely male attributes/characteristics through use of outdated materials and teaching thus reinforcing all the barriers against equal opportunities in this field.

1050 Smith S. and Saunders S. Costing part-time provision *Open Learning* Vol 4 No 3 1989 28-34

Examines the ways in which the provision of part-time higher education has been costed and considers the implications of the different models which have been used.

1051 Smithers A. and Robinson P. *Increasing participation in higher education* London BP Educational Service August 1989 43 pages
This report was originally prepared as a briefing document for the Further and Higher Education Board of British Petroleum, which asked that the material should be made more widely available. It sets out in an accessible way, ideas for increasing participation in higher education. The first 5 chapters summarize the numerical context and the following discuss the ideologies behind widening access, how the system can be improved and individual motivation to study.

1052 Smithers A. and Griffin A. *The progress of mature students* Manchester Joint Matriculation Board 1986 177 pages
An excellent research study which followed the progress of mature students at various stages in their application to higher education and later graduation. Considers background of the students, reasons why they dropped out at any stage, and the students' own viewpoint of courses. The Recommendations offered are succinct and most informative.

1053 Smithers A. *The vocational route into higher education* Manchester University of Manchester 1991 90 pages
Describes the existing vocational routes into higher education and discusses developments leading towards the establishment of a vocational path. Argues that such a vocational route will give young people more marketable skills and strengthen the skill base of the nation but its acceptance will require major attitudinal and cultural changes.

1054 Sowers J. and Powers L. (Ed) *Vocational preparation and employment of students with physical and multiple disabilities* London Paul Brookes Publishing Company 1991 213 pages
Whilst this book is based predominantly on experiences in America, it is an important source and points to a significant gap in the British literature on special needs and vocational training for adults. Identifies the types of tasks that students with multiple disabilities can be trained to perform when

developing vocational programmes. Critical work related issues are clearly discussed. The case studies are of particular value.

1055 Sparkes J.J. *On the design of effective distance teaching courses* Paper presented to the Annual Conference of the International Council on Distance Education 17 pages
This paper offers pragmatic guidance for designing effective distance education courses. Discussion of a brief taxonomy of types of learning-knowledge, skills, understanding and attitudes is followed by descriptions of corresponding educational strategies.

1056 Spencely N. The college prospectus *Journal of Further and Higher Education* Vol 12 No 3 1988 73-79
Discusses the inadequacies of many prospectuses and draws up criteria for a more effective prospectus. Describes the efforts of one college in producing a new prospectus.

1057 Spencer D. Short courses waste the potential of young blacks *Times Educational Supplement* No 3781 2nd Oct 1987 page 14
Quotes from Linbert Spencer of Project Fullemploy which criticises the low cost, high volume approach of MSC which he argues wastes the potential of young blacks.

1058 Spencer L. TECs and the training requirements of minority ethnic communities *TEC Director* Issue 5 1990 14-15
Discusses the role of TECs in meeting the training needs of ethnic minorities. TECs should reflect the ethnic composition of the locality and involve all interested groups, ensuring that good practice in equal opportunities underpins all their activities. Discusses the ways that TECs in Oldham and Sheffield are meeting these needs.

1059 Spencer L. and Taylor R. Universities and the provision of Access courses *Adults Learning* Vol 2 No 4 December 1990 99-100
Reviews the progress of Access and institutional commitment; discusses the role of Departments of Adult and Continuing Education; and the consortium validation system. Concludes by reinforcing the

importance of staff development if further support for Access is to materialise.

1060 Spink M. and Thompson Q. The cost of (further education) courses *Education* Vol 171 No 1 1988 14-15

Reports on an initiative which aimed to develop a framework for assessing the costs of courses in further education. Argues that this is crucial to improving efficiency in the further education sector.

1061 Spurling A. *Women in higher education - research project* Cambridge Kings College May 1990 143 pages

This is a valuable and readable report of the Women in Higher Education project based in the King's College Research Centre. It consists of two parts: the first contains the findings and recommendations of the project, and the second presents material on the background to the project and the College's response to it. Using action research, the report highlights negative aspects of academic life at King's and its function is to serve as a basis for change within the College although the problems of women in higher education are considered in a wider context and the report will therefore be of interest to those concerned with higher education and education in general.

1062 Squires G. *Modularisation* Manchester CONTACT September 1986

A study of the development of modular courses in four of the CONTACT institutions : the universities of Manchester and Salford, UMIST and Manchester Polytechnic, commissioned by CONTACT and funded by the DES.

1063 Stamper A. Education and the women's insititutes *Adult Education* Vol 59 No 1 1986 33-38

Shows how the scope of WI's traditional provision of education for rural women has extended beyond crafts and domestic skills to encompass the changing needs and roles of women.

1064 Stanley D. Value for money in further education *BACIE Journal* Vol 40 No 4 July/Aug 1985 110-111

Discusses the issues which need to be considered by colleges, employers, LEAs and the DES to ensure that resources are used effectively in further education.

1065 Stanton G. The contribution of further education colleges to delivering NVQs *Competence and Assessment* No 9 1989 11-13

Describes the central role played by the further education sector in enabling students to gain NVQs and the changes of emphasis this involves for further education colleges.

1066 Statistical Bulletin Mature students in higher education *Statistical Bulletin* No 2 February 1991

Presents the latest statistics on, and trends in, home domiciled, first year, full-time and part-time mature students at publicly funded higher education institutions in Britain, excluding the Open University.

1067 Steele M. et al *Women returners to Scottish labour market* Strathclyde Department of Organisation Management & Employment Relations 1990 79 pages

This report discusses the scope for encouraging women back into the labour market and the opportunities that will be available to such women and considers whether they are likely to be able to fill the jobs that will be available.

1068 Stephen W. A year of NORSWAP - North of Scotland consortium of the Scottish wider access programme *Journal for Further and Higher Education in Scotland* Vol 15 Part 2 1991 11-12

Describes the function of Norswap, the youngest of the Scottish SWAP consortia. A policy is to keep tight control over the number of Access courses and make them as multi-exit as possible. Looks at some of the problems facing students returning to study and the importance of a guidance system which takes account of the special needs of adult returners.

1069 Stephens M. *Adult Education* London Cassell Education Ltd. 1990 132 pages

This is a comprehensive guide to key developments in education for adults starting from the premiss of 'lifelong learning'. There is a good section on guidance including a listing of computerised databases.

1070 Stern E. and Turbin J. *Case study evaluation of the Enterprise in Higher Education (EHE) initiative: employer involvement in EHE* London Tavistock

Institute of Human Relations 1989 32 pages

This is one of a series of Working Papers prepared by a team located at the Tavistock Institute of Human Relations, responsible for the case study evaluation of the first year of the Enterprise in Higher Education Initiative (EHE). Discusses employer/HEI links prior to the scheme; the advent of EHE and early impact. The most frequently mentioned benefit of EHE is recruitment advantage.

1071   **Stevens J. and MacKay R. (Ed)** *Training and competitiveness* Kogan Page 1990 214 pages

The central focus of this varied and informative collection of papers is intended to be on how the training of adults may contribute to increasing the competitiveness of individual companies and of British industry as a whole. This book should stimulate debate on how the needs of the individual, employer and the economy may best be accommodated.

1072   **Steward T.G. and Alexander D.J.** *Information and guidance on adult learning opportunities in Scotland: a study of issues and current provision* Edinburgh Edinburgh University 1987 141 pages

An appraisal of the current state of adult education and guidance in Scotland, focusing on issues and problems and suggesting methods of helping more adults take advantage of educational opportunities.

1073   **Stone M. and Thompson S.** How far can marketing be applied within the FE sector? *Quarterly Review of Marketing* 1987 16-19

1074   **Storan J.** *Making experience count* London LET January 1988 14 pages

'Making Experience Count' (MEC) is the first systematic attempt in this country to tackle the academic assessment of prior experiential learning with adults. The report is based on a postal questionnaire distributed to students who have attended the 'MET' courses held at Goldsmiths' College and Thames Polytechnic over the four year period the courses have been operating from 1982-1986.

1075   **Strachan R.** Adult education and scientific literacy: an innovation with workshops *Adult Education* Vol 61 No 2 1988 109-114

Describes the organisation and running of a series of workshops which aimed to give adults the opportunity to develop scientific literacy and bridge the gap between amateur and professional scientific understanding.

1076   **Strachan R. et al** Raising interest in science through novel adult education courses: a stepping stone to access *Journal of Access Studies* Vol 4 No 1 1989 62-70

Describes a project, the aim of which, was to design a short adult education course to encourage adults to delve into science. At a general level the course illustrated a range of issues relevant to the successful development of Access courses in science.

1077   **Stradling D. and March C.** A degree of partnership *Personnel Management* Vol 21 No 6 June 1989 44-48

The construction industry faced with a shortfall of suitably qualified graduates accepted Salford University's invitation to build its own degree course in construction management. The authors describe how the course has grown up from firm foundations into a blueprint for future industry/education partnerships.

1078   **Straw J.** *Equal opportunities: the way ahead* London Institute of Personnel Management 1989 220 pages

This is a valuable book which reviews the equal opportunities movement in the UK to date. The author incorporates the legislative framework and considers possible future developments and the influence of Europe.

1079   **Stuart M.** Working and training opportunities for people with mental health problems *Educare* No 38 November 1990 10-11

This article addresses some of the issues that emerged from research carried out at MIND into work and training opportunities for people with mental health problems. The original objective was to enable MIND's information workers to advise people on ways back into employment.

1080   **St. John-Brooks C.** What price prison education *New Society* 6th June 1986 page 18

This article argues education for prisoners does not have a high priority for most officers and when it does, they argue for the strictly utilitarian: literacy and numeracy, rather than further education or degree level work.

1081 Summers D. 'Glass ceiling' stops female managers reaching the top *Financial Times* 9 Apr 1991 page 16
Examines the arguments for and against separate training for women. Concludes women-only training must be seen as an adjunct to, rather than a substitute for more traditional training to guard against accusations of sex discrimination.

1082 Sunday Times *Sunday Times* 3 March 1991 page 15
An informative discussion on TECs and the new advertising campaign. It is noted that many employers continue to lack professional advice and guidance on training and many do not know what TECs are.

1083 Sutcliffe J. *Adults with learning difficulties: education for choice and empowerment* Leicester NIACE/OU 1991 189 pages
This handbook is concerned with highlighting good practice in continuing education for adults with learning difficulties. A variety of innovative practice is described, drawn from settings where students are actively involved in choosing what and how they learn.

1084 Sutcliffe J. Education for adults with learning difficulties: a second rate service *NATFHE Journal* Vol 15 No 6 1990 12-13

1085 Sutcliffe J. Prejudice or participation? *Adults Learning* Vol 2 No 3 November 1990 66-67
An interesting article in which the author asserts adult educators must look critically at their provision to assess the quality of opportunity that is available to disabled people. Reviews some developments in services for people with learning difficulties based on a set of values called 'the five accomplishments' (choice, competence, respect, community presence, community participation) coined by John O'Brien.

1086 Swann P. Subsidising students *Economic Review* Vol 6 1988 19-21

1087 Symonds T. TECs faulted over basic skills training *Financial Times* 10 Jan 1991 page 7
Overview of the survey by Apex which asked 2,500 UK employers the qualities they most look for on recruiting. More emphasis was placed on personal attitudes such as honesty and positive attitude than on formal education or vocational training. TECs however are geared towards providing vocational qualifications rather than these basic skills which employers want. This would support the view that the prison sentence has a valuable part to play in encouraging the development of personal skills through discussion groups, education and counselling.

1088 Syrett M. Europe's view of women at work *Professional Engineering* January 1991 32-34
Reviews the findings of the Price Waterhouse Cranfield project (1989-1990) which was a survey of working women in 5 European countries. Considered the attitudes to women in employment, initiatives to encourage women returners to professional jobs with retraining courses and careerbreaks. Found Britain leads in training women returners and offering part-time work. Most careerbreak schemes are offered in the public sector, and where offered in the private sector, they are predominantly within retail or financial enterprises.

1089 Tait A. The politics of open learning *Adult Education* Vol 61 No 4 1989 303-313
Discusses the contribution which adult education has made to the development of open learning. Examines the future role of adult education in open and distance learning and spells out some of the possible pitfalls.

1090 Taking Liberties Collective *Learning the hard way: women's oppression in men's education* reviewed in *Gender and Education* Vol 2 No 3 1990 370-371
This article makes some interesting points about access courses and discusses the issue of transferability concluding that access courses should not be geared to one specific higher education institution which has been the case in some areas which may mean those women who move area with their husband have to drop-out before completing a course.

1091 Tallentyre F. *Women at the crossroads : 10 years of new opportunities for womens courses in the northern district* Edinburgh Workers Educational Association 1985 37 pages

Using a 'case study' approach highlights in some detail the thinking which has informed the shaping of one course New Opportunities for Women, as the centre of one women's educational programme in the WEA Northern district over 10 years. The course was designed to act as a bridge by which an individual woman may cross into new territories.

1092 Tasker M.E. and Packham D.E. Freedom, funding and the future of the universities *Studies in Higher Education* Vol 15 No 2 1990 181-195

Argues that the autonomy of universities is being eroded by the UGC, the CVCP and the increasing involvement of government and industry. As such, the author argues that the role of universities within society as centres of free thinking is being compromised. The universities are facing a philosophical as well as a financial crisis.

1093 Taylor D. et al *Articulation of 16+ national development programme* Glasgow Jordanhill Scottish School of Further Education 1989

Examines the extent to which policy is achieving the objectives of the 16+ Development Programme. The main aim is that the non-advanced modular provision should articulate with school and higher education or advanced further education and work-based training. Illuminates areas requiring further development.

1094 Taylor G. *Initial assessment in employment training* ALBSU Newsletter No 36 Winter 1990 11-13

Reports on an initial assessment programme developed on the Community Programme and Employment Training schemes. Describes the objectives and operation of the scheme.

1095 Taylor R. The Queen's University of Belfast: the liberal university in a divided society *Higher Education Review* Vol 20 No 2 1988 27-45

Describes the non-sectarian stance adopted by Queen's University Belfast since its foundation in 1845. Gives some figures for the religious affiliations of staff and students. However,

from the authors account of student life at the University religious divisions still appear to be present.

1096 Taylor R. Universities and access: adult education practice at the University of Leeds *Journal of Access Studies* Vol 3 No 2 Autumn 1988 29-37

Describes and analyses one particular access model as an example of a fairly typical extramural response to access needs from within a large civic university with a long history of university adult education involvement.

1097 TEC Director Career Development Loans *TEC Director* Issue 9 1991 16-17

Relates the successful story of a woman who financed her studies by borrowing money from the Career Development Loan scheme.

1098 TEC Director Childcare and TECs *TEC Director* Issue 5 1990 16-17

Discusses the Women's Institute Group TEC has formed to generate plans that will encourage women in the country to enter and remain in employment. Also discusses Day Care Trust and 'Childminding in Business'.

1099 TEC Director Discussion document *TEC Director* Issue 5 1990 4 pages

Useful fact sheet which sets out key objectives for TECs on women and strategies for implementing equal opportunities and childcare facilities.

1100 TEC Director Investors in People *TEC Director* Issue 7 1990 38 pages

Effective training and development is to be the key to business success and this notion forms the base of 'Investors in People'. The articles give an overview of the many initiatives now taking place to enable the education system, employers and TECs to work together for effective training strategies and enterprise.

1101 TEC Director Standards and qualifications: keys to quality and success *TEC Director* Issue 4 1990 20-21

Describes the background to the introduction of national standards and qualifications. Considers the implications of this for the work of the TECs.

1102 TEC Director Tending tomorrow's workforce *TEC Director* 1991 34 pages

The underlying theme of this issue is TEC partnerships with business and education. The articles which appear are both concise and informative and are recommended reading to all with an interest in opportunities for the emerging workforce of tomorrow.

1103   Temple H. Starting them young: flexible learning in the TVEI programme *Open Learning* Vol 6 No 2 June 1991 28-35
Attempts to pick out some of the features of the Technical and Vocational Education Initiative which have contributed to the sum of open learning activity in Great Britain.

1104   Tennant A. The rise and fall of Great Britain *Director* August 1991 66-68
An interesting article comparing Britain's generally negative attitude towards industry and the concept of 'ambition' to other nations. Argues the problem faced is primarily a cultural one and the solution must lie in effecting change through education.

1105   Theodossin E. College companies *Coombe Lodge Reports* Vol 20 No 9 1988 539-603
Report on a workshop run in May 1988 on the theme of college companies. The contributors provide an overview of the British scene and stress the need for effective marketing in an era of skills shortages. There are contributions from the managing directors of college companies discussing their experiences.

1106   Theodossin E. The modular market: studies in further education Further Education Staff College Blagdon, Bristol *Coombe Lodge* 1986 138 pages
An indepth analysis of the role of modularisation and issues of credit transfer and marketing in further and higher education. Five case studies which show the diversity surrounding modularisation and structure are usefully included.

1107   Thompson C. Client satisfaction: monitoring quality *Coombe Lodge Reports* Vol 20 No 12 1988
The whole issue looks at the notion of client satisfaction as a measure of quality. Models and mechanisms are suggested which can be used to implement such a quality control system within further education courses.

1108   Thompson C. Marketing FE *NATFHE Journal* Vol 13 No 6 1988 19-21
The author stresses the need to view marketing as a challenge and an opportunity. Argues that those involved in education have great scope for anticipating and preparing for change in a proactive fashion rather than merely reacting to events. To achieve this the involvement of all staff is crucial.

1109   Thompson P. The meaning of vocational qualifications *Education and Training* Vol 31 No 3 1989 13-15
Written by the chief executive of the NCVQ. The author explains the main aims of the organisation, how it has developed since 1986 and the implications of its work for education and training.

1110   Thomson I. Why the SEB must now take account of adults *Times Educational Supplement Scotland* No 1111 19 February 1988 page 2
Reviews the policies of the Scottish Education Board in relation to adult learners.

1111   Thorp J. et al *Training needs in major economic developments* London FEU/PICKUP 1989 33 pages
Reviews the project set up to investigate the issues arising in relation to the training needs of companies involved in major economic developments. Stansted Airport and Dartford International Ferry Terminal. Training needs for managers, supervisors, secretaries and clerical staff.

1112   Thorpe M. et al Open for business: delivering the goods in management education *Open Learning* Vol 1 No 1 February 1986 5-9
Reports on the Open University's array of short courses in business for managers.

1113   Tight M. Access and part-time undergraduate study *Journal of Access Studies* Vol 2 No 1 1987 2-24
This paper explores the scope and variety of part-time undergraduate provision, reviews the available evidence on the characteristics of part-time undergraduate students and discusses the different kinds of access arrangements to be found. Concludes access courses and part-time higher education have a fundamental aim in common - the opening up of opportunities for study and

self-development to people who have not followed the conventional route. An expanded, flexible system of part-time higher education provision is therefore required.

1114   **Tight M.** Access - not access courses *Journal of Access Studies* Vol 3 No 2 1988 6-13

Briefly reviews the educational objectives which can be levelled at access courses. Stresses the importance of maintaining a broad view of the access issue and believes the tendency to equate 'access' with 'access courses' is too narrow and harmful for future developings in opening up higher education.

1115   **Tight M.** *Higher education: a part-time perspective* Buckingham SRHE/OU press 1991 170 pages

This book provides a comprehensive analysis of the past, present and future of part-time higher education in the UK. The main thrust is while part-time higher education has been seriously under-valued in recent years, it offers the only viable model for a significantly expanded, more flexible and more relevant higher education system.

1116   **Tight M.** Part-time higher education as open learning *Open Learning* Vol 4 No 2 1989 3-6

Explores the close conceptual and practical links between part-time study and open learning. Describes the development and current state of open learning provision in the UK.

1117   **Times Educational Supplement** Scotland The time is not right to ditch HNC and HND *Times Educational Supplement Scotland* No 1073 29 May 1987 page 4

Discusses the importance and relevance of the HNC and HND and why these qualifications are sought after by employers.

1118   **Times Higher Education** Supplement Scotland's strays come home *Times Higher Education Supplement* No 987 4 October, 1991 page 12

Reports on Scottish system of higher education and major changes.

1119   **Titmus C. (Ed)** *Widening the field: continuing education in higher education*

SRHE and NFER-Nelson 1985 121 pages

Widening the field takes up the case for post-21 year old degree level education. Explains what continuing education is, what can be made of it and why we need to broaden education as a whole. Appraises the market, the curriculum, the cost, benefits economically and socially and use to be made of new technologies in distance learning.

1120   **Todd F.** The key to competence *Pickup in Progress* Summer 1989 16-20

1121   **Todd R.** Skills towards 2000 In **Stevens J. and Mackay R. (ed)** *Training and Competitiveness* London Kogan Page 1991 243-259

This paper sets out the need for national qualification targets, a national skills framework, and especially for joint action at workplace level between employers and unions. It is intended as a starting point for debate, and a contribution to the growing consensus on training in Britain.

1122   **Togneri C.** *Open learning: a student perspective* Glasgow Scottish Council for Educational Technology May 1985 60 pages

This is a valuable survey which considers the system of open learning from the learners' viewpoint. Little research has emerged from the students' perspective so this report is most appropriate. Charts the experience of students through a number of key areas from pre-enrolment, tutorial support, delivery of materials and general information. Considers weaknesses as well as strengths of the system and posits a number of recommendations.

1123   **Tolley H. and Thomas K.** Access training as a means of recruiting ethnic minority police officers *Adult Education* Vol 61 No 4 1989 314-318

Describes an initiative between the West Midlands Police force and Nottingham University in which ethnic minority applicants who narrowly failed the initial police assessment tests were given a second chance through attendance on a special Access course.

1124   Tope P. Education for women in prison *WEA Women's Studies* Dec 1986 page 15

This article looks at existing provision for relevance to women's needs and interests and suggests that traditional interpretations for women's concerns should give way to self defence and non-traditional skills training as well as advice before their return to the outside world.

1125   Toyne P. Achieving wider access *In Access and alternative futures* Parry and Wake (Ed) London Hodder and Stoughton 1990

A highly informative overview of the developments which should facilitate wider access by making learning more open and flexible. Discusses CATs, modularisation and the need for attitudinal change towards issues such as staff development and marketing.

1126   Trades Union Congress *Skills 2000* London TUC August 1989 15 pages

A statement intended to stimulate discussion on the framework which individuals, unions, employers, education/training providers and government can use to meet the training challenges of the 21st century. TUC supports proposals for a system that, by emphasising the role of broad-based qualifications as a motor for progress, encourages individuals to develop their skills based on a sound foundation. Argues obstacles that prevent workers from their potential must be tackled.

1127   Trades Union Congress *Education, vocational training and work women and prison: a TUC report* London TUC 1987 22-26

Describes provision of Holloway and Cookham Wood Prisons including basic education, general education, home economics courses, skills training, ESL work and correspondence study.

1128   Trade Union Research Unit Employee development and assistance programme (EDAP) *Occasional paper* no. 101 London Trade Union Research Unit March 1991 16 pages

This is a joint initiative by the trade unions and Ford of Britain which offers a description and preliminary evaluation of EDAP and the potential for its transferability. The paper offers a basis of guidance, encouragement and support for unions wishing to consider the negotiation and implementation of a similar scheme. The emphasis is upon returning to learning, the process of learning and the experience of study as providing an appetite

for and entry route into adult education and development and should not be confused with paid educational leave.

1129   Trades Union Congress *The education and training of girls and women* Bristol University of Bristol 1987 25 pages

This report describes the position of girls and women in education and training and considers some of the causes of inequality. Forwards recommendations for action by various agencies aimed at removing sex discrimination from education and training services.

1130   Training Agency *Accreditation of prior learning: a Training Agency perspective* Sheffield Department of Employment 1990 17 pages

The Training Agency has played an important role fostering the development of systems for the Accreditation of Prior Learning. This document presents the background to APL and NVQ and definitions of competence and vocational qualifications. Also asks key questions to stimulate feedback, looks at the many current developments and research on APL.

1131   Training Agency *The core skills project and work-based learning* Sheffield Training Agency 1987 23 pages

Considers the main features of work-based learning and uses examples to illustrate the benefits of work-based learning.

1132   Training Agency *Development of assessable standards for national certification: assessment of competence* Sheffield Training Agency 1989 12 pages

Guidance notes to inform the work of standards development. Will appeal in particular to those concerned with the technical aspects of standards development in ILBs and Awarding Bodies.

1133   Training Agency *Employment training and educational needs of refugees from Vietnam in Leeds and Bradford* Sheffield Training Agency 1989

Aimed to identify the training undertaken by Vietnamese adults in the Leeds/Bradford area and to assess the training needs and particular barriers which still exist.

1134 **Training Agency** *Literacy and numeracy: a guide to good practice* Sheffield Training Agency 1989 30 pages

Guide aimed at YTS and ET providers for improving the quality of literacy and numeracy training within the programmes. Also useful for those working with literacy and numeracy problems within the workplace.

1135 **Training Agency** *Market Research: an overview* Sheffield Employment Department 1990 20 pages

Part of a series of good practice guides which advises on how to make effective use of market research in TECs. Includes models on which the market research function could be based and gives examples of good practice.

1136 **Training Agency** *Marketing employment training: open learning pack* Sheffield Training Agency 1989

A loose leafed pack dealing with all aspects of marketing for use in staff development and training. Contains nine modules, flash cards, a video, an audio tape and workbooks.

1137 **Training Agency and Training Research Advisory Consultancy Enterprises Ltd** *Marketing training: open learning pack* London TRACE 1990

For use with the TA/TRACE workbook. Contains text based modules, a video, an audio tape and flash cards covering all aspects of marketing. For use in staff development and training.

1138 **Training Agency and Training Research Advisory Consultancy Enterprises Ltd** *Marketing training: workbook* London TRACE 1990

A collection of materials for use with the TA/TRACE open learning pack in staff development and training. Contains project ideas and places to record achievements and assessments. Covers all aspects of marketing.

1139 **Training Agency** *Research Annual Report 1990* Sheffield Employment Department 1990 40 pages

Research will continue to play a vital part in assisting the Training Agency (now Training, Enterprise and Education Directorate) in its role as the country's national training authority. Stresses the need to look ahead and

to use, build on information gained. This Report reviews current and future research projects which will help to improve efficiency and effectiveness of TA programmes.

1140 **Training Agency** *TEC: developing good practice: equal opportunities* Moorfoot, Sheffield Training Agency Aug 1990 28 pages

A guide offering practical advice for TEC staff and training providers on how to develop and implement effective equal opportunities strategy. Shares some examples of good practice.

1141 **Training Agency** *Total quality management and BS 5750: the links explained* Sheffield Training Agency 1990 14 pages

1142 **Training Agency** *Training and enterprise: priorities for action 1990/91* Sheffield Employment Department 1989 25 pages

Offers strategic guidance from the Secretary of State for employment and describes the relevant labour market and demographic trends. Raises some issues which those involved in training and enterprise will want to consider in developing their plans.

1143 **Training Agency** *Training in Britain: a study of funding activity and attitudes: the main report* London HMSO 1989 99 pages

A wide ranging survey of vocational education and training in Britain. Chapter 3 deals with the funding of training and attempts to chart and measure the flow of the funding involved. Figures are presented on training costs and some evaluation of the economic benefits of training are summarised.

1144 **Training Agency** *Training in Britain: a study of funding, activity and attitudes: summary* London HMSO 1989 6 pages

Summarises the main report above.

1145 **Training Agency** *The use of ASE basic skills tests* Sheffield Training Agency 1988

Reports on the results of administering literacy and numeracy tests on people entering employment training schemes. The need for further development to make such testing more occupationally relevant was identified.

1146 Training and Enterprise Council *Developing good practice TEC information and advice services* Sheffield DE 1990 19 pages

Reaffirms the importance of a coherent strategy of high quality information and advice about employment which is accessible to individuals and businesses. Points out that information and advice services can help provide the 'feedback loop' which is essential if training and education programmes are to be effectively delivered in response to local needs.

1147 Training, Enterprise and Education Directorate and NIACE *New Approaches to adult training* Leicester NIACE/REPLAN 1991 64 pages

This study reports on good practice in current adult training, including Employment Training Programmes. Focuses on staff development and training: initial assessment and action planning; the planning and delivery of training; accreditation and evaluation. Interspersed with illustrative case study material.

1148 Training, Enterprise and Education Directorate *The skills link: higher education developments* Sheffield Employment Department Group November 1990 106 pages

Research projects are illustrated (pages 34-37) which are specifically concerned with access to science, technology and engineering. These projects are either near completion or due to finish in the next couple of years. Contact names are given for further information. This document also lists other research projects currently being carried out on higher education and employment.

1149 Transition The BS 5750 debate *Transition* Vol 91 No 7 1991 10-11

Discusses the appropriateness of applying the British standard for quality assurance to training.

1150 Tribe K. The accumulation of cultural capital: the funding of UK higher education in the twentieth century *Higher Education Quarterly* Vol 44 No 1 1990 21-34

The author considers the long term development of British higher education and argues that the experience of Europe and the USA shows that reliance on the private financing of higher education will not sustain the system.

1151 Trollope K. The price is right *Personnel Today* 20th Nov 1990 page 34

Reports on employers views of open learning as a cost effective method of training.

1152 Troth J. People, quality and business success *TEC Director* Issue 7 1991 20-21

Managing director of a large firm describes the strategy of its success which is based on a commitment to quality in all aspects of the organisation. Discusses the role that Investors in People can play in business success.

1153 Trow M. Academic standards and mass higher education *Higher Education Quarterly* Vol 41 No 3 1987 268-292

Discusses the reconciliation of academic standards and mass education. The author sees a truly mass system arising out of further education. He concludes that higher education must be viewed not as a separate system but as an important part of the broad continuing education system which is characterised by a variety of standards, aims and costs.

1154 Troyna B. Selection and learning: framework for anti-racist initiatives in education *Multicultural Teaching* Summer 1988 5-7

Identifies two elements in anti-racist work. That ensuring fair representation and sharing of resources and that combatting racist attitudes and practices. In all white settings such as the author's further education college the emphasis must be on the latter. Describes initiatives aimed at developing an understanding of racism.

1155 Tudor C. The Employment Service and inner cities *Employment Gazette* August 1990 395-398

An interesting article which considers the Employment Department's Employment Service which now has a variety of outreach staff in inner cities including Restart counsellors who conduct interviews with the long-term unemployed on non-employment service sites. The article discusses Job Interview Guarantee (which includes feedback and assessment) and Programme Development Funds.

1156 **Tumelty C.** A balanced approach to retraining *Personnel Management* Vol 20 No 5 May 1988 40-43
GEC-Avery was one of 1987's top three winners of annual National Training Awards. The firm, threatened by international competition, introduced strategic business and product planning techniques creating a need for a massive personnel retraining effort. Line managers have been made responsible for retraining and have been provided with a set of tools to help them.

1157 **Turner D. and Pratt J.** Bidding for funds in higher education *Higher Education Review* Vol 22 No 3 1990 19-33
Describes and examines the implications of the PCFC's bidding system for the funding of the polytechnics and colleges. Offers advice to institutions on how to make successful bids.

1158 **Twentyman T.** Take ten: Sheffield's paid educational leave scheme *Adults Learning* Vol 1 No 8 1990 218-220
Reports on the Take Ten which is an invitation to Sheffield council employees to take ten days paid educational leave provided through 3 adult education departments which is related to the world of work and the experiences of council workers but is not employer led. The aim of this scheme is to enable students to build self confidence, practise communication skills and develop the ability to work in a group.

1159 **Twining J.** Smart cards for training credits *Educa* No 112 1991 9-10
Discusses training credits and how these may be adapted for those with special needs.

1160 **Twining J.** Treasury rules OK?: media reports suggest that British training is facing a crisis: an analysis of cause and effect *Educa* No 104 1990 10-11
Considers reports in the media which suggest that British training is in crisis mainly due to underfunding and the influence of the Treasury rather than the DES and the DTI. The author argues however that the problems are due to other factors such as the decline of youth unemployment and the proliferation and incoherence of different training bodies.

1161 **Twining J. et al** An open learning delivery system *British Journal of*

Educational Technology Vol 20 No 2 May 1989 129-34
Discusses the Resourced Open Learning Facility (ROLF), which was developed by the Skills Training Agency as a means of delivering off-the-job skill training for the unemployed. Employment training is discussed and an evaluation of ROLF is described, including management issues and types of trainees.

1162 **Twinning J.** Updating and retraining initiatives in the UK *World Yearbook of Education* 1987 174-186
This is a special issue on vocational education. Argues greater emphasis on the need for systematic opportunities for updating, retraining and career change. Goes on to discuss initiatives such as PICKUP and Training Access Points and the issues surrounding motivation of adults. Concludes adults must have a full choice and the need for comprehensive and coherent information is therefore essential.

1163 **Tysome T. and O'Neill S.** Ministers warned of 'kite marks' for colleges *Times Higher Education Supplement* No 975 12th July 1991 page 1
Reports on the criticism which has arisen out of the application to higher education of measures such as Total Quality Management and BS5750

1164 **Unemployment Unit** *Square pegs in round holes: employment training: quality or workfare?* London Unemployment Unit 1988 12 pages

1165 **Unit for the Development of Adult Continuing Education** *An Agenda for Access - a strategy paper* Leicester NIACE/UDACE January 1990 24 pages
This paper outlines the challenge of access and offers a view of what a truly accessible service of education and training for all adults would be like. It then offers a strategy for development, and concludes with specific recommendations for action directed to Government, LEAs, education and training providers.

1166 **Unit for the Development of Adult Continuing Education** *Black community access* Leicester NIACE 1990 33 pages

Aimed at those involved in further and higher education and black community groups this paper examines how collaboration between the two can improve access for the black community. Includes 7 case studies showing how collaboration has worked from both sides.

1167 Unit for the Development of Adult Continuing Education *The challenge of change: developing educational guidance for adults* Leicester NIACE 1986 106 pages

This report which follows on from UDACE 1985 has been a major influence for later research. It is about helping adults to learn, whether this is denoted as education, training, on the job, open learning or independent study. It is addressed to every agency concerned with improving the skills, knowledge, creativity and flexibility of the adult population. The report follows the premise that for the national, economic and social survival of our society, we must improve the match between learning needs of adults and the learning opportunities available.

1168 Unit for the Development of Adult Continuing Education *Developing Access: the discussion paper* Leicester UDACE 1988 11 pages

This paper is both a developmental tool, for use in discussion, or individually, by those wishing to improve access to education and training for adults and as a framework for consultation, to enable those concerned with these issues to respond to UDACE with their views on priorities for access development.

1169 Unit for the Development of Adult Continuing Education *Helping adults to learn* Leicester UDACE May 1985

In 1984 the DES asked UDACE to investigate and make recommendations on the development of educational guidance for adults. The results which make up this consultative document, which was widely circulated, give a high priority to the development of guidance. This report laid the foundations for many other UDACE surveys.

1170 Unit for the Development of Adult Continuing Education *Open college networks and national vocational qualifications* Leicester NIACE 1990 14 pages

This paper is written for all involved in the implementation of the National Vocational Qualification framework or the development of Open College Networks and sets out the similarities and differences between the aims and processes of both and identifies the potential for developing the relationship between them, in order to improve access to qualification and progression in education and training for adults.

1171 Unit for the Development of Adult Continuing Education *Open college networks - current developments and practice* Leicester NIACE 26 pages

This paper describes what Open College Networks are, how they work, and the current national state of development and presents a range of strategic issues for future exploration and development. The aim of the paper is to stimulate wider debate on how Open College Networks can contribute to improving education and training opportunities and provision for adult learners.

1172 Unit for the Development of Adult Continuing Education *What can graduates do? A consultative document* Leicester NIACE February 1991 61 pages

This document is introduced as 'work in progress' and its aim is to explore ways of describing and assessing the outcomes of degree level study, in the belief that this will make the purposes of higher education more widely understood by learners and employers and thus help to make the system more accessible and of higher quality. The project's overall aim therefore is to help in the development of a more outcome based education and training system.

1173 University of Warwick *Increasing part-time degree opportunities* Coventry University of Warwick (in progress)

New part-time degree provision is being developed and introduced at the University in order to improve access to higher education. To support the introduction of the part-time degrees new procedures for credit accumulation and transfer, a system of certification through open studies, recognition of in-company experience for academic credit, flexible forms of course delivery will be amongst the areas necessary for development during the course of the project. Research ends May 1992. Contact name Prof. Chris Duke.

1174   **Unwin L.** NVQs and the man-made fibres industry: a case study of Courtalds Grafil Ltd In: *Change and intervention: vocational education and training* Raggatt P. and Unwin L. (Ed) London Falmer Press 1991 220 pages

Reports on a case study which examined the consequences of a company's decision to restructure its training programme and introduce NVQs.

1175   **Urwin L.** Staff development, competence and NVQ *Journal of Further and Higher Education* Vol 14 No 2 1990 26-37

Discusses the response of colleges to the introduction of NVQs. Looks at the staff development needs associated with a move from offering vocational education and training to supplying vocational qualifications.

1176   **Usher G.** Employment training: Britain's new Bantustans *Race and Class* Vol 32 No 1 1990 46-56

Traces the growth of ET from MSC to TA to TECs. Argues that these agencies are trying to deal with unemployment in the context of restrictive social security legislation. Argues that the involvement of the educational and training agencies affect the rights and roles of students and staff and will create a black underclass who are produced and regulated by the state agencies.

1177   **Usher R.S.** Reflections and prior work experience: some problematic issues in relation to adult students in university studies *Studies in Higher Education* Vol 11 No 3 1986 245-256

The primary concern in this paper is adult part-time study. The author discusses issues surrounding access and prior experience. Argues that emphasis should be on the quality of learning derived from work experience and procedures need to be constructed which facilitate, through reflective activity, the specification of the perceived learning outcomes of work experience.

1178   **Varlaam C. and Bevan S.** *Gaining access to training and jobs* No 132 Brighton Institute of Manpower Studies 1987 146 pages

Based on the work for the Manpower Commentary programme undertaken by IMS for Dept of Employment and MSC.

1179   **Vaughan P.** *Maintaining professional competence: a survey of the role of the professional bodies in the development of credit bearing CPD courses* Hull University of Hull 1991 83 pages

Reports on a research project which explores the role of Credit Accumulation and Transfer Schemes and the modularisation of higher education courses in continuing professional development. The role and interest of Professional Bodies in these issues was examined through an extensive postal questionnaire and interviews.

1180   **Vickers A.** An open learning system for careers guidance *Open Learning* Vol 6 No 1 Feb 1991 59-64

A review of careers guidance at a distance. For those studying at a distance, access to a careers adviser is not always possible. It is essential therefore to develop a first rate set of printed materials with targeted individual support to assist students and make the best use of the facilities available to them within and outside the Open University.

1181   **Waddington P.** Access: a rich man's market *Education* Vol 174 No 5 1989 101-102

Suggests that the outcome of current access policies may be the opposite of that intended. That is, elite institutions will become more autonomous, less accountable and less accessible whilst institutions striving to become more accessible will not have the funds needed.

1182   **Waddington P.** Access: the name of the game *Education* Vol 174 No 4 1989 80-82

A concise and informative discussion on the issues surrounding the term 'access' and the need for higher education reform generally. Concludes higher education must open its doors to more mature students and socially disadvantaged in order to re-establish its political support and rediscover a sense of mission.

1183   **Waddington P.** Buddy can you spare a paradigm? Wider access for

non-traditional students in HE *Education* Vol 177 No 24 1991 504-505
Argues that more commitment from academic institutions and more resources from government are needed if access to higher education is to be widened to non-traditional students.

1184 **Waddington P.** Does you does or does you don't give access? *NATFHE Journal* Vol 15 No 3 May/June 1990 18-20
Looks at the problems surrounding the development of access to higher education because 'extending access' means such different things to different people.

1185 **Wagner L.** Adults in higher education: the next five years *Adults Learning* Vol 2 No 4 December 1990 94-96
Warns that the mild triumphs of the last few years in the development of Access and increase in the number of mature students could easily be reversed, and adults forced to resume their role as the reserve army of students, unless government and institutional rhetoric is turned into reality.

1186 **Wagner L.** Continuing education: retrospect and prospect *Journal of Access Studies* Vol 3 No 1 1988 81-91
This is the text of a keynote address given to the annual conference of the Polytechnic Association for Continuing Education at the Polytechnic of Wolverhampton 4 March 1988. Reviews the progress of Access, PICKUP and the importance of continuing education as a central part of higher education.

1187 **Wake C.** Access courses and the universities *Journal of Access Studies* Vol 3 No 1 1988 8-16
Discusses mature student admission to universities and the various efforts made to raise awareness of access courses among Admissions Tutors and teachers. Stresses the importance of cultural change in the whole educational structure.

1188 **Walby S.** (Ed) *Gender segregation at work* Milton Keynes OU Press 1988 190 pages
An excellent volume whose contributors explore explanations of gender segregation at work, the changing forms and levels of segregation, and deliberate attempts to reduce

it. They provide the general theoretical and historical background, a number of specific case studies and a discussion of such issues as part-time work, the role of trade unions, sex discrimination, sexual harassment and racism in relation to gender segregation.

1189 **Walker A. and Wright G.A.** The funding of higher education in the UK: a contribution to the debate *Higher Education Quarterly* Vol 44 No 3 1990 230-244
Reviews the arguments of the last 20 years relating to the funding of higher education and the introduction of student loans. Four funding proposals are assessed in terms of their efficiency and effectiveness.

1190 **Wallis E.** Job obsolescence in the nineties *Education and Training* Sept/Oct 1987 14-15
Considers the effects of declining manufacturing industry and movement towards service sector occupations. Education and training will be a growth industry helping people cope with technology and develop thinking and communication skills. Consequently, there will be no need for most semi and unskilled jobs and many people who cannot adapt will suffer. For the relatively educated and adaptable vast opportunities will open out, hence the author reinforces the need for re-training strategies.

1191 **Ward K.** From public to private? Employer-financed general education opportunities *Adults Learning* Vol 1 No 2 October 1989 43-45
An account of the new Ford-Trade Unions joint employee development programme (EDAP). The programme aims to offer employees a wide range of personal and career development through broad educational opportunities, and make available a variety of employee assistance services to encourage healthier life-styles.

1192 **Warner-Weil S. and McGill I.** (Ed) *Making sense of experiential learning: diversity in theory and practice* Society for Research into Higher Education 1989 280 pages
Appraises the multiplicity of meanings and practices associated with experiential learning in an international context and incorporating theoretical and practical frames of reference.

Reflects depth, breadth and complexity of current developments.

1193   **Warren C.E.** British women with interrupted technological careers: societal attitudes and patterns of childhood socialisation *International Journal of Lifelong Education* Vol 6 No 2 Apr-Jun 1987 125-151
Data collected from 94 British women enroled in 'Women in Technology', a course for women returning to the work force, focused on societal attitudes, childhood socialisation patterns, and this group's attitudes towards interrupted careers.

1194   **Warren J.** Training by open learning *Scottish Journal of Adult Education* Vol 7 No 2 Autumn 1985 30-36
Discusses the growth of open learning and the advantages companies find with it as a training method.

1195   **Warwick J.** *Planning human resource development through equal opportunities* London FEU 1991 34 pages
This handbook particularly refers to and examines gender issues in relation to equal opportunities policies and practices. The paper draws heavily on the experiences which practitioners have recorded, very often making positive recommendations for the supplementation of equal opportunities having learned from earlier deficiencies they had to report.

1196   **Waterhouse R.** The access possibility: barrier or bridgehead? *Journal of Access Studies* Vol 2 No 2 1987 15-21
This article contributes to the debate surrounding Access as A-level substitute and therefore an additional barrier for non-conventional students; versus Access as a route into higher education for those who would not have otherwise entered. The author favours Access courses as a bridgehead into higher education and shows why.

1197   **Watson D.** EC-level developments in the 1980s affecting the industry-higher education interface *Industry and Higher Education* Vol 5 No 2 June 1991 87-91
Sets in the context of more general conditions, the various EC policies and initiatives which have direct or indirect impact on the industry-higher education interface. Reviews

specific developments in education and training and speculates on the future.

1198   **Weatherall D.** New technology skills shortage *Management Services* Vol 33 No 4 April 1989 38-41
Skills shortages due to demographic and technological change are discussed. The main strategies open to employers are reviewed, most notably retrain existing staff, widening the hiring net to include types of people not usually considered.

1199   **Webb S.** Access, credit levels and the learner: a rejoinder *Journal of Access Studies* Vol 6 No 2 1991 205-209
Offers some thoughts on the operation and educational consequences of accreditation and current perceptions of learners within Access and Open College Federations.

1200   **Webb T.** Negotiating for training *Industrial and Commercial Training (UK)* Vol 21 No 5 Sept/Oct 1989 18-22
The Manufacturing, Science and Finance union MSF believes that details of access to training and retraining should be a basic part of an employee's contract of employment. This article discusses trade unions growing commitment to training.

1201   **Weimer W.A.** Planning for lifelong education: cooperation between industry and education in continuing education *Industry and Higher Education* Vol 2 No 2 June 1988 91-97
Argues continuing education is a business higher education must enter and exploit if they are to compete with the industrial sector and other training providers. Concludes, preconceived views surrounding industry have meant failure of many educational institutions to enter the continuing education field.

1202   **Weir D.** *Current issues and concerns in Scottish vocational education research and development.* Occasional paper number 118. Ohio, USA National Center for Research in Vocational Education 1986 28 pages
A research paper which appraises the Scottish initiatives which have been directed at improving the vocational relevance of education.

1203 **Wells A.** Staff development in the provision of adult literacy and basic skills *Adults Learning* Vol 2 No 5 1991 157-158

Looks at staff development issues relating to those working in the area of adult literacy and basic skills. Describes the existing structures and training and suggests future developments.

1204 **Welsh L. and Woodward P.** *Continuing professional development: towards a national strategy* Glasgow Planning Exchange 1989

1205 **West H. and Woffinden R.** *Literacy problems of Restart clients* Sheffield Employment Department Group 1990 81 pages

Reports on the first stage of a two part survey to find the extent and nature of literacy problems amongst Restart clients. It outlines methods for identifying clients with literacy problems during Restart interviews. Attempts are made to characterise clients with such difficulties and links are made between literacy problems and the length of unemployment, sex, age and health.

1206 **Weston C.** Training go-slow puts the brake on skill factor *The Guardian* 26 October 1991 page 6

Reports on the slow progress being made in updating the skills of the present workforce and states the case for investment by employers in the quality and quantity of training. Discusses various strategies for increasing the proportion of employees receiving job-related training.

1207 **Wheale J.W.** Managing marketing: a checklist *Education Management and Administration* Vol 17 No 3 1989 387-395

Provides a checklist for senior managers on the development of structures to enable the implementation of a marketing strategy. Describes such a project at Warwick University.

1208 **White, D.** Midland's Anne Watts - equality for all *Banking World* No 5 May 1990 9-10

This article illustrates the success of appointing Ann Watts as its Group Equal Opportunities Director. She initiated the establishment of workplace nurseries for staff and improvements in opportunity for all women. Shows this bank's commitment to equal opportunity.

1209 **Whyte A.** Community prisoning and the long sentence offender workshop *Scottish Journal of Adult Education* Vol 7 No 4 1986 24-25

Discusses parallels between unemployment and imprisonment and how adult education can respond to imprisonment. A six point strategy is presented which stresses the importance of offering training in transferable skills.

1210 **Whyte A.** Images of success *Times Educational Supplement* No 3858 8th June 1990 page B2

Report from North London College on a project in which black people in a trade or profession become mentors to black people in further education.

1211 **Whyte J.** Transition from school to labour market: the Northern Ireland youth training programme In: Osborne R.D. et al (Ed) *Education and policy in Northern Ireland* Belfast Policy Research Institute 1987 191-206

Describes and evaluates the aims and effectiveness of the youth training programme in Northern Ireland. Some attempt is made to assess the socio-economic status of the participants.

1212 **Wickham A.** *Women and training* Milton Keynes Open University Press 1986 147 pages

Examines sexism in education and training and looks at the present provision for school leavers and women returners. Compares training facilities with those in the USA, USSR and Sweden and analyses the relationship between education, training and the labour market.

1213 **Wilkinson C. and Morris A. (Ed)** *The post-release experience of female prisoners: women and the penal system.* Papers presented to 19th Cropwood Round-Table Conference Cambridge 1988

The rhetoric of 'treatment and training' is more readily embraced in women's prisons and whilst the purposes of prison for women are the same as men: to assist prisoners to retain links with the community and help prepare them for their return to it, education and training for women prisoners is a drastically under-researched area.

1214 **Williams J.** *Words or deeds? A review of equal opportunities in higher education* London CRE 1989 28 pages
Questionnaires were sent to all polytechnics and universities to provide an overview of equal opportunities policies in higher education in the mid 1980s. Findings show that well over half had given very little thought to and showed little commitment to the issues.

1215 **Williams M.** *Credit transfer: in-course credit recognition* Manchester CONTACT/Leverhulme Trust March 1988 75 pages
A discussion paper from the project on in-course credit recognition funded by the Leverhulme Trust. This project proposed ways in which credit transfer can be facilitated so that their largely complementary resources can be combined more easily in joint programmes responding to emerging needs for training, retraining and updating.

1216 **Willman B.** Women and the skill gap *Training and Development* Vol 8 No 5 May 1990 31-32
Looks at what companies are doing to attract women into the workplace. Illustrates with examples of retraining, career breaks and flexible working at NATWEST Bank and also job change at Financial Times Offices whereby women have been admitted to previously non-traditional areas of work.

1217 **Wilson C. and West D.** A modular argument *Education* September 1989 228-230
Investigates the reasons behind the urgent need for a radical reform of educational provision for post 16-year olds. Supports the need for unified learner centred system of education and training throughout life. The gap between education and work may be bridged by actively promoting training at all levels.

1218 **Wilson L.** The costs of developing and implementing competence based standards *Competence and Assessment* No 10 1990 6-10

Addresses the issue of costing the implementation of competence based standards. Discusses a Training Agency project to develop a framework for analysing such costs.

1219 **Wilson P.** Access and quality: the debate re-opened? *Journal of Access Studies* Vol 6 No 1 1991 16-31
Gives an overview of the debate about access and quality. Presents a model of quality assurance for Access courses derived from elements of good practice in further and higher education and industry.

1220 **Wilson P.** The future funding of access studies *Journal of Access Studies* Vol 4 No 1-2 1989 71-78
Discusses the funding of Access courses in the light of recent legislation. Recognises the value of the government's recognition of Access courses as a route to higher education but is not convinced that the necessary funding will be forthcoming.

1221 **Wilson S.** The door that never closes: Open University in Scotland *Times Scottish Educational Supplement* No 1285 June 1991 page 25

1222 **Wilson V.** The training needs of women in rural areas *Training and Development* Vol 7 No 9 9th Jan 1989 page 6
Reports on a pilot study funded by the MSC which investigates the training needs of women living in rural areas and the specific problems they face when attempting to return to work.

1223 **Windess R.** *Information technology in the delivery of distance education and training* London Peter Francis Publishers 1988 192 pages
This book gives examples of successful innovation in the use of information technology for distance learning. A variety of techniques is considered including audio and video conferencing, computer applications and the use of satellites.

1224 **Windle R.E.** *Undergraduate income and expenditure survey 1988/89* Middlesex Research Services Limited 1989 130 pages

A detailed survey to obtain information about student income and expenditure upon which NUS policy could be based. Conducted by questionnaire the survey looked at student expenditure on accommodation, food, leisure, travel and equipment and books needed for study and collected data on income from grants and awards, parental contribution, earnings, social security and other sources.

1225   Wisker G. Facilitating the learning of mature women students: a British perspective *Studies in Continuing Education* Vol 1 No 1 1989 66-85
Addresses issues involved in increased numbers of mature women students in higher education: (1) reasons for past low participation; (2) models of good practice, such as Access courses and the Open University; and (3) institutional and instructional concerns such as course design and content, teaching and learning strategies, funding, hours, assessment, day care and counselling.

1226   Witcher H. Let's accentuate the positive: sex stereotypes *Times Educational Supplement* Scotland No 1165 3 March 1989 page A18
Stresses men and women have to take up the issue of equal opportunities and tackle sexism at both personal and professional levels.

1227   Withnall A. Celebrating informal learning: from theory to practice *Adults Learning* Vol 2 No 4 Dec 1990 102-104
Many learners monitor and evaluate their own learning activity but may not know how to improve it or how to transfer their newly acquired skills to other spheres. The need for some method of validation of learning effort urgently needs to be developed.

1228   Wolfson B. Winning with people: why Investors in People matters *TEC Director* Issue 7 1991 16-17
Introduces the new national standard 'Investors in People' and discusses the role of TECs in implementing it and developing it into a valuable tool for encouraging businesses to recognise the value of investing in people.

1229   Women and Training Workshop Report Recruitment,retraining and retaining women returners *Women and Training* 22 May 1990 33 pages

This is a valuable report which examines issues of the recruitment process, support and training for women returners, ways of changing attitudes in the work place and changes to working practices. Women and Training are now known as Catalyst for Change.

1230   Women of Europe Supplement *Child care in the European Communities 1985-1990* Aug 1990
This report deals with reconciling employment and training, equality and children. It analyses some of the main developments in this area in the European Community between 1985-1990. The inequality of childcare is one of the fundamental causes of women's unequal position in the labour market. In UK, childcare has gained priority on the political and economic agenda. To date, the government's main response is to encourage employers to make employment measures but otherwise look to the private market to provide childcare services.

1231   Women Prisoners Resource Centre Basic 'fact sheet' London NACRO Feb 1990
Describes the work of WPRC which was set up to help identify and meet the re-settlement needs of women prisoners, who would be returning to London on their release. WPRC liaise constructively with prison education departments.

1232   Women Returners Network *Returning to work: education and training for women* London Longman 1987 296 pages
A directory of courses for women who want either to return to work after a break or to improve their career prospects by following a course of training, including linked access, preparatory, community studies, and women's studies foundation courses.

1233   *Women Returning to work* London
Information pack covering a variety of pertinent issues: looking for a job, childcare, new technology and better employment.

1234   Wood S. (Ed) *Continuous development: the path to improved performance* London Institute of Personnel Management 1988 191 pages
An incisive and practical guide covering all aspects of continuous development. The

authors explore what is meant by the concept and look at learning needs and styles. The book provides valuable case histories of top companies who have been inspired by the continuing development philosophy to achieve excellent results.

1235 **Woodhall M.** *Financial support for students, grants, loans or graduate tax?* London Kogan Page 1989 126 pages

A collection of six papers which examines the Government's proposals for student loans. Considers the experience of other countries in this area and examines common trends and responses.

1236 **Woodhall M.** Loans for learning: the loans versus grants debate in international perspective *Higher Education Quarterly* Vol 43 No 1 1989 76-87

Reviews the arguments for and against student loans and considers alternatives to the proposed system. The British experience is put into context with comparisons of the experience in Sweden, Germany and the USA.

1237 **Woodley A.** Has the Open University been an unqualified success? *Journal of Access Studies* Vol 2 No 2 1987 7-14

In this paper the contribution made by the Open University to widening access to education, especially for those with lower qualifications is reviewed. The authors conclude from the evidence presented that there has been little improvement over the years in the proportion of students with low qualifications. Stresses the need for better admissions counselling and preparatory courses and ongoing educational guidance from tutors and counsellors.

1238 **Woodley A.** et al *Choosing to learn - a study of adults in education* Milton Keynes OU Press 1988 228 pages

1239 **Woodrow A.** *Skills assessment and vocational guidance for the unemployed* London FEU 1989 44 pages

This document describes a REPLAN programme to help unemployed adults articulate and record in a personal portfolio their experience relevant to employment or education in order to help them convince employers or educators that they can do the job or benefit from the training.

1240 **Woolfe R. et al** *Guidance and counselling in adult and continuing education: a developmental perspective* Milton Keynes Open University 1987 211 pages

Presents the case for counselling as an essential part of the role of many in adult continuing education. Counselling is discussed in terms of a helping relationship and as a non-directive partnership. A rather different interpretation of the relationship of guidance and counselling is given from that developed through the UDACE and NICEC work.

1241 **Working Brief** TECs tackle TEED *Working Brief* July 1991 page 1

Reports on a meeting between representatives of the TECs and the DE in which the TECs complained of inadequate funding and unnecessary bureaucracy.

1242 **Working Mothers Association** *The employer's guide to childcare* London The Working Mothers Association 1990

This guide is intended as an introduction to existing childcare provision for working parents and discusses why and how employers should develop their childcare options. Looks at government policy on childcare and examples of good practice followed by various trade unions, local authorities and companies. Each chapter ends with a summary and action plan to assist employers turn the theory into practice.

1243 **Wrench J.** Employment and the labour market *New Community* Vol 17 No 4 1991 617-623

Reviews a number of recent (90/91) instances concerning racial inequality in access for black and ethnic minority people to higher level jobs in for example, universities, the civil service and the medical and legal professions.

1244 **Wrench J.** New vocationalism, old racism and the careers service *New Community* Vol 16 No 3 1990 425-440

Examines the implications of the increasing importance of vocational education for the careers service in its work with ethnic minorities. Argues that the careers service has a role in ensuring that employers work within the Race Relations Act.

1245 **Wright A.** Prison education runs out of whitewash *Times Educational*

Supplement Scotland No 1092 9th October 1987 page 4

Discusses the recent report produced by Scottish Home and Health Department on education in prisons. Draws on some of the perceptions of ex prisoners. Stresses the importance of education as anything that creates opportunities for personal growth.

1246   **Wright P.W.G (Ed)** *Industry and higher education: collaboration to improve students learning and training* Buckingham Open University Press 1990 93 pages

This book sets out the contexts in which higher education and industry now find themselves and examines possible spheres of joint activity. It concentrates primarily on the contribution that both partners can make to improving the quality of student's learning and to increasing its relevance to the needs of employment.

1247   **Yorke M.** *Performance indicators: observations on their use in the assurance of course quality* London CNAA 1990 42 pages

1248   **Zaklukiewicz S.** *Special needs after 16: priorities for development* Edinburgh SCRE 1987

This project covered the whole of Scotland, highlighting educational provision within the main services available to school leavers who have special needs. In addition to further education and the Youth Training Scheme, this covered day services for handicapped adults, and continuation at special schools. The main findings will be available in a single volume published by SCRE, *'Continuing Education for Special Needs'*.

SUBJECT INDEX

The numbers refer to the numbers of the entries *not* to page numbers.